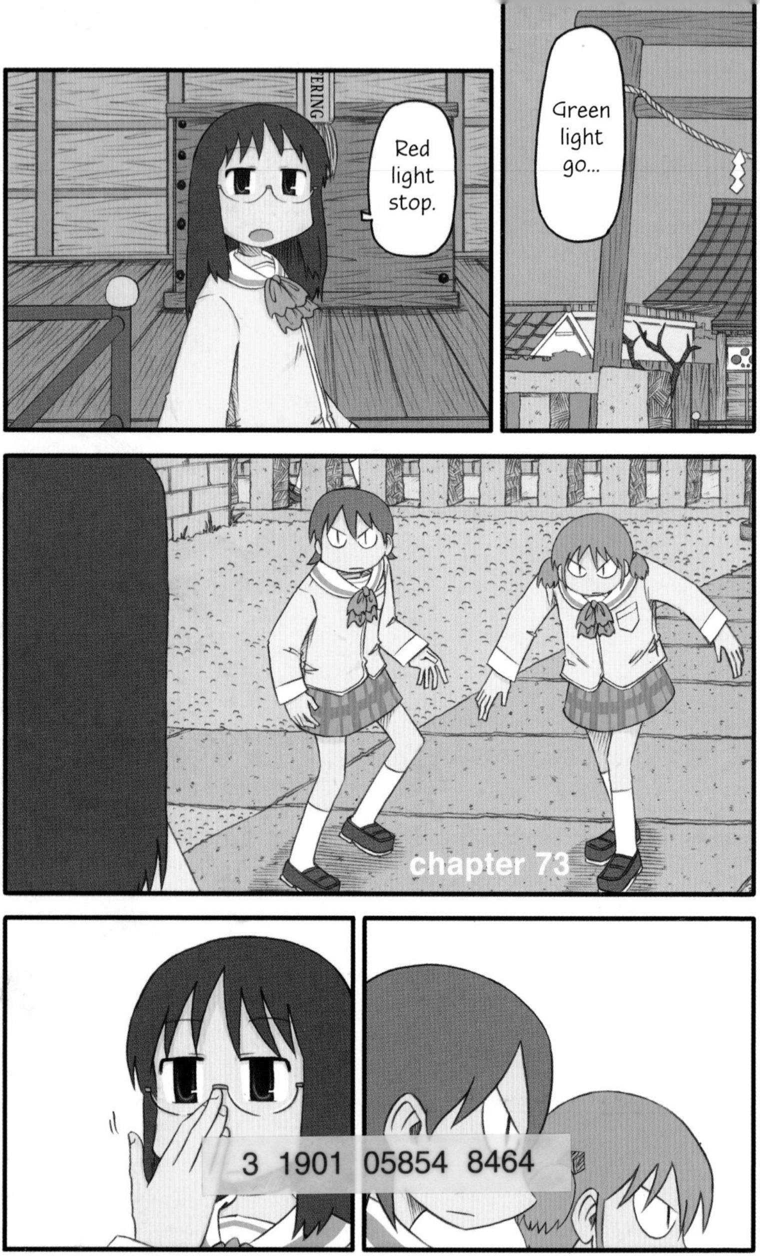
Green light go...
Red light stop.
chapter 73

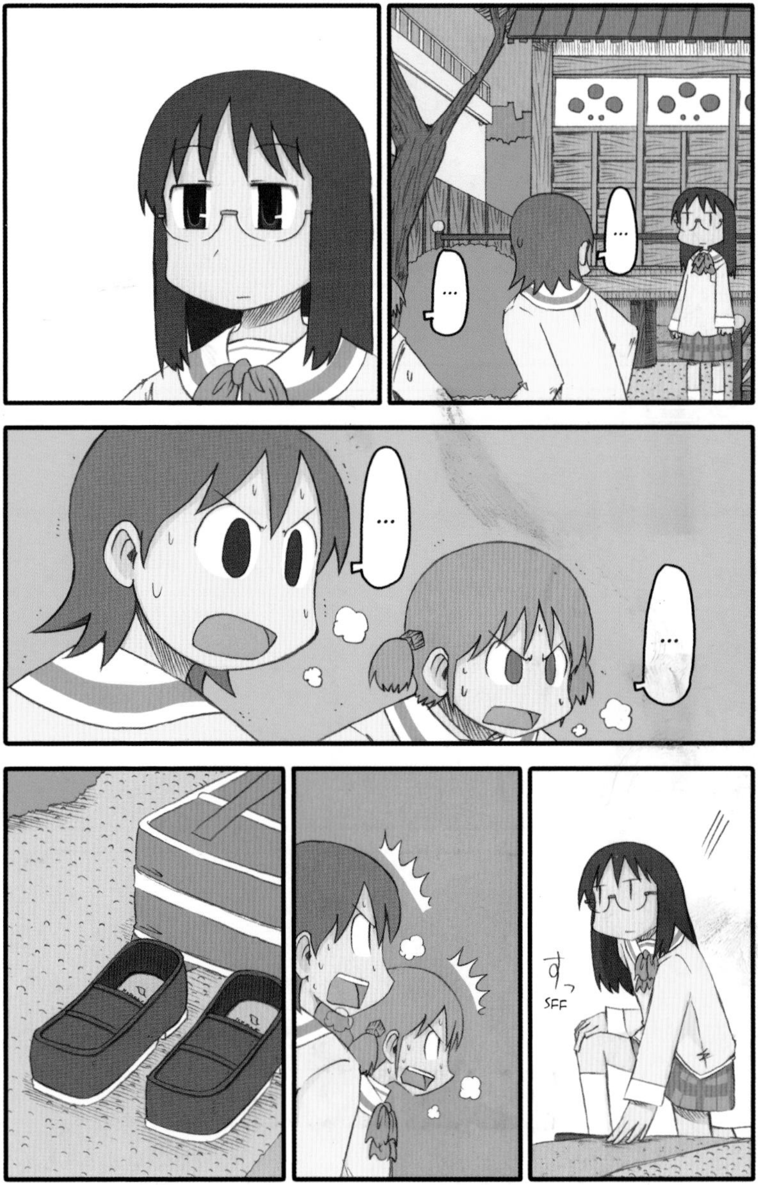
...
...
...
...
すっ
SFF

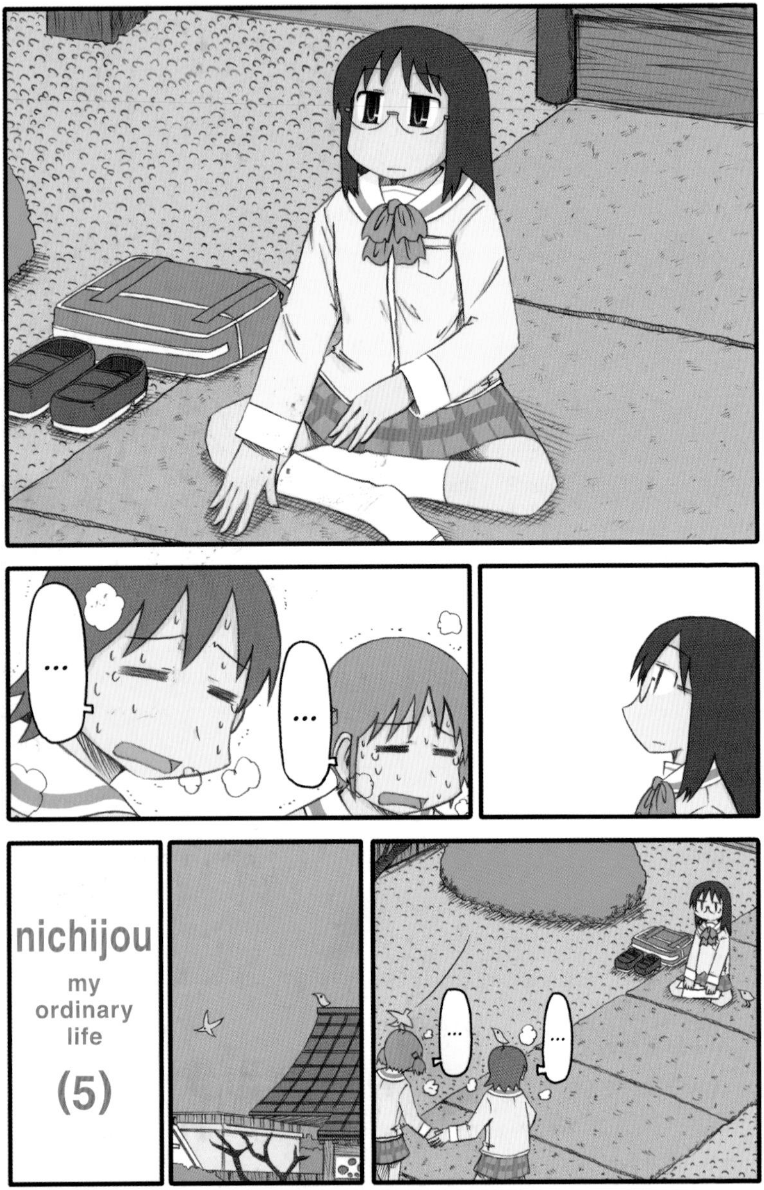
...
...
...
...
nichijou
my ordinary life
(5)

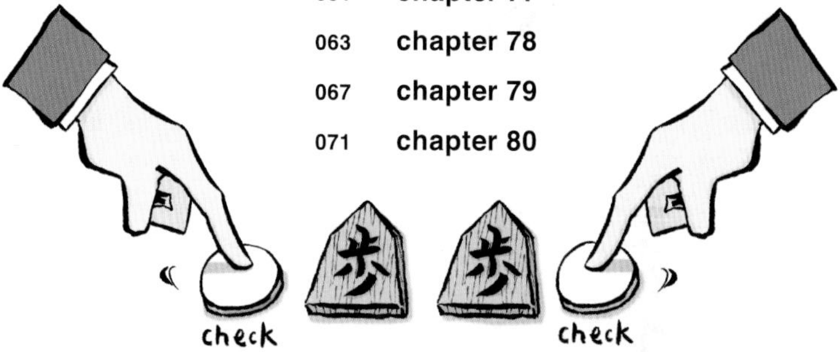
check
check

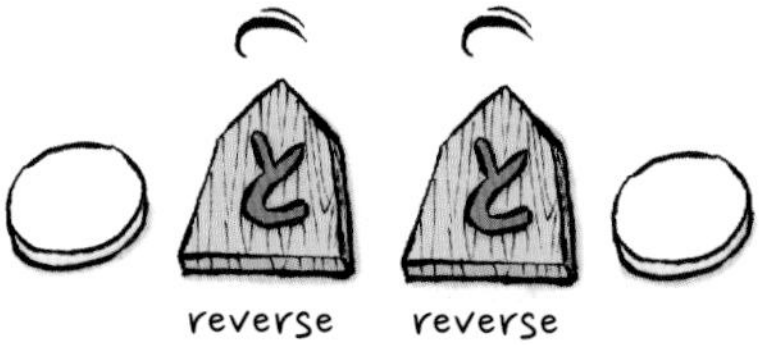
reverse
reverse

ordinary shorts 6

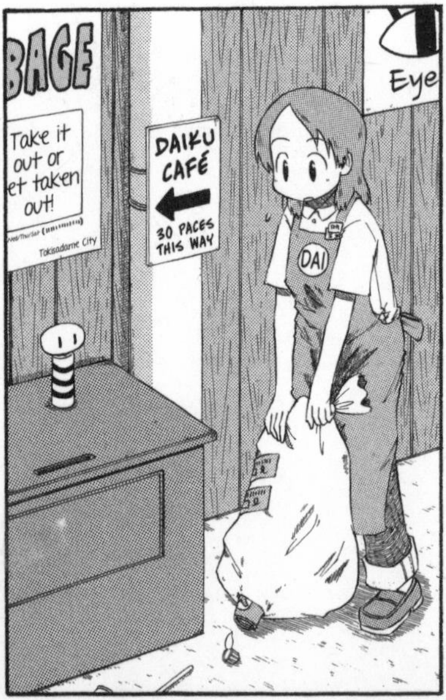
Eye
BAGE
DAIKU
CAFÉ
30 PACES THIS WAY
Take it out or et taken out!
Tokisadame City

boredom game

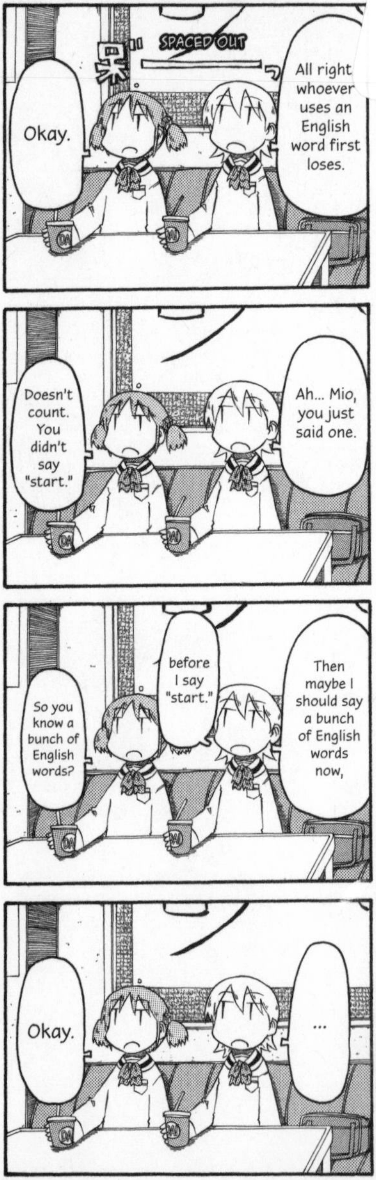
All right whoever uses an English word first loses.
SPACED OUT
Okay.
Ah... Mio, you just said one.
Doesn't count. You didn't say "start."
Then maybe I should say a bunch of English words now,
before I say "start."
So you know a bunch of English words?
...
Okay.

daiku power

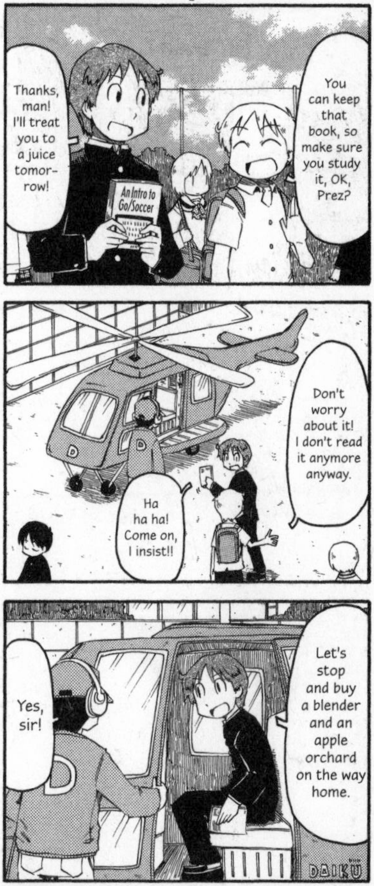
You can keep that book, so make sure you study it, OK, Prez?
Thanks, man! I'll treat you to a juice tomorrow!
An Intro to Go/Soccer
Don't worry about it! I don't read it anymore anyway.
Ha ha ha! Come on, I insist!!
Let's stop and buy a blender and an apple orchard on the way home.
Yes, sir!
DAIKU
So that's...
ZWOOOOMM
the power of the Daiku Conglomerate...

ms. nakamura

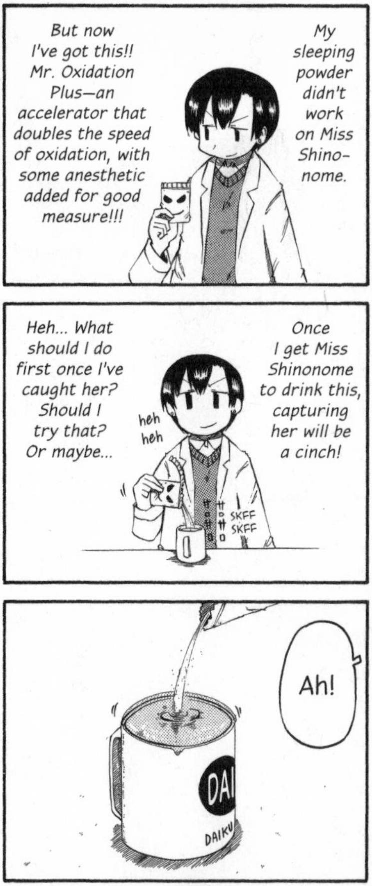
My sleeping powder didn't work on Miss Shinonome.
But now I've got this!! Mr. Oxidation Plus—an accelerator that doubles the speed of oxidation, with some anesthetic added for good measure!!!
Once I get Miss Shinonome to drink this, capturing her will be a cinch!
Heh... What should I do first once I've caught her? Should I try that? Or maybe...
heh heh
SKFF SKFF
Ah!
DAI
DAIKU
Oopsie ...
SSLURP

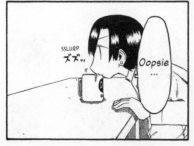

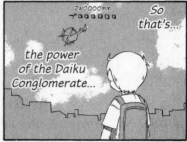

the 15-year secret revealed

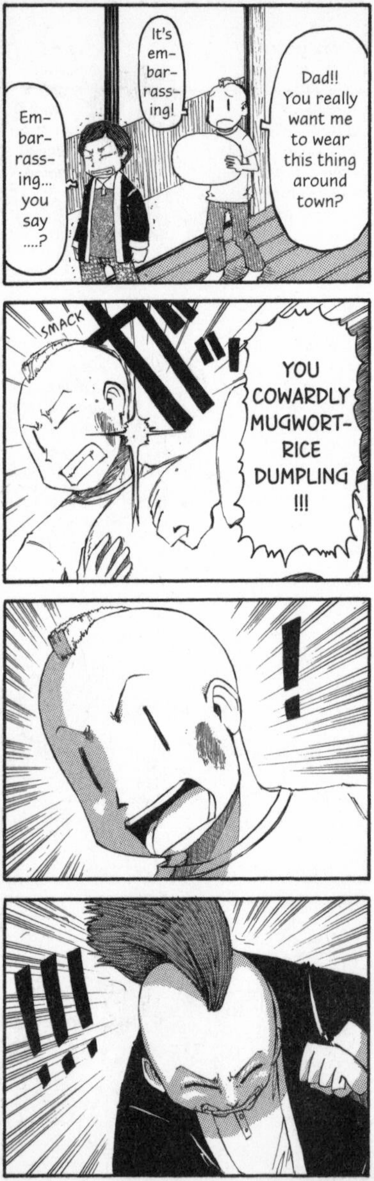
Dad!! You really want me to wear this thing around town?
It's em-bar-rass-ing!
Em-bar-rass-ing... you say ....?
SMACK
YOU COWARDLY MUGWORT-RICE DUMPLING !!!
!

birthday present

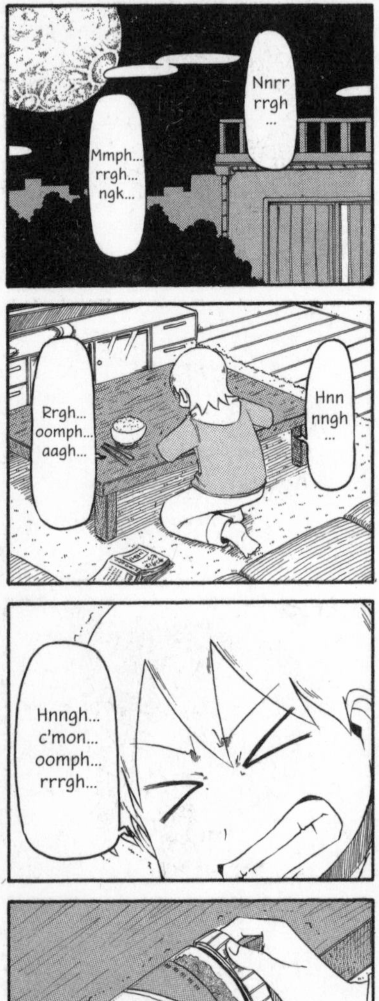
Nnrr rrgh ...
Mmph... rrgh... ngk...
Hnn nngh ...
Rrgh... oomph... aagh...
Hnngh... c'mon... oomph... rrrgh...
OCTOPUS WASABI

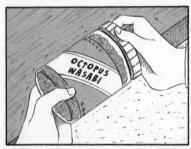

ms. nakamura's weakness

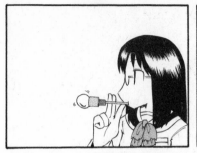

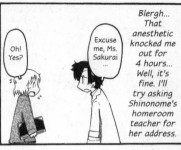

Blergh... That anesthetic knocked me out for 4 hours... Well, it's fine. I'll try asking Shinonome's homeroom teacher for her address.
Excuse me, Ms. Sakurai ...
Oh! Yes?
Ah, Ms. Naka-mura... your hair...
You have bed head ...
Oh, yeah.
I just woke up, so...
It's kind of cute, really!
Argh !!
I'll try again later!
Huh? Ah... uhm...
Ms. Naka-mura?
TROT TROT
TROT

mai

ordinary shorts 6: end

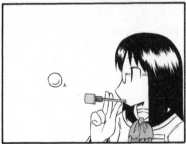

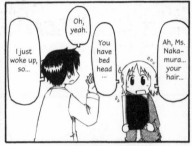

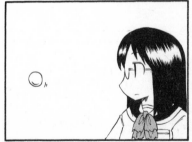

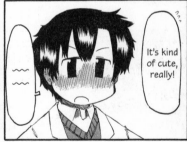

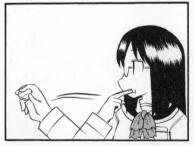

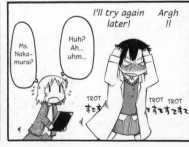

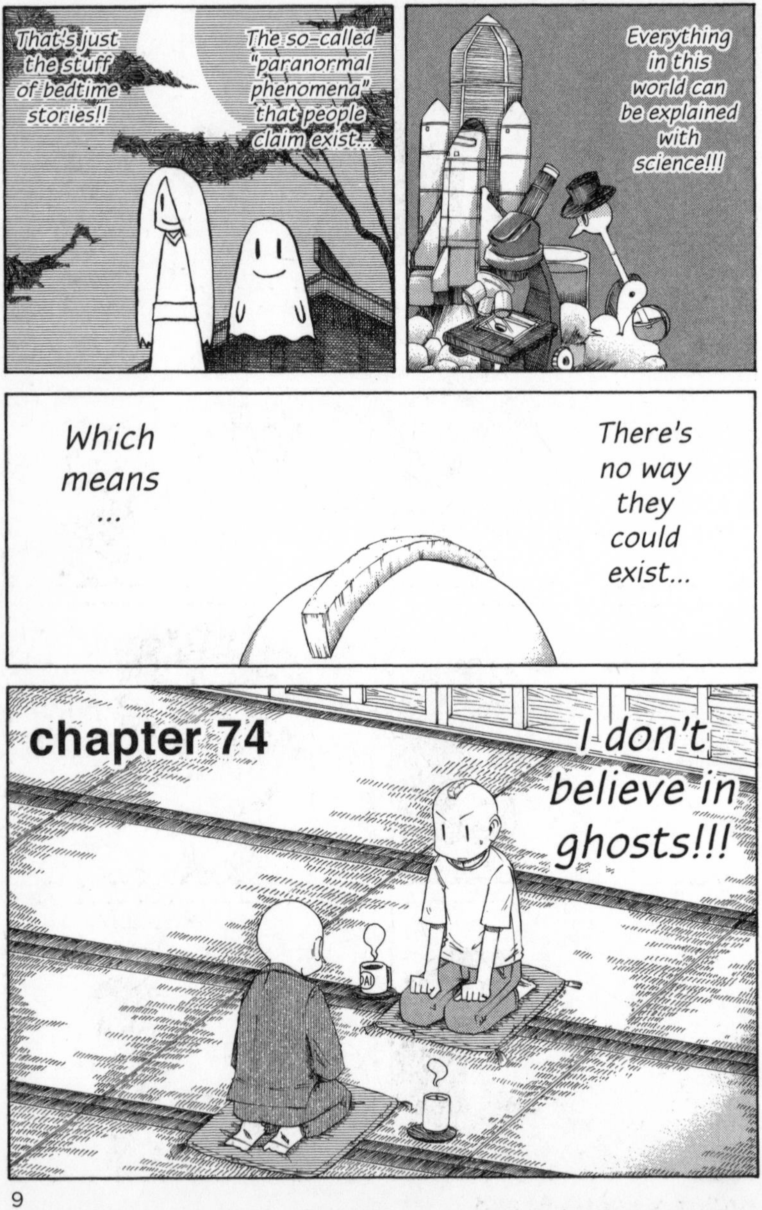
Everything in this world can be explained with science!!!
The so-called "paranormal phenomena" that people claim exist...
That's just the stuff of bedtime stories!!
There's no way they could exist...
Which means ...
I don't believe in ghosts!!!
chapter 74

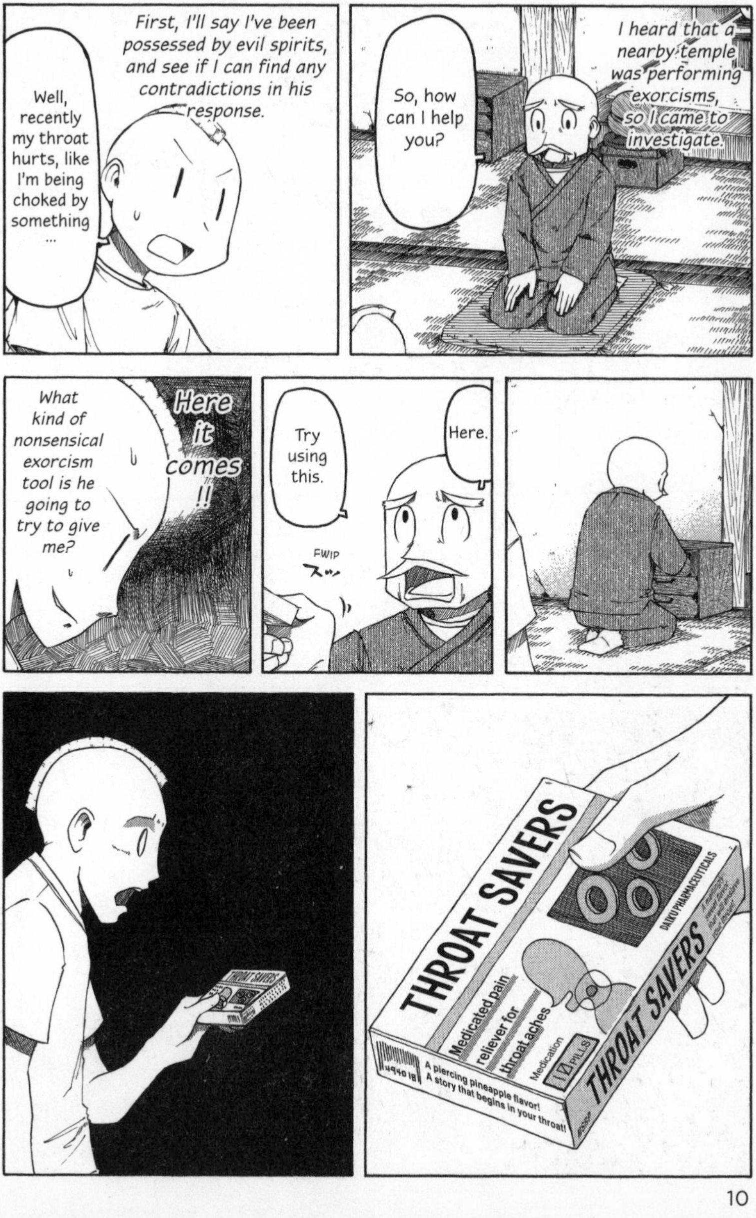

I heard that a nearby temple was performing exorcisms, so I came to investigate.
So, how can I help you?
First, I'll say I've been possessed by evil spirits, and see if I can find any contradictions in his response.
Well, recently my throat hurts, like I'm being choked by something ...
Here.
Try using this.
FWIP
スッ
Here it comes!!
What kind of nonsensical exorcism tool is he going to try to give me?
THROAT SAVERS
DAIKU PHARMACEUTICALS
Medicated pain reliever for throat aches
Medication
PILLS
A piercing pineapple flavor!
A story that begins in your throat!
THROAT SAVERS
THROAT SAVERS

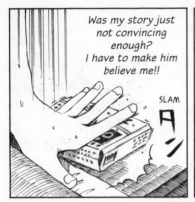

This product is said to help sore throats.
Th... That's actually pretty sensible!!
Was my story just not convincing enough? I have to make him believe me!!
SLAM
Listen, it's not like I just have any sore throat...
It's as if someone is trying to strangle me...
And some-times I'll make these strange sounds...
To be frank, it seems like I'm pos-sessed!
Well, isn't it just that ...
you've been reading too many weird books?
That's kinda
creepy.

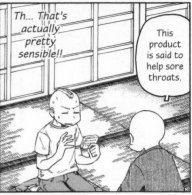

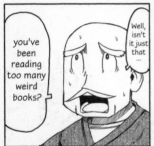

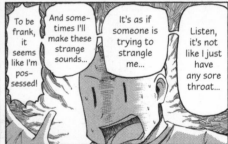

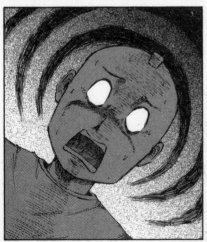

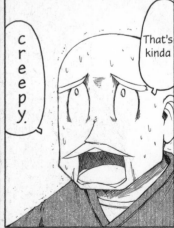

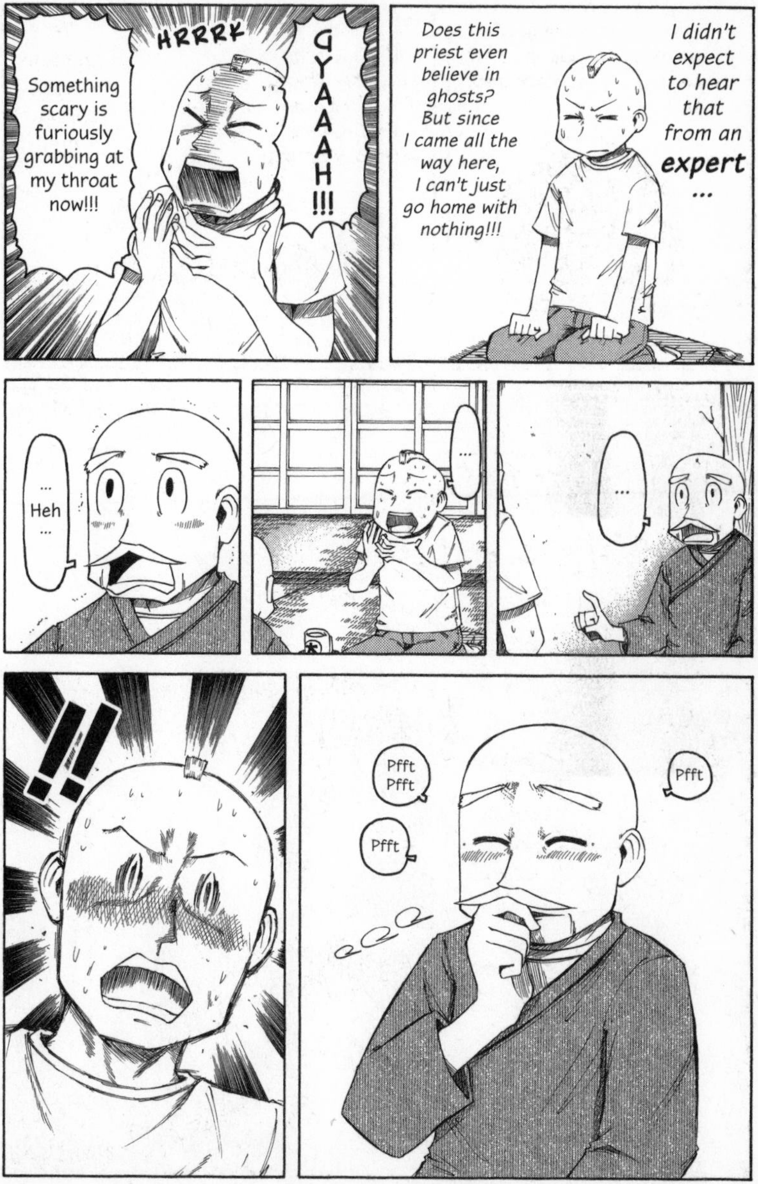
I didn't expect to hear that from an **expert**...
Does this priest even believe in ghosts? But since I came all the way here, I can't just go home with nothing!!!
GYAAAAH!!!
HRRRK
Something scary is furiously grabbing at my throat now!!!
...
...
... Heh ...
Pfft
Pfft Pfft
Pfft
!!

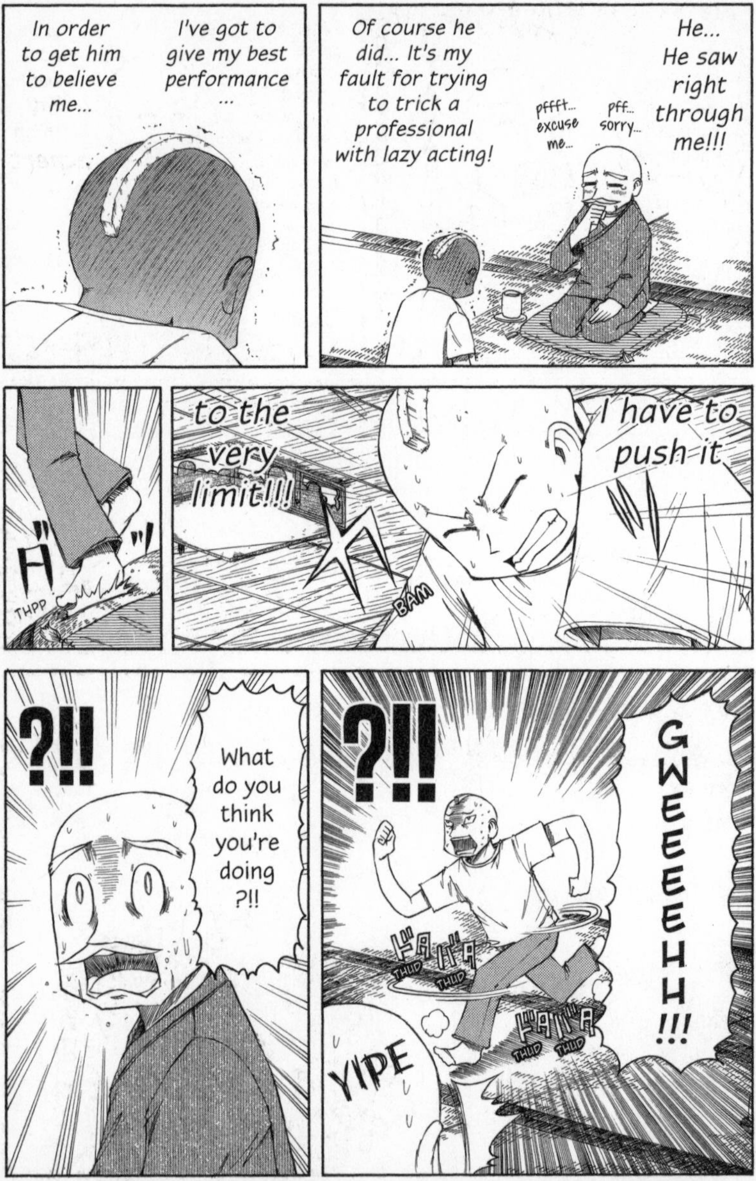

He...
He saw right through me!!!
pff... sorry...
pffft... excuse me...
Of course he did... It's my fault for trying to trick a professional with lazy acting!
I've got to give my best performance ...
In order to get him to believe me...
I have to push it
to the very limit!!!
BAM
THPP
?!!
GWEEEEEHH!!!
THUD THUD
THUD THUD
YIPE
?!!
What do you think you're doing ?!!

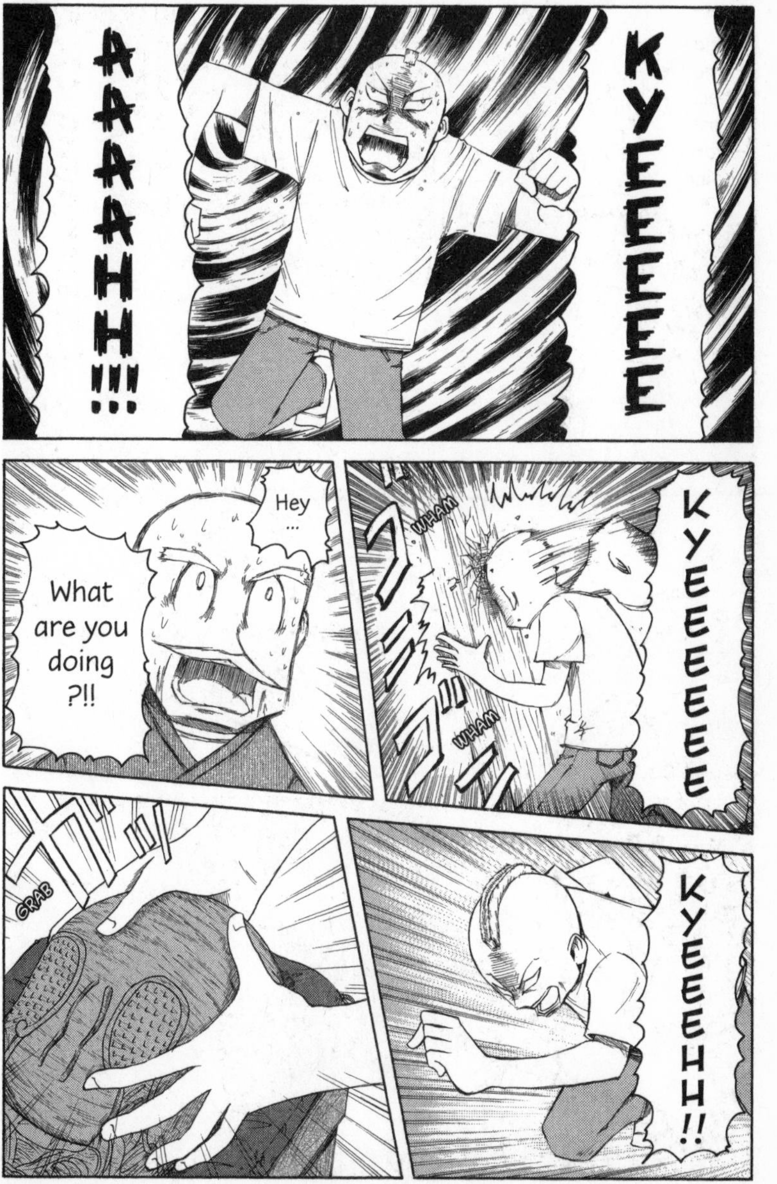

KYEEEEEE
AAAAHH!!!
KYEEEEEEEE
WHAM
WHAM
Hey ...
What are you doing ?!!
KYEEEEHH!!
GRAB

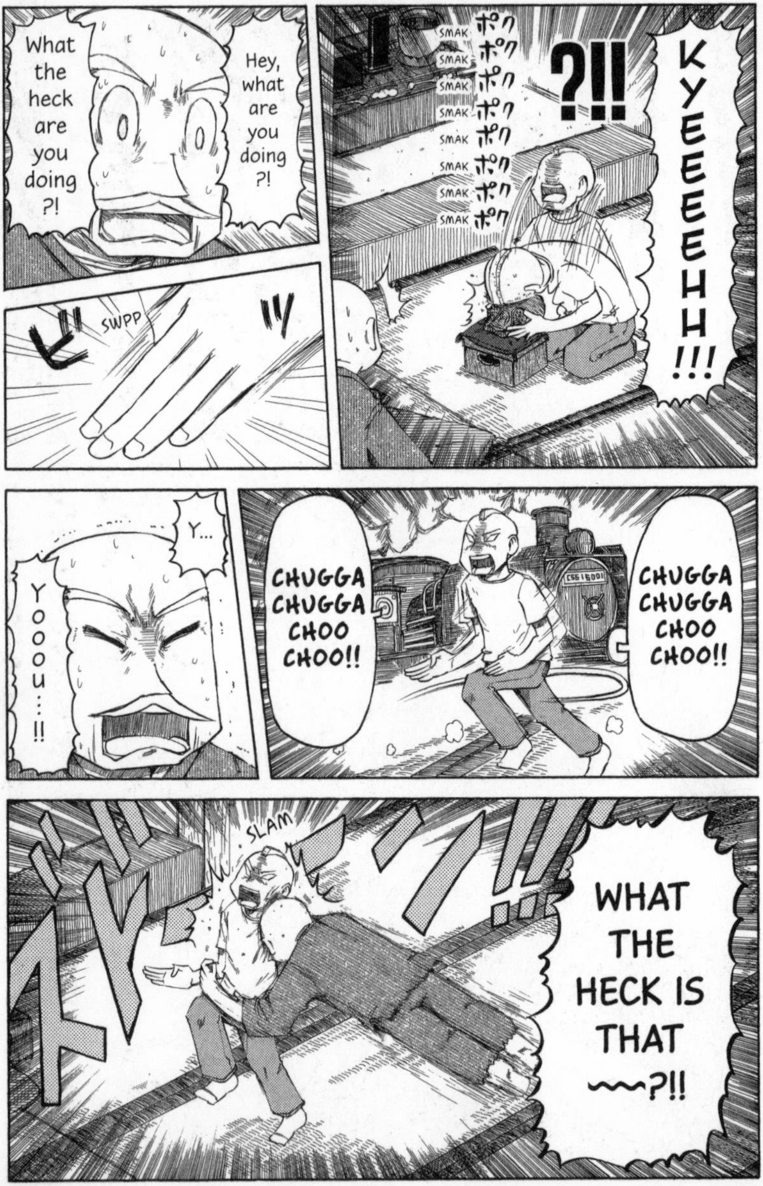
KYEEEEEHH!!!
?!!
SMAK ポク
SMAK ポク
SMAK ポク
SMAK ポク
SMAK ポク
SMAK ポク
SMAK ポク
SMAK ポク
Hey, what are you doing?!
What the heck are you doing?!
SWPP
CHUGGA CHUGGA CHOO CHOO!!
CHUGGA CHUGGA CHOO CHOO!!
Y...
Yoooou…!!
SLAM
WHAT THE HECK IS THAT ~~?!!

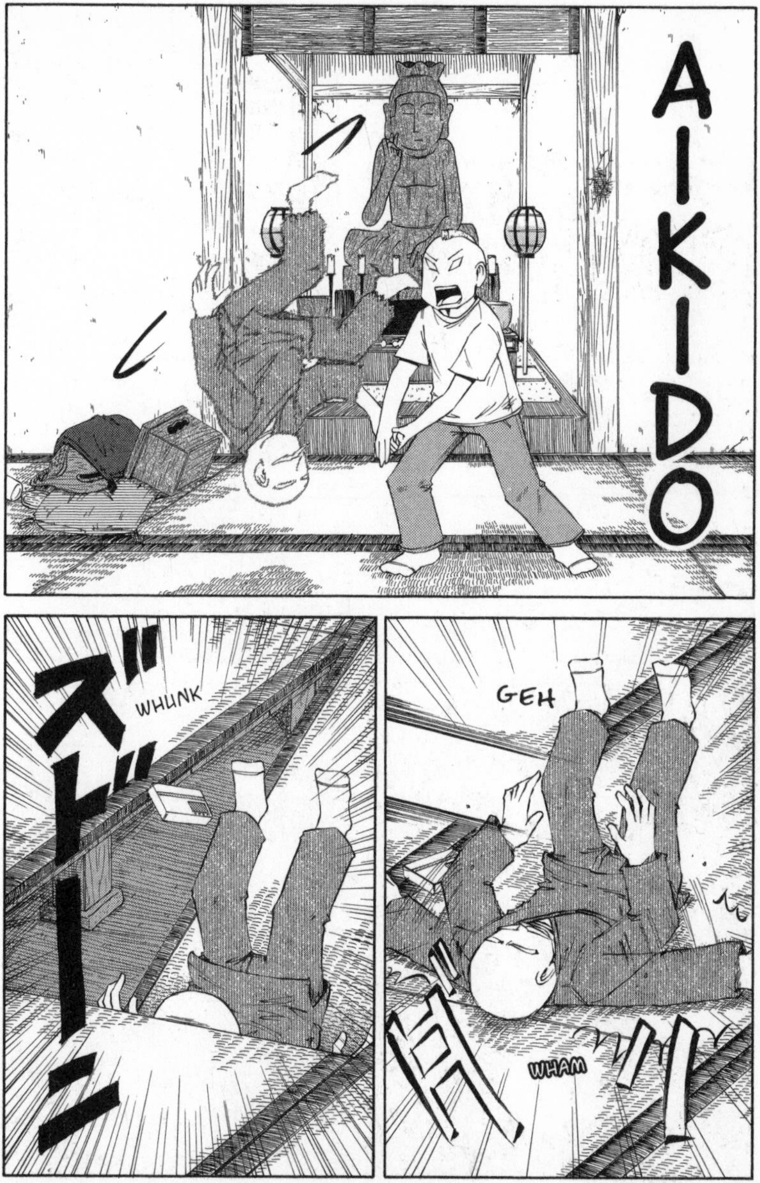
AIKIDO
GEH
WHAM
ズドーン
WHUNK

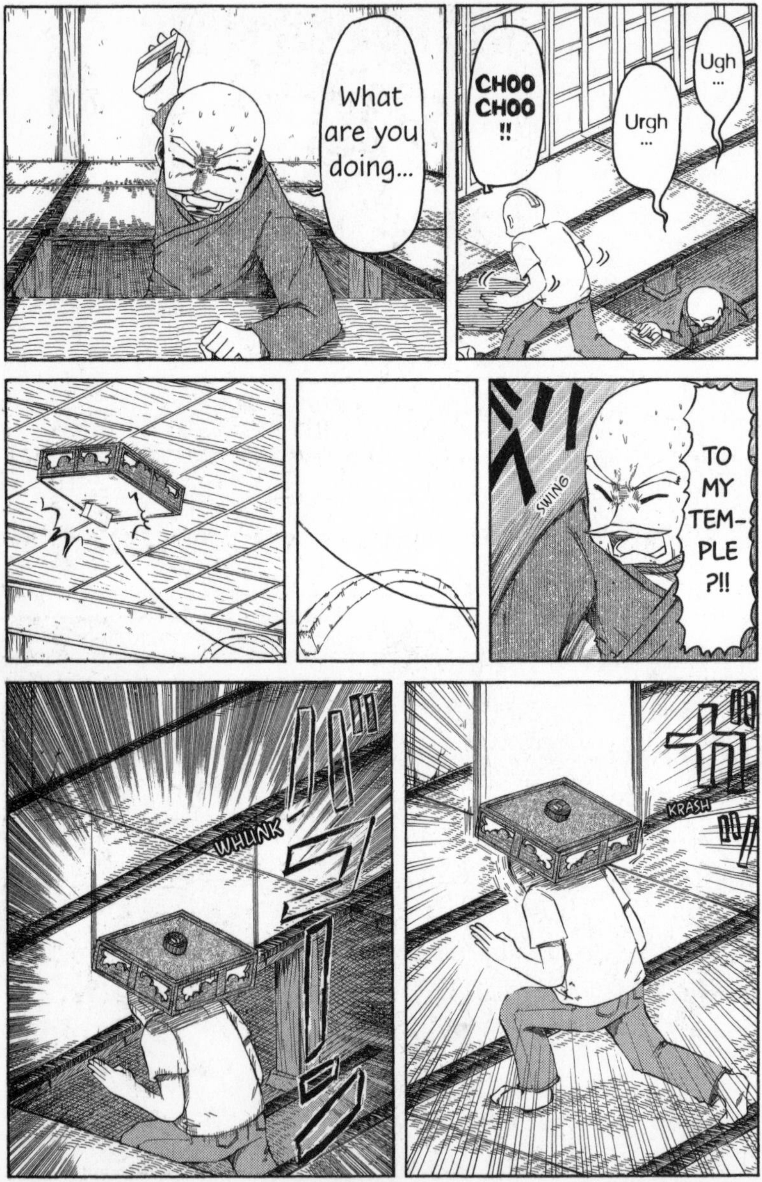
Ugh...
Urgh...
CHOO CHOO!!
What are you doing...
TO MY TEMPLE?!!
SWING
KRASH
WHUNK

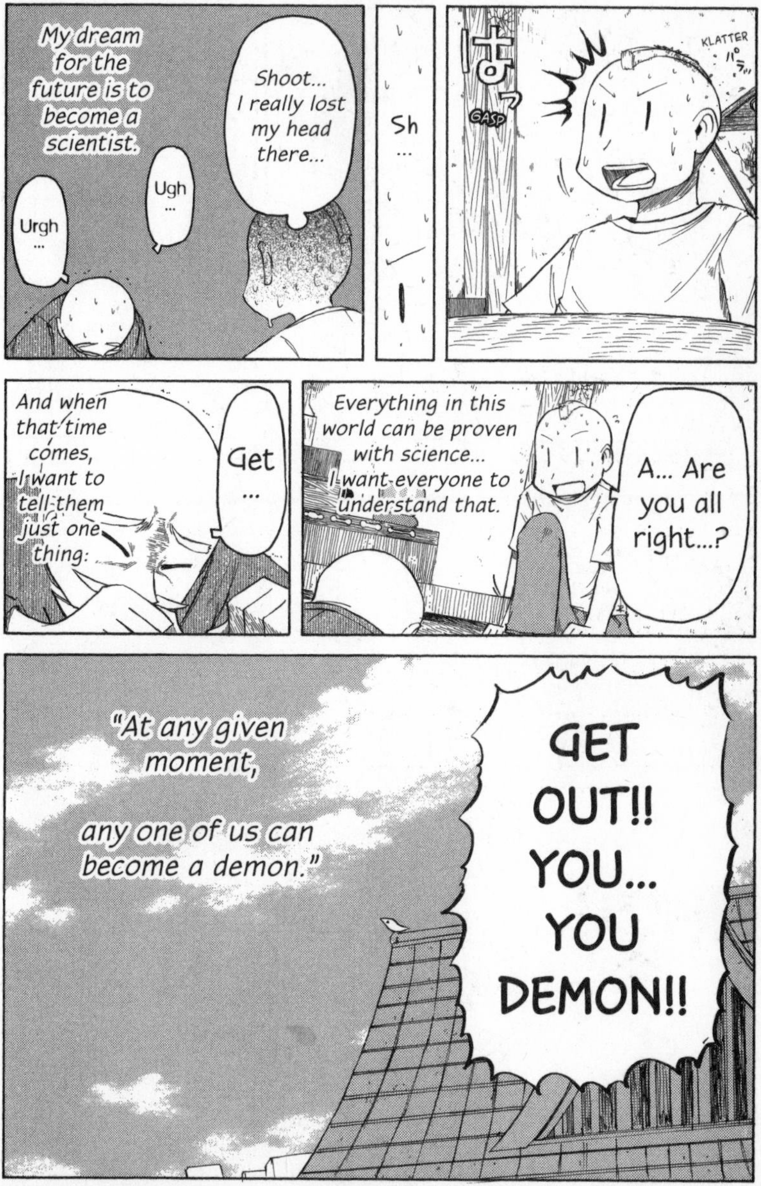
KLATTER
はっ
GASP
Sh
...
Shoot... I really lost my head there...
My dream for the future is to become a scientist.
Ugh ...
Urgh ...
A... Are you all right...?
Everything in this world can be proven with science... I want everyone to understand that.
Get ...
And when that time comes, I want to tell them just one thing:
GET OUT!! YOU... YOU DEMON!!
"At any given moment,
any one of us can become a demon."

chapter 74: end

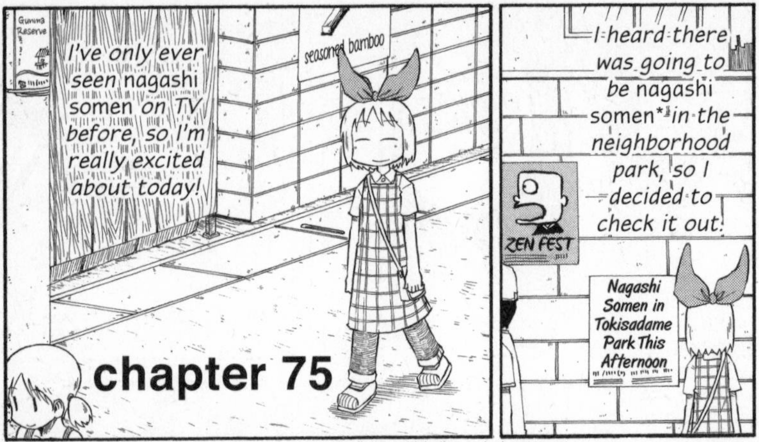
I heard there was going to be nagashi somen* in the neighborhood park, so I decided to check it out.
ZEN FEST
Nagashi Somen in Tokisadame Park This Afternoon
seasoned bamboo
Gunma Reserve
I've only ever seen nagashi somen on TV before, so I'm really excited about today!
chapter 75

* "flowing noodles." chilled noodles are sent down a water flume, which diners pluck out to eat.

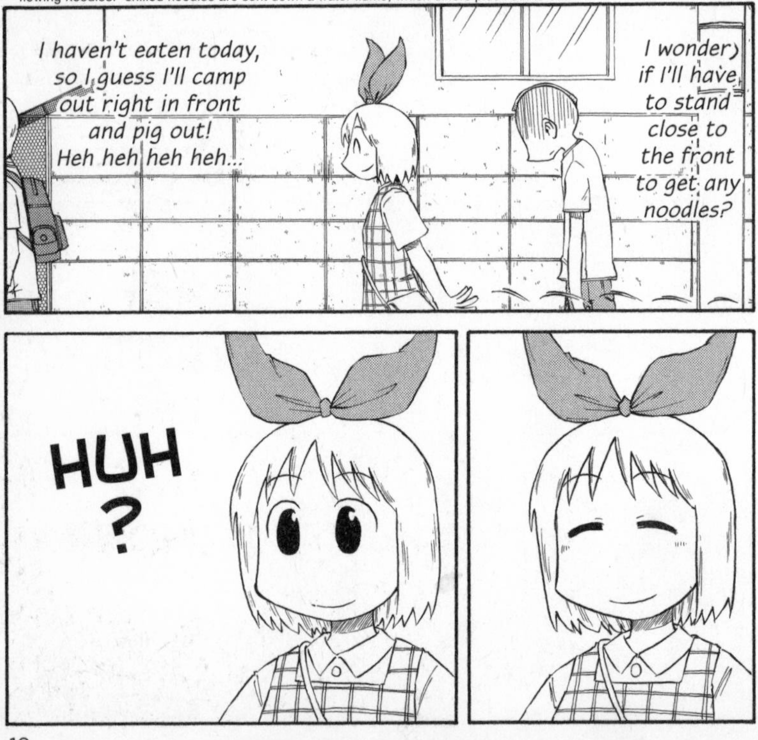
I wonder if I'll have to stand close to the front to get any noodles?
I haven't eaten today, so I guess I'll camp out right in front and pig out! Heh heh heh heh...
HUH ?

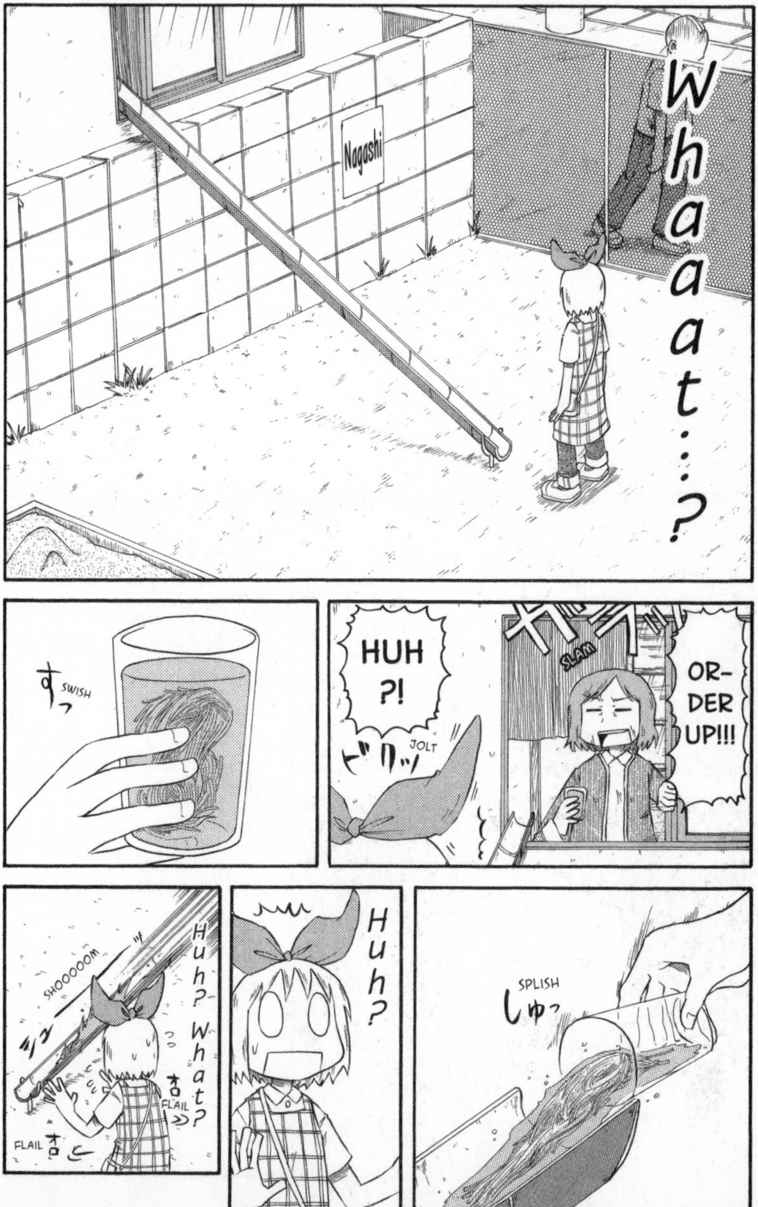
Nagashi
Whaaat...?
OR-
DER
UP!!!
SLAM
HUH
?!
ビクッ
JOLT
すっ
SWISH
SPLISH
しゅっ
Huh?
SHOOOOOM
Huh? What?
FLAIL
FLAIL

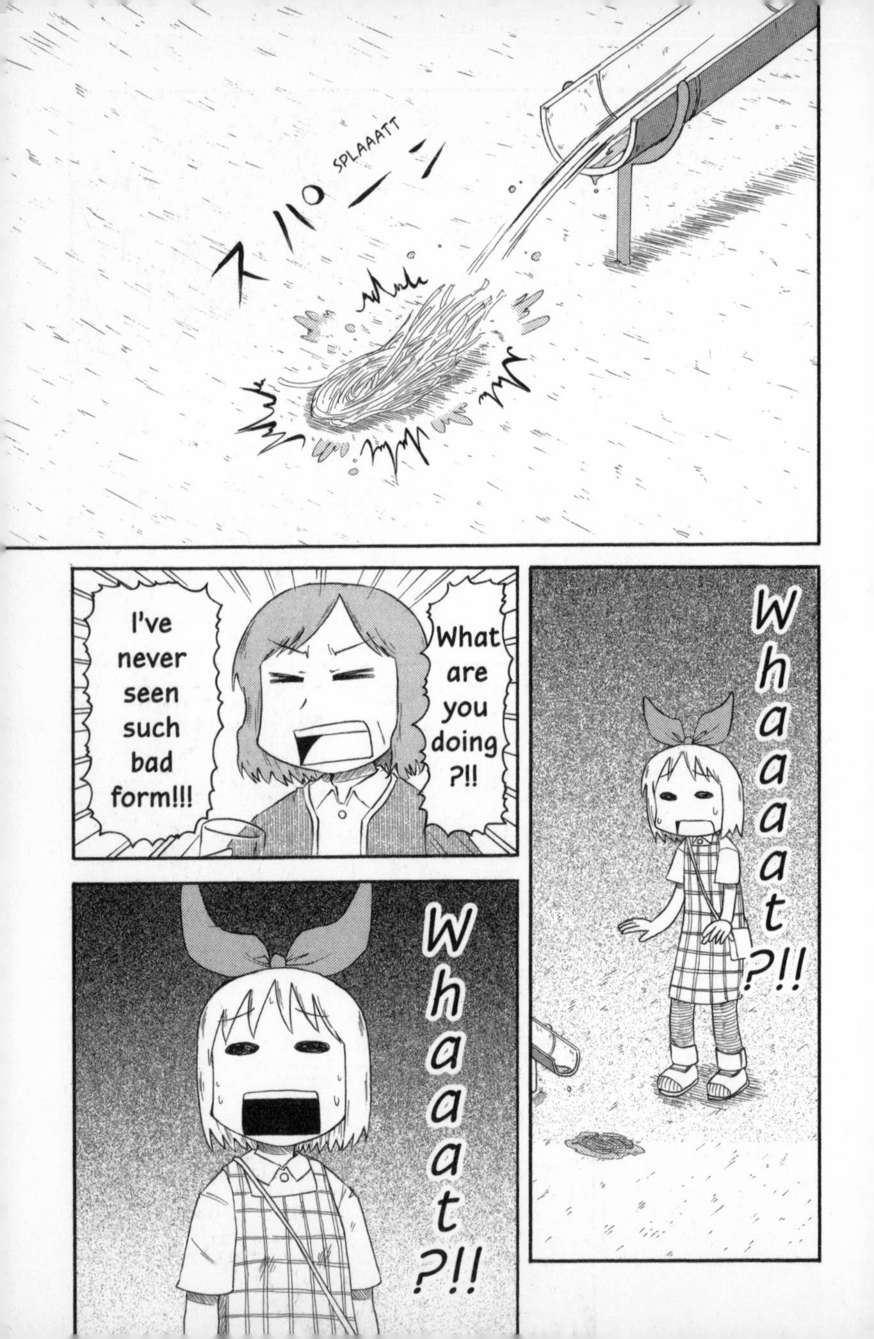
スパーン
SPLAAATT
Whaaaat?!!
What are you doing?!!
I've never seen such bad form!!!
Whaaaat?!!

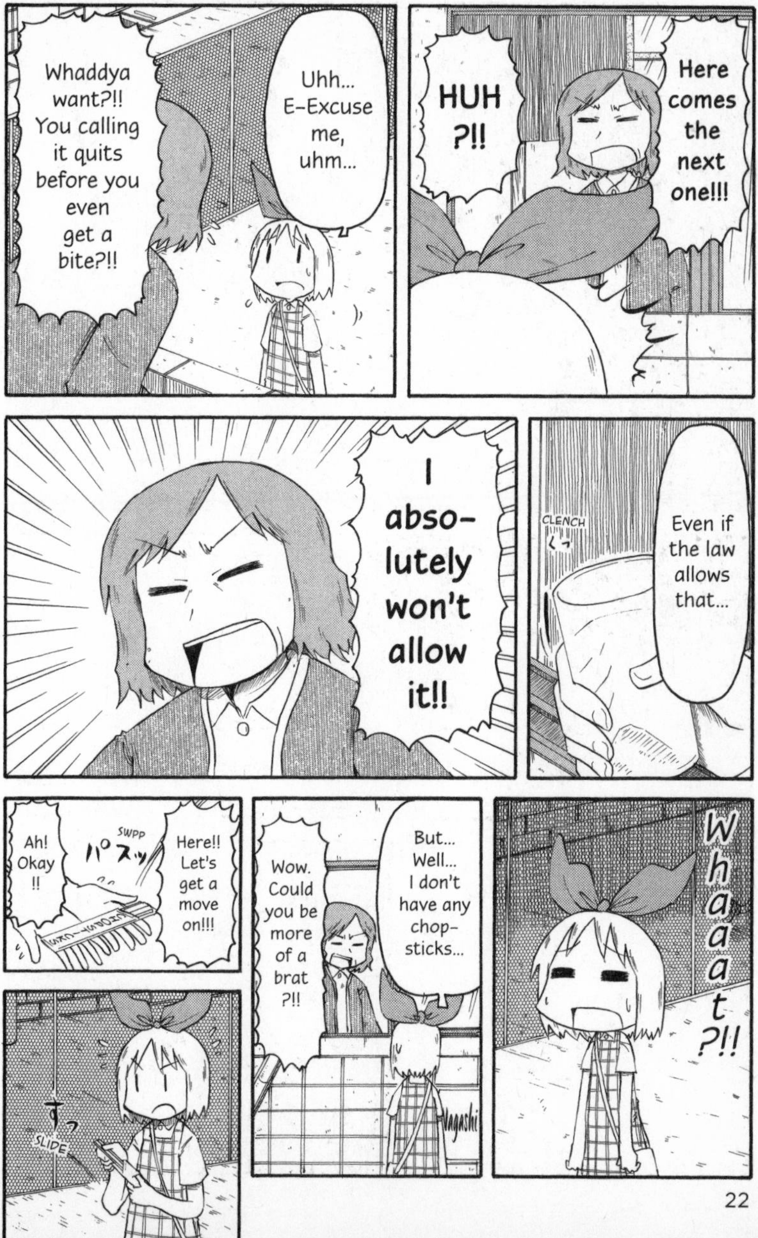
Here comes the next one!!!
HUH ?!!
Uhh... E-Excuse me, uhm...
Whaddya want?!! You calling it quits before you even get a bite?!!
CLENCH
くっ
Even if the law allows that...
I absolutely won't allow it!!
Whaaaat ?!!
But... Well... I don't have any chopsticks...
Wow. Could you be more of a brat ?!!
Nagashi
Here!! Let's get a move on!!!
SWPP
パスッ
Ah! Okay !!
すっ
SLIDE

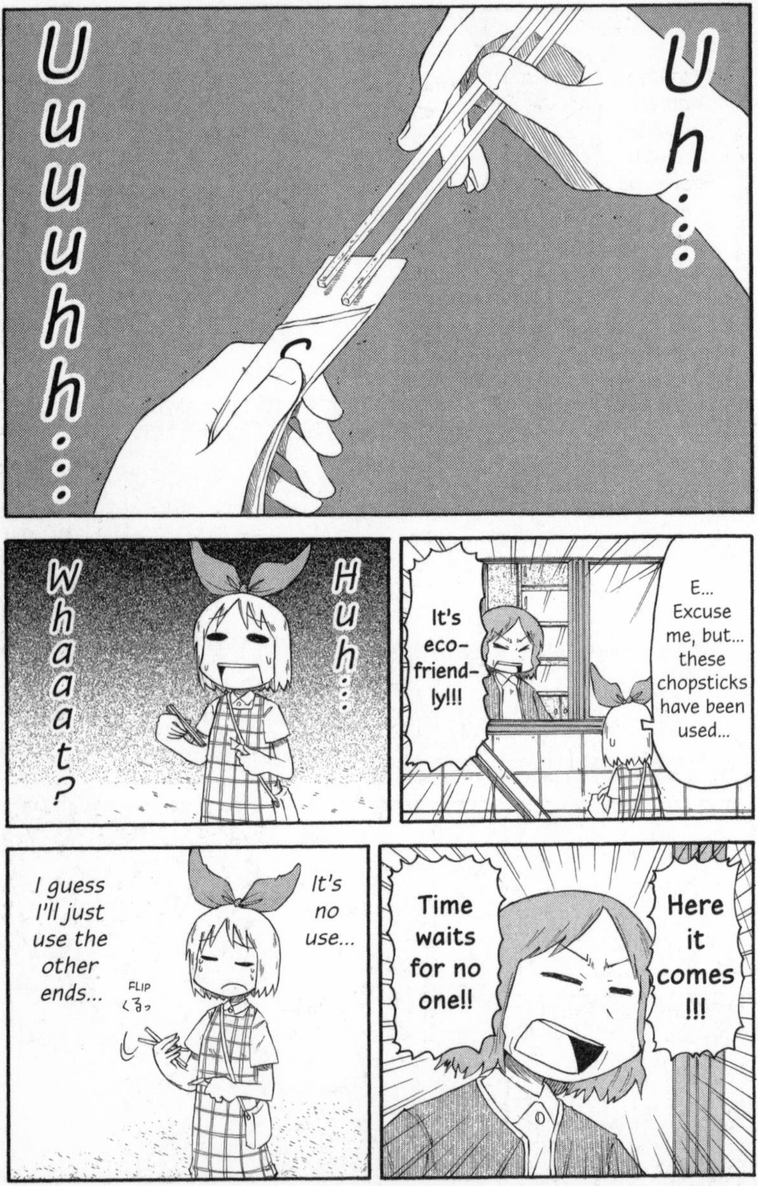

Uh...
Uuuuhh...
E... Excuse me, but... these chopsticks have been used...
It's eco-friendly!!!
Huh...
Whaaaat?
Here it comes!!!
Time waits for no one!!
It's no use...
FLIP くるっ
I guess I'll just use the other ends...

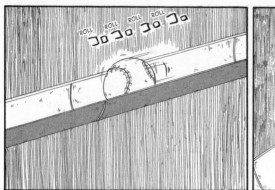
ROLL ROLL ROLL ROLL
コロ コロ コロ コロ

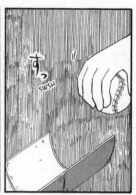
すっ
SWISH

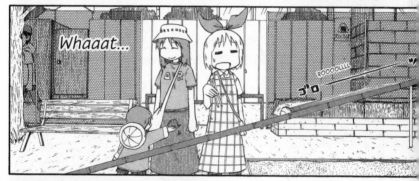
Whaaat...

ROOOOLLL
ゴロ

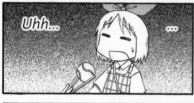
Uhh... ...

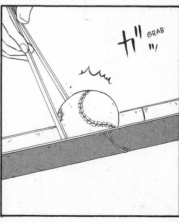
ガ GRAB
"

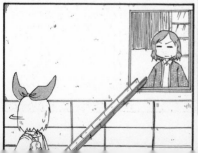

24

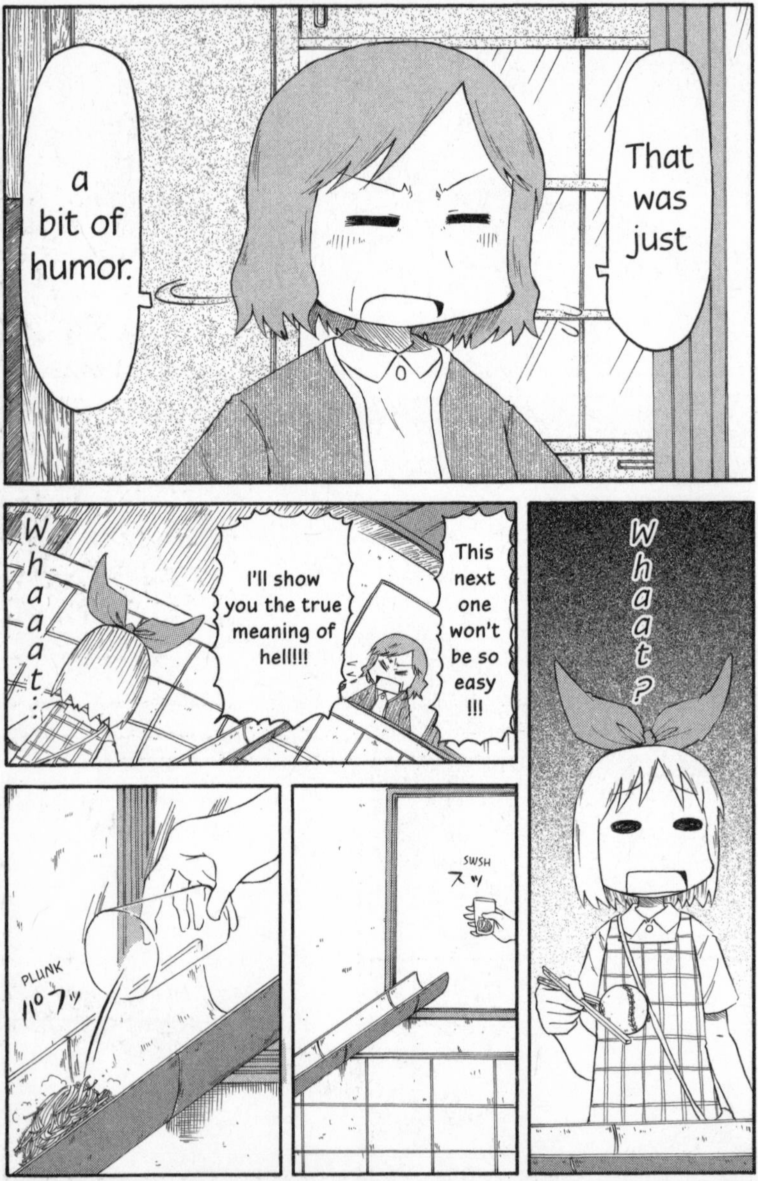
That was just
a bit of humor.
Whaaat?
This next one won't be so easy!!!
I'll show you the true meaning of hell!!!
Whaaat...
SWSH
スッ
PLUNK
パフッ

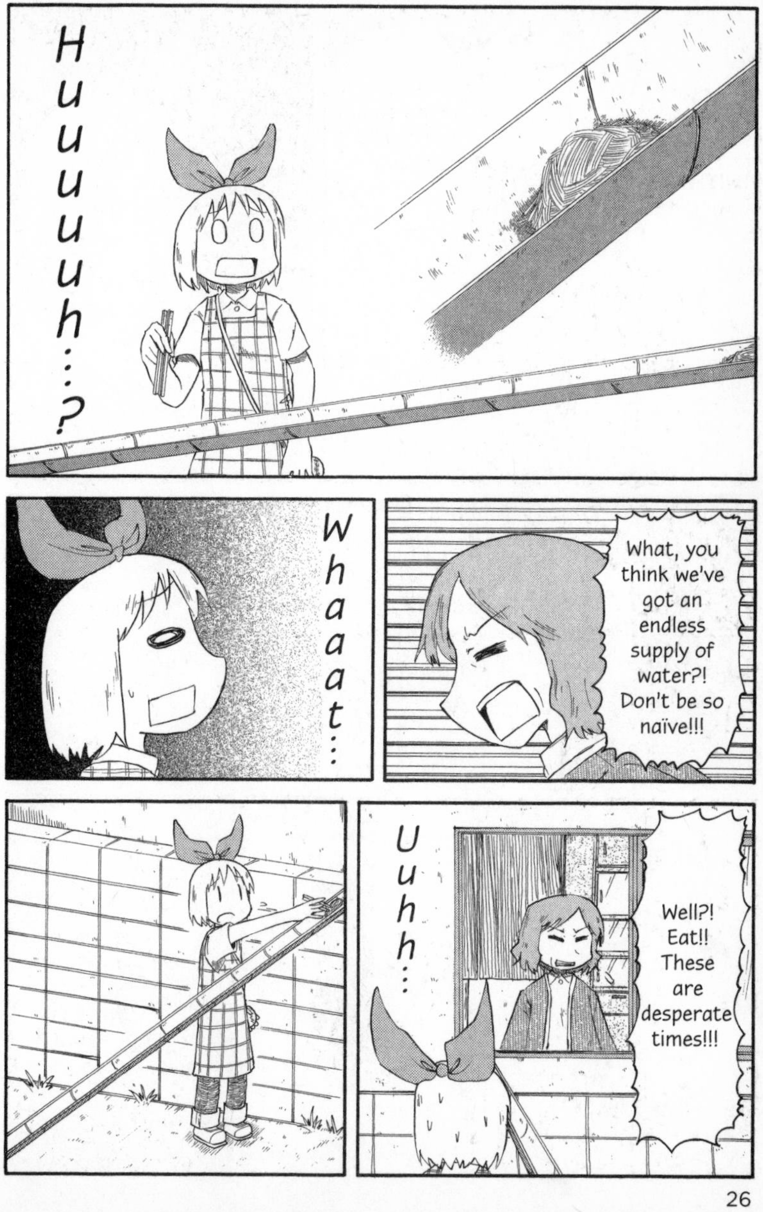
Huuuuuh...?
What, you think we've got an endless supply of water?! Don't be so naïve!!!
Whhaaat...
Well?! Eat!! These are desperate times!!!
Uuhh...

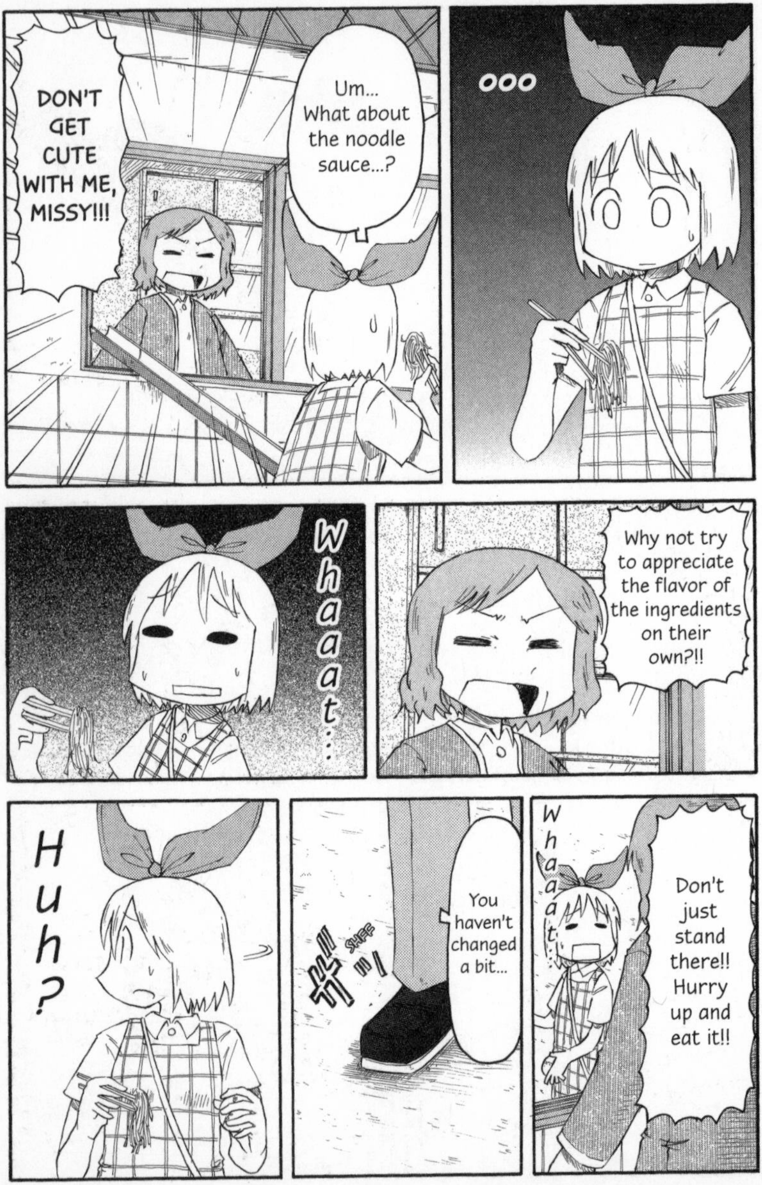

ooo
Um... What about the noodle sauce...?
DON'T GET CUTE WITH ME, MISSY!!!
Why not try to appreciate the flavor of the ingredients on their own?!!
Whaaaat...
Don't just stand there!! Hurry up and eat it!!
Whaaaat...
You haven't changed a bit...
SHUFF
Huh?

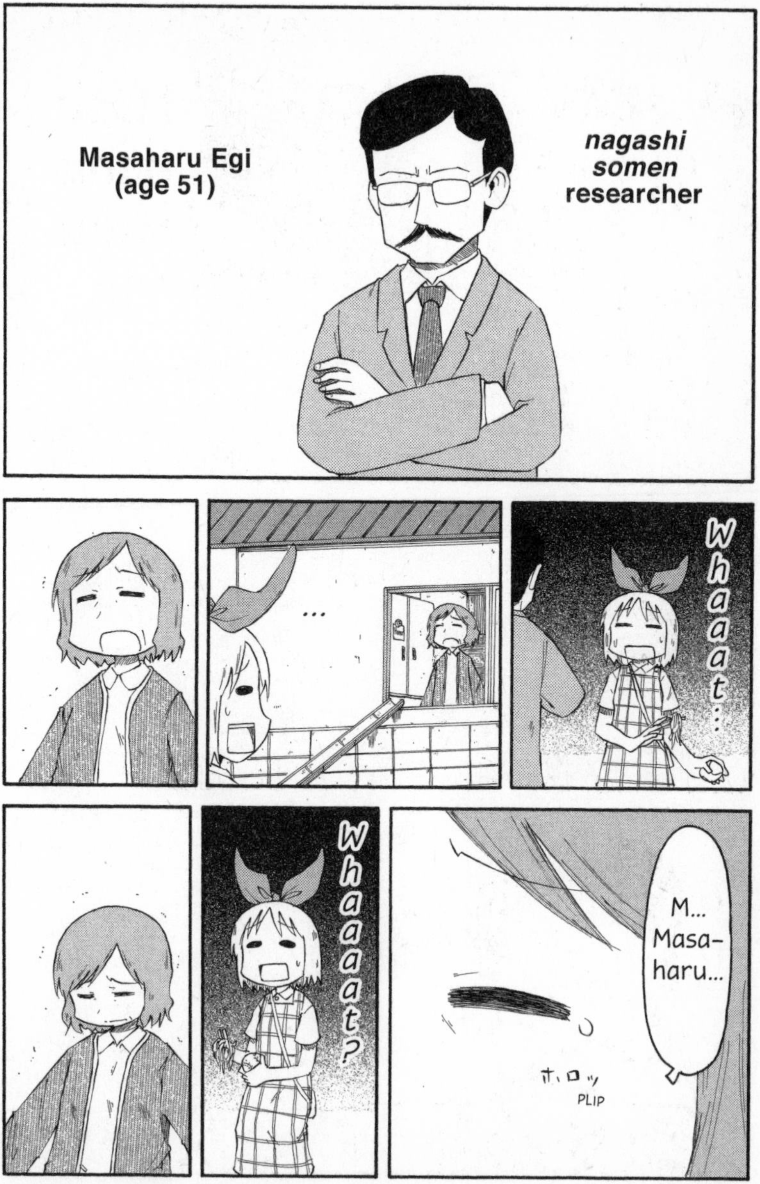
nagashi somen researcher
Masaharu Egi (age 51)
Whaaaat...
...
M... Masa-haru...
ホロッ
PLIP
Whaaaaat?

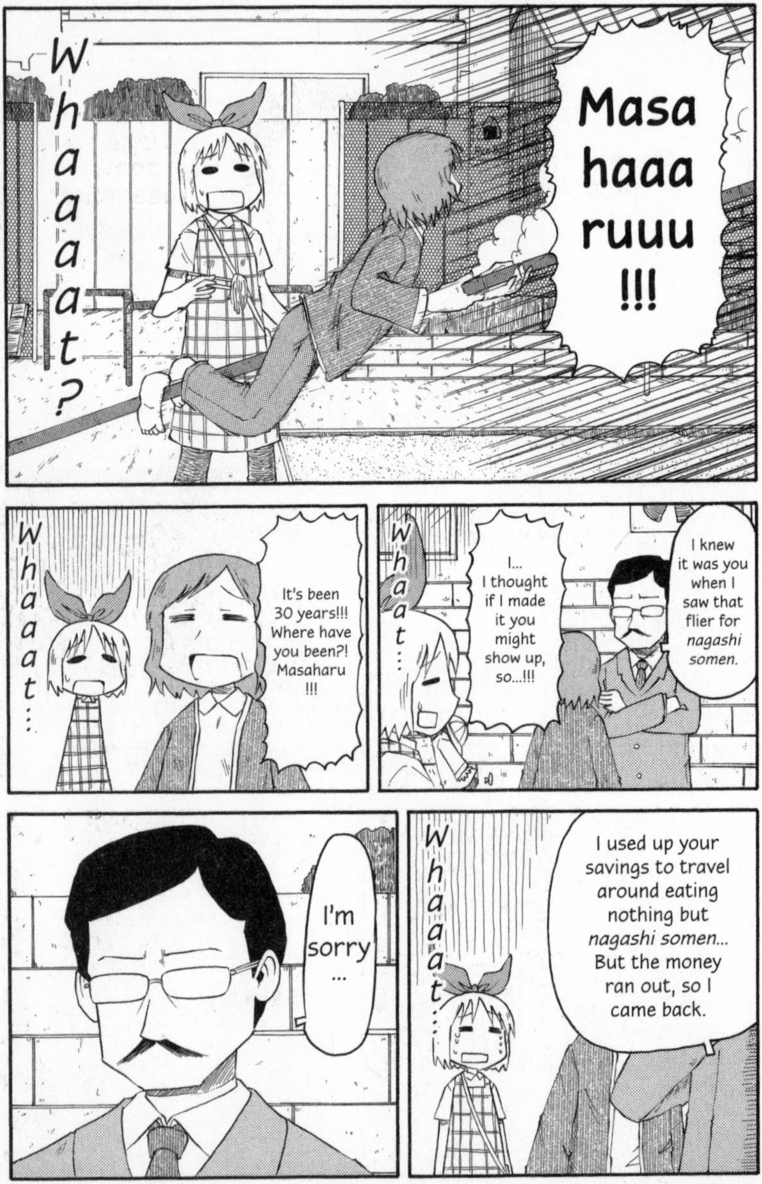
Masa haaa ruuu !!!
Whaaaat?
I knew it was you when I saw that flier for *nagashi somen.*
I... I thought if I made it you might show up, so...!!!
Whaaat...
It's been 30 years!!! Where have you been?! Masaharu !!!
Whaaaat...
I used up your savings to travel around eating nothing but *nagashi somen*... But the money ran out, so I came back.
Whaaaat...
I'm sorry ...

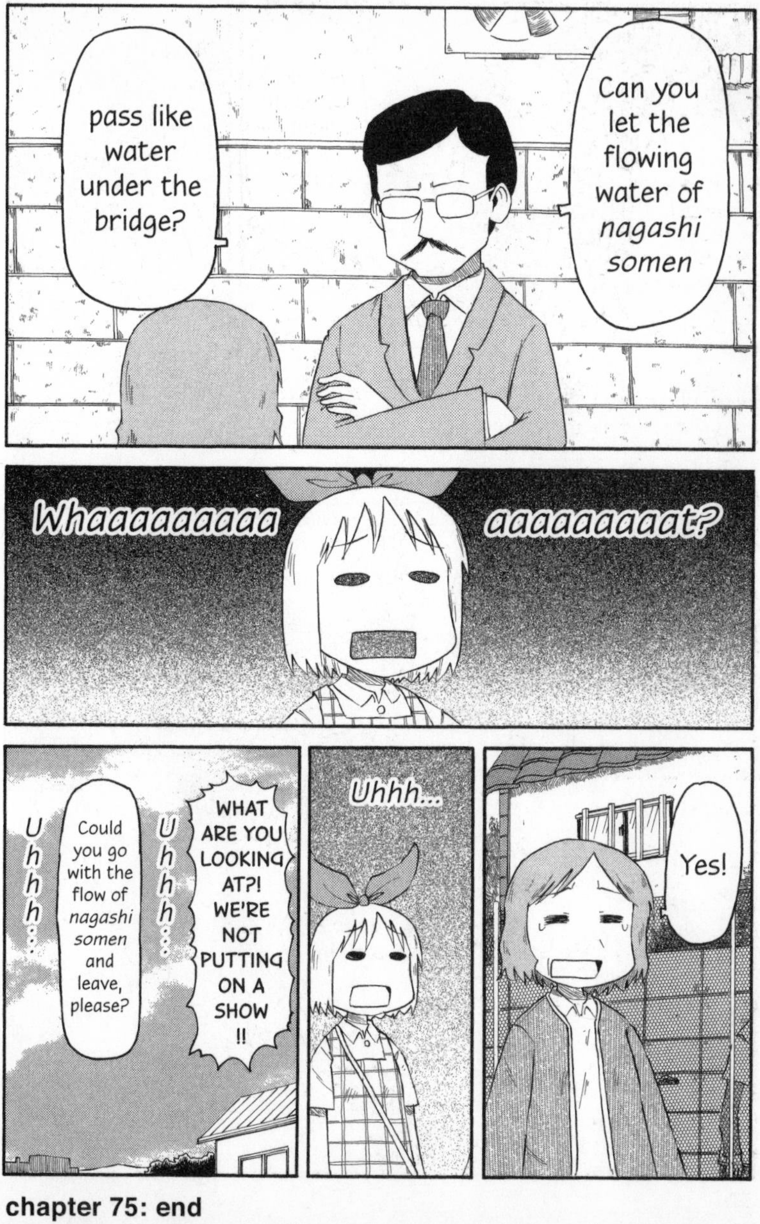
Can you let the flowing water of *nagashi somen*
pass like water under the bridge?
Whaaaaaaaaaa
aaaaaaaaat?
Yes!
Uhhh...
WHAT ARE YOU LOOKING AT?! WE'RE NOT PUTTING ON A SHOW !!
Uhhh...
Could you go with the flow of *nagashi somen* and leave, please?
Uhhh...

chapter 75: end

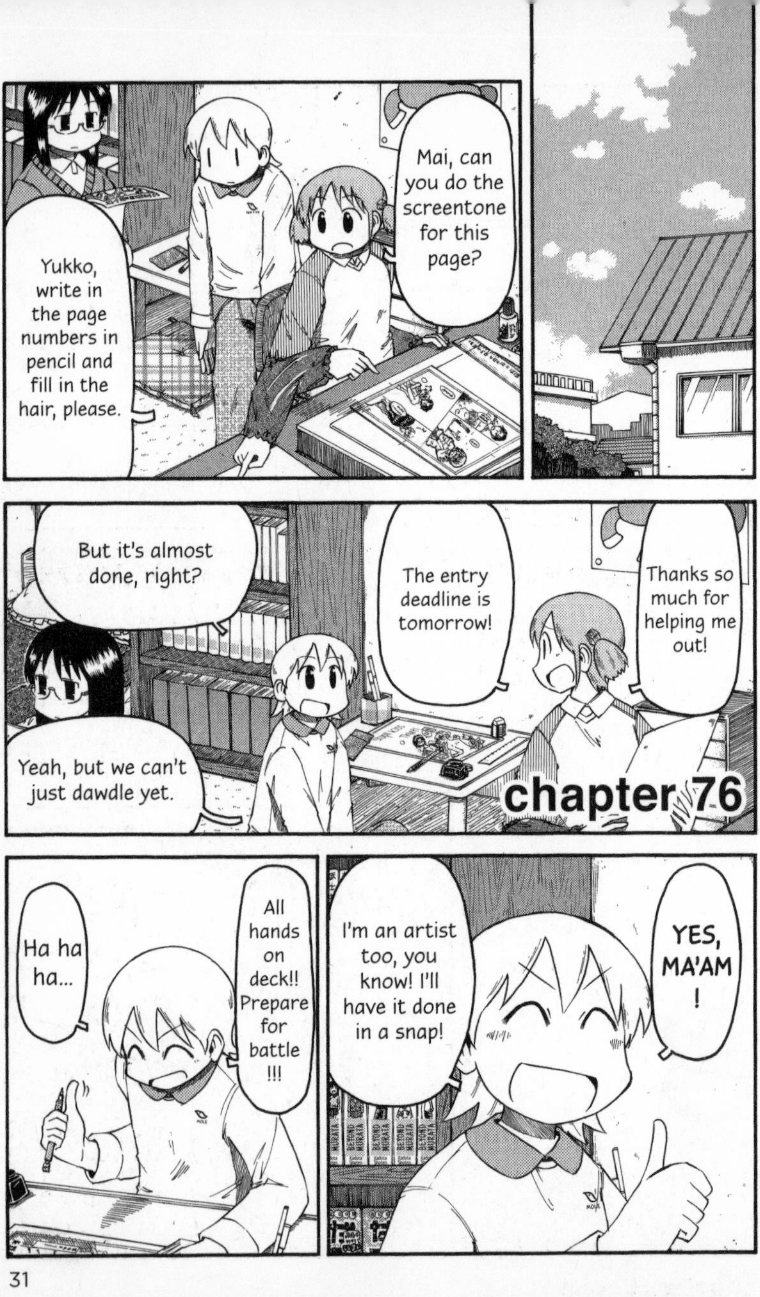
Mai, can you do the screentone for this page?
Yukko, write in the page numbers in pencil and fill in the hair, please.
Thanks so much for helping me out!
The entry deadline is tomorrow!
But it's almost done, right?
Yeah, but we can't just dawdle yet.
chapter 76
YES, MA'AM!
I'm an artist too, you know! I'll have it done in a snap!
All hands on deck!! Prepare for battle!!!
Ha ha ha...

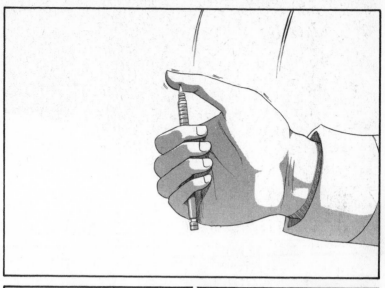

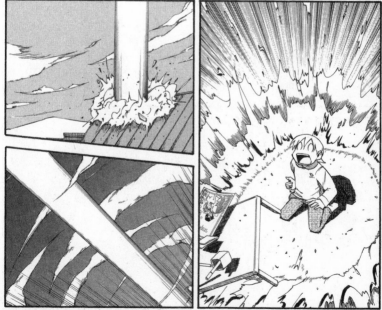

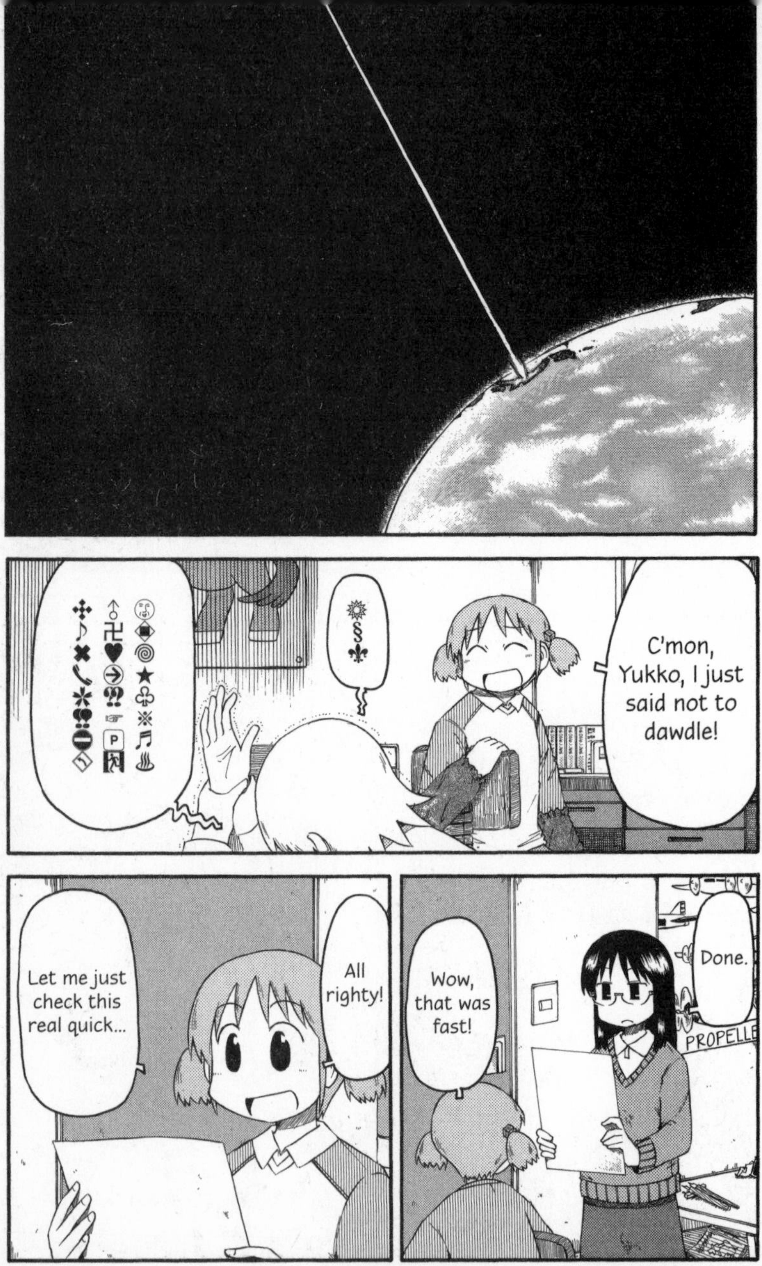
C'mon, Yukko, I just said not to dawdle!
Done.
Wow, that was fast!
PROPELLE
All righty!
Let me just check this real quick...

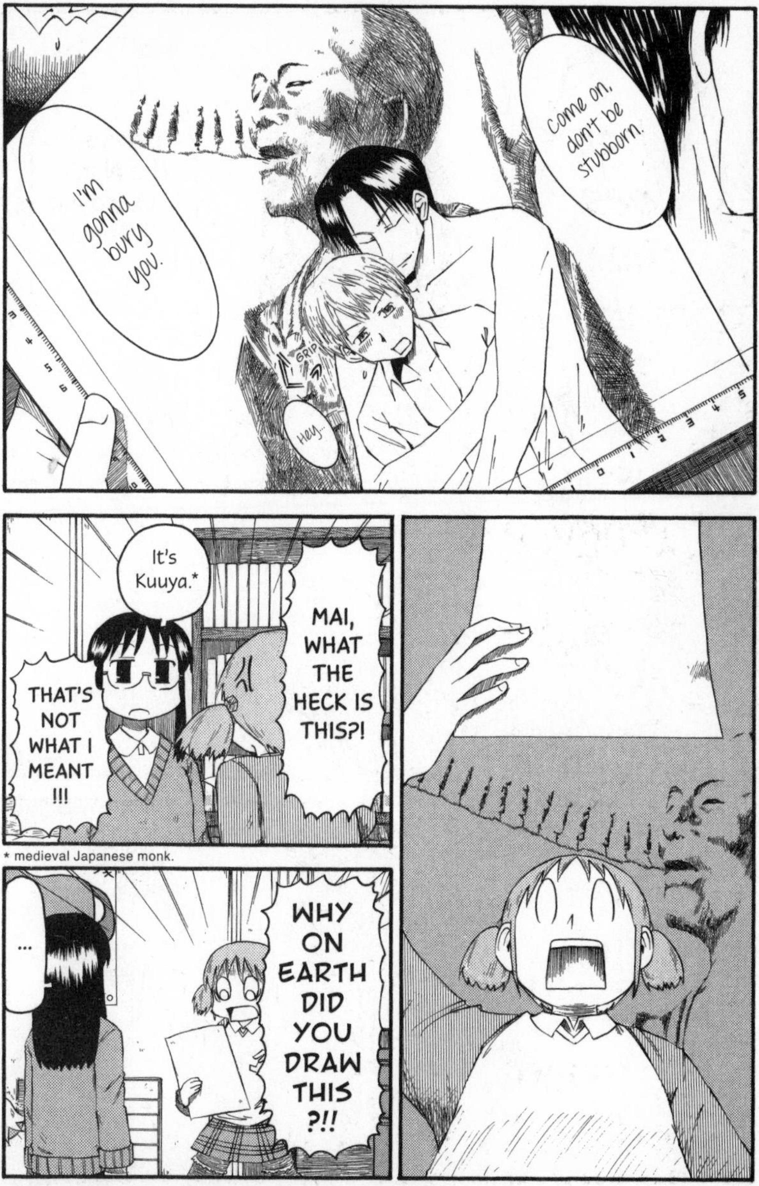
Come on, don't be stubborn.
I'm gonna bury you.
GRIP
Hey...
MAI, WHAT THE HECK IS THIS?!
It's Kuuya.*
THAT'S NOT WHAT I MEANT !!!
WHY ON EARTH DID YOU DRAW THIS ?!!
...

* medieval Japanese monk.

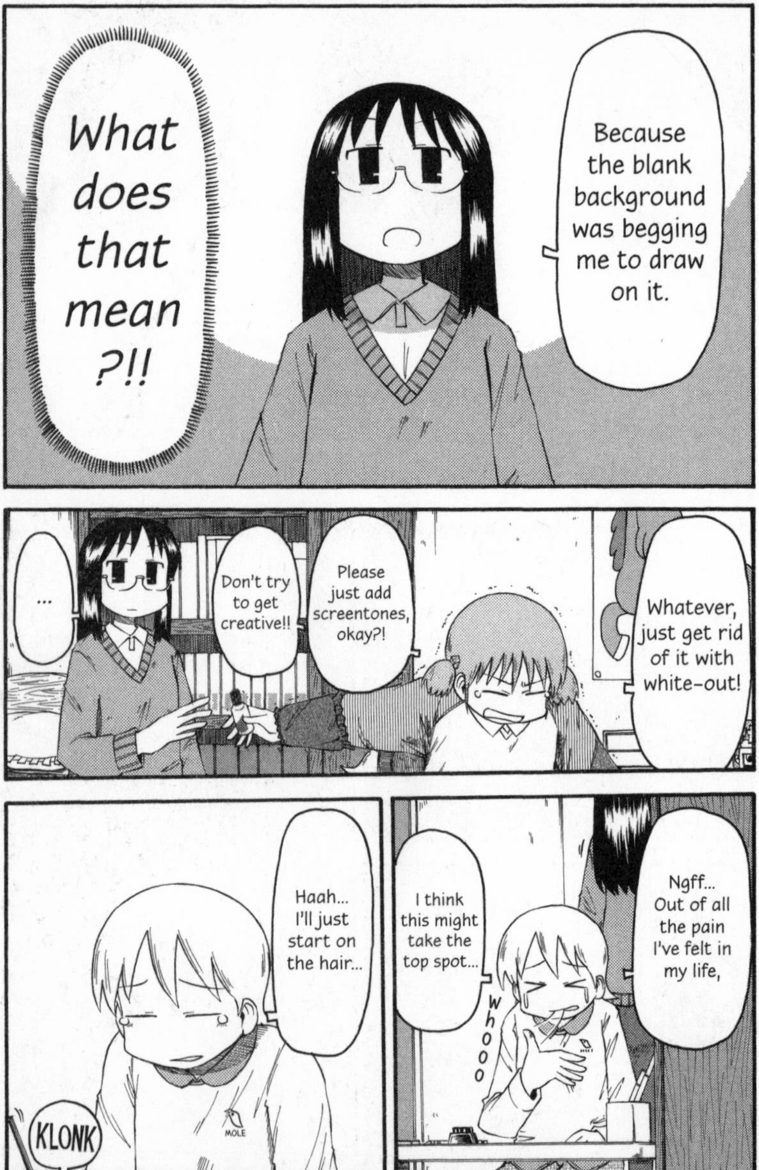
Because the blank background was begging me to draw on it.
What does that mean ?!!
Whatever, just get rid of it with white-out!
Please just add screentones, okay?!
Don't try to get creative!!
...
Ngff... Out of all the pain I've felt in my life,
I think this might take the top spot...
Whoooo
Haah... I'll just start on the hair...
MOLE
KLONK

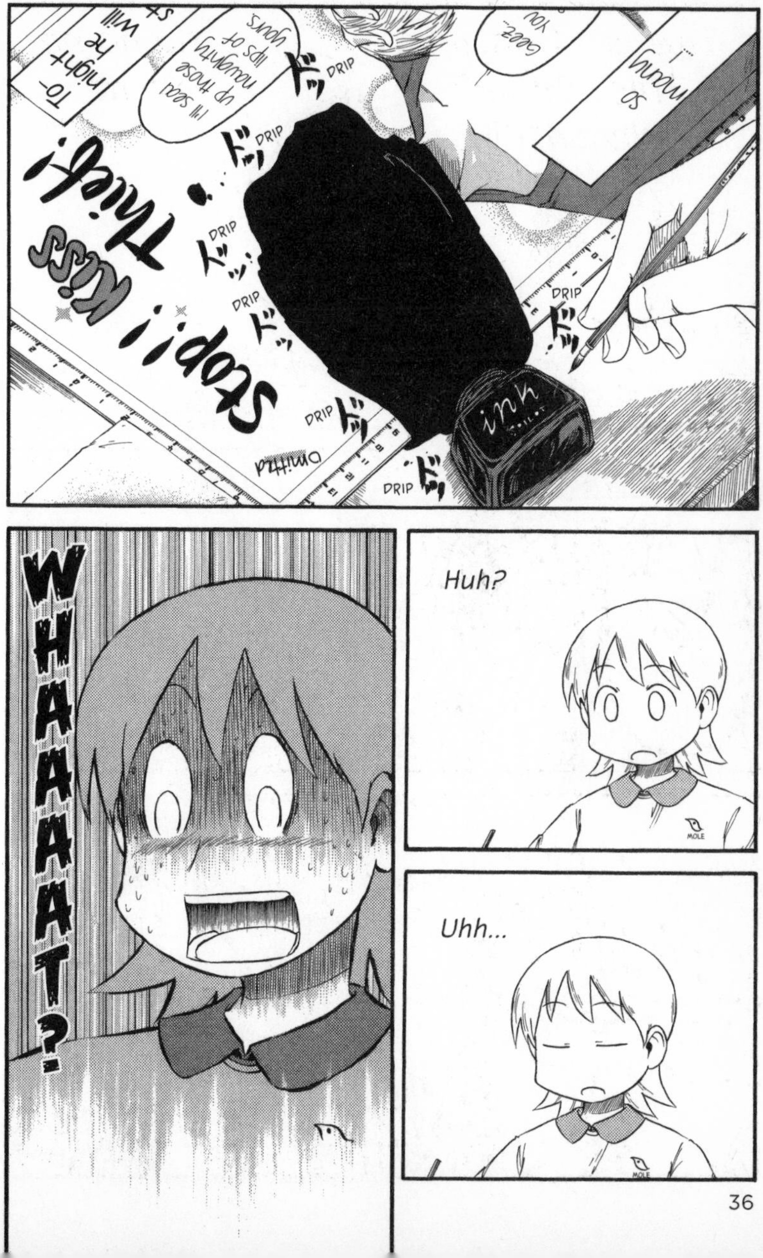
Stop!! Kiss Thief!
I'll seal up those naughty lips of yours.
To-night he will
Geez... you
DRIP ドッ
DRIP ドッ
DRIP ドッ
DRIP ドッ
DRIP ドッ
DRIP ドッ
ink
Huh?
Uhh...
WHAAAAAT?!

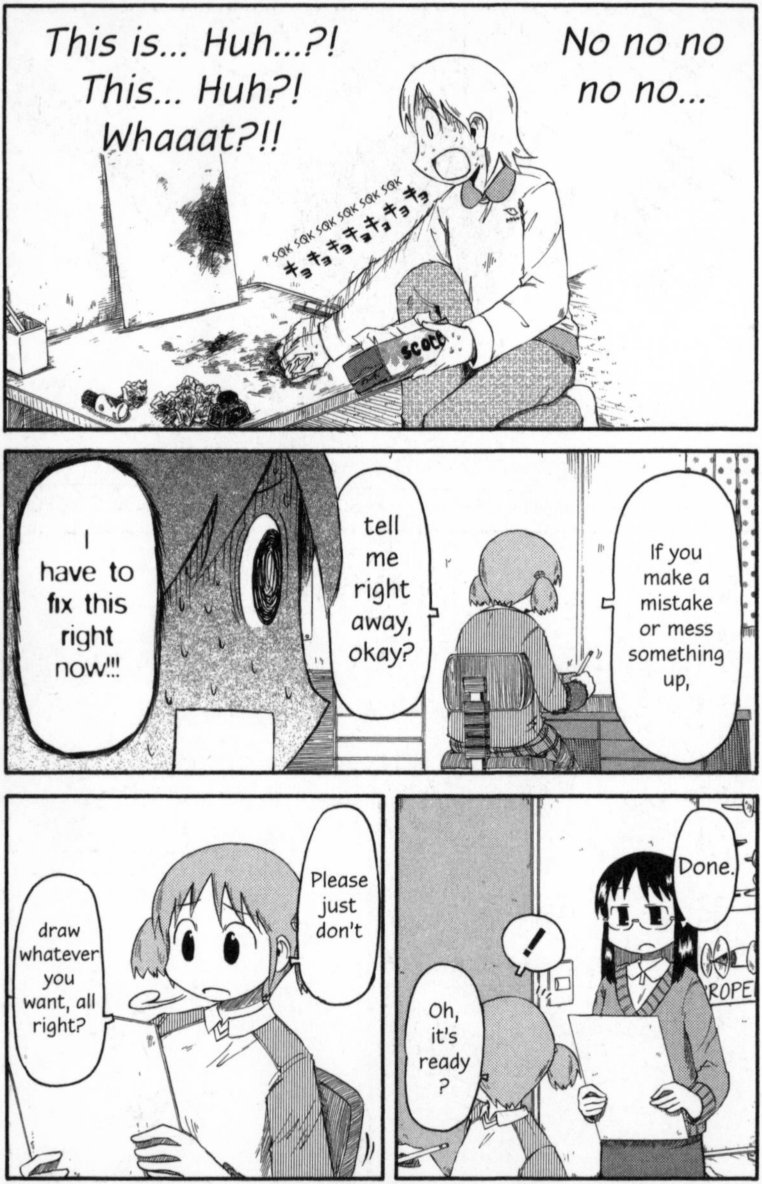
No no no no no...
This is... Huh...?! This... Huh?! Whaaat?!!
sqk sqk sqk sqk sqk sqk
scott
If you make a mistake or mess something up,
tell me right away, okay?
I have to fix this right now!!!
Done.
!
Oh, it's ready?
Please just don't
draw whatever you want, all right?
PROPE

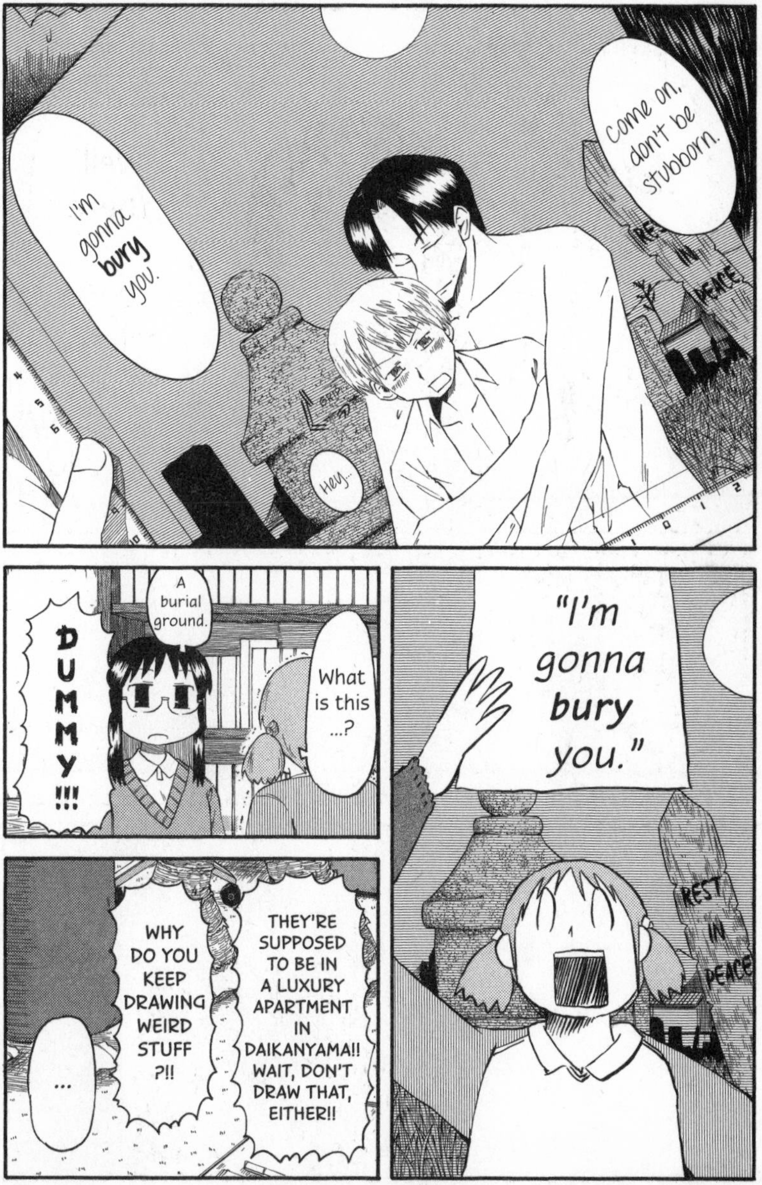

Come on, don't be stubborn.
REST IN PEACE
I'm gonna bury you.
Hey...
"I'm gonna bury you."
REST IN PEACE
What is this ...?
A burial ground.
DUMMY!!!
THEY'RE SUPPOSED TO BE IN A LUXURY APARTMENT IN DAIKANYAMA!! WAIT, DON'T DRAW THAT, EITHER!!
WHY DO YOU KEEP DRAWING WEIRD STUFF?!!
...

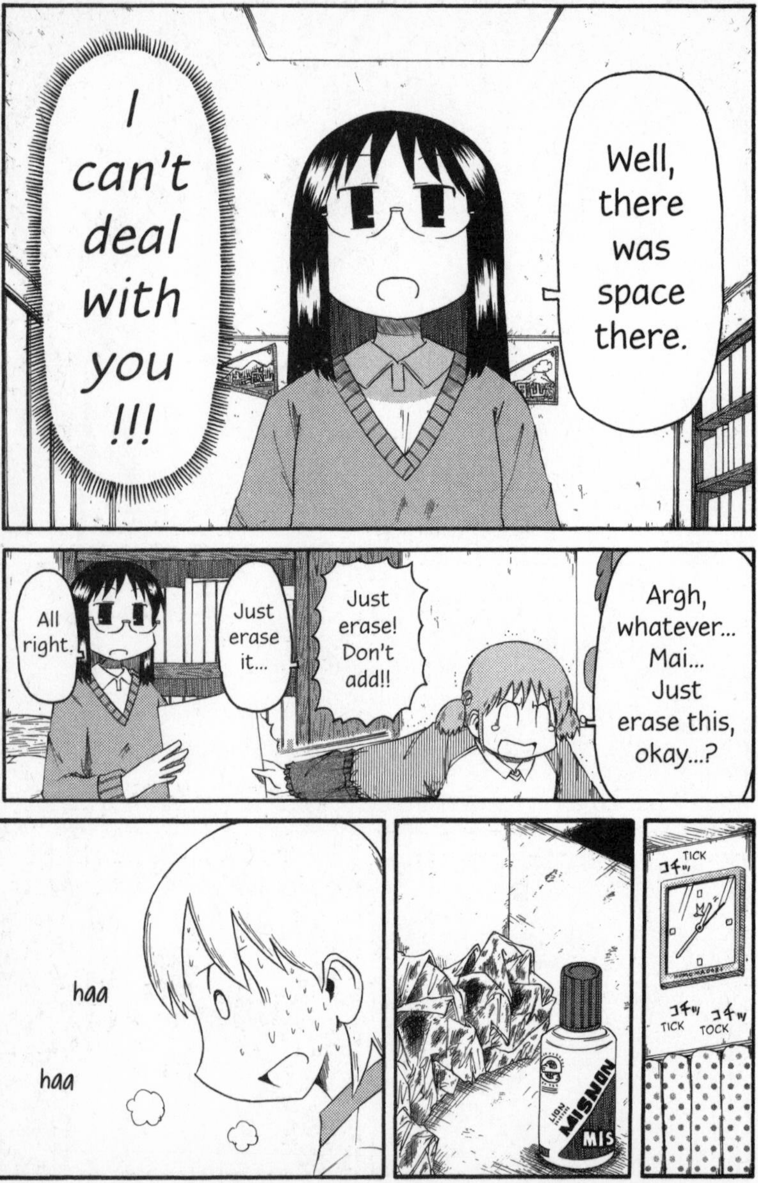
Well, there was space there.
I can't deal with you!!!
Argh, whatever... Mai... Just erase this, okay...?
Just erase! Don't add!!
Just erase it...
All right.
コチッ TICK
コチッ TOCK
コチッ TICK
LION
MISNON
MIS
haa
haa

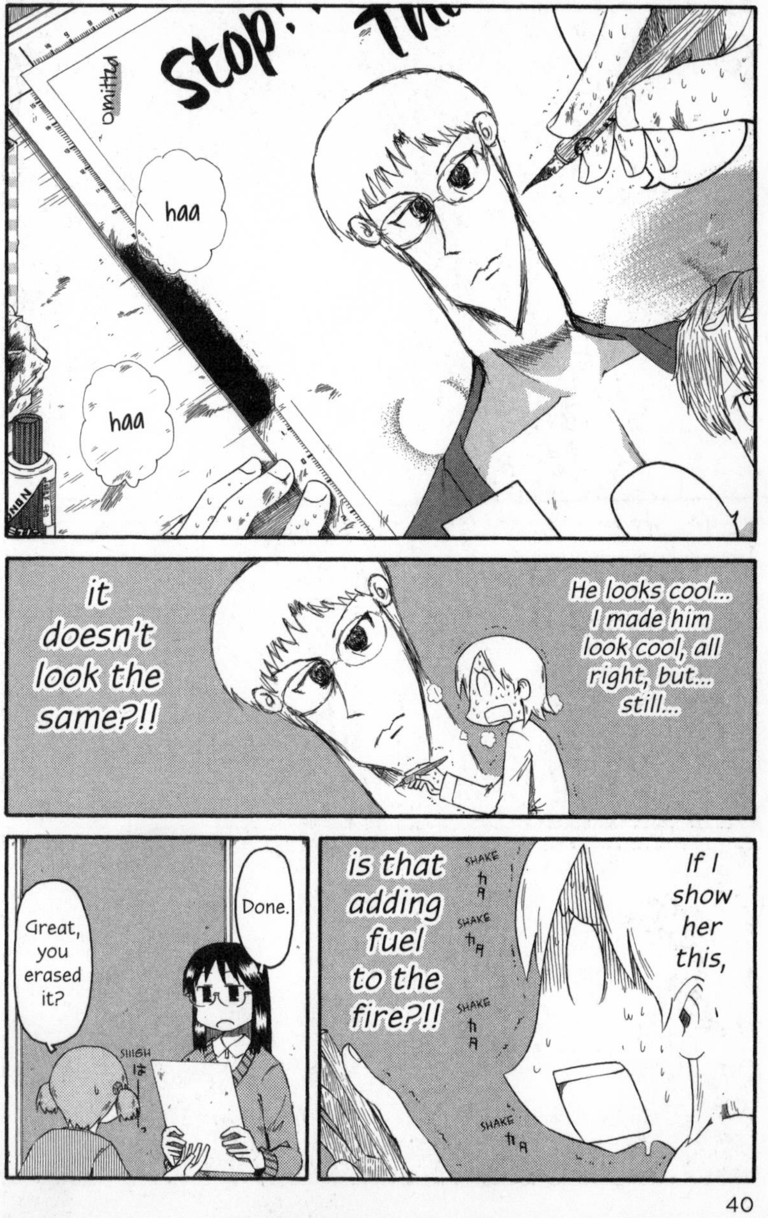
Stop!
Omitted
haa
haa
He looks cool... I made him look cool, all right, but... still...
it doesn't look the same?!!
If I show her this,
SHAKE カタ
SHAKE カタ
SHAKE カタ
SHAKE カタ
is that adding fuel to the fire?!!
Done.
Great, you erased it?
SIGH は

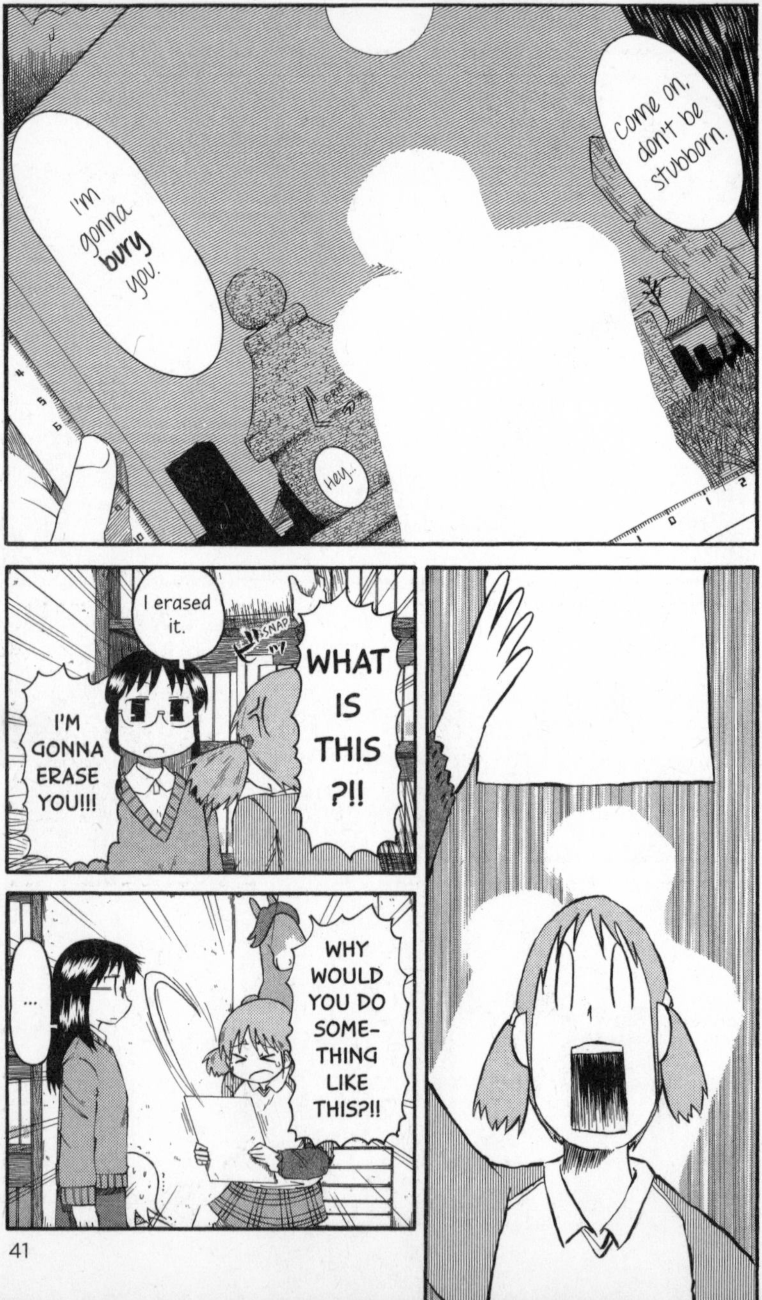
Come on, don't be stubborn.
I'm gonna bury you.
Hey...
SNAP
WHAT IS THIS?!!
I erased it.
I'M GONNA ERASE YOU!!!
WHY WOULD YOU DO SOME-THING LIKE THIS?!!
...

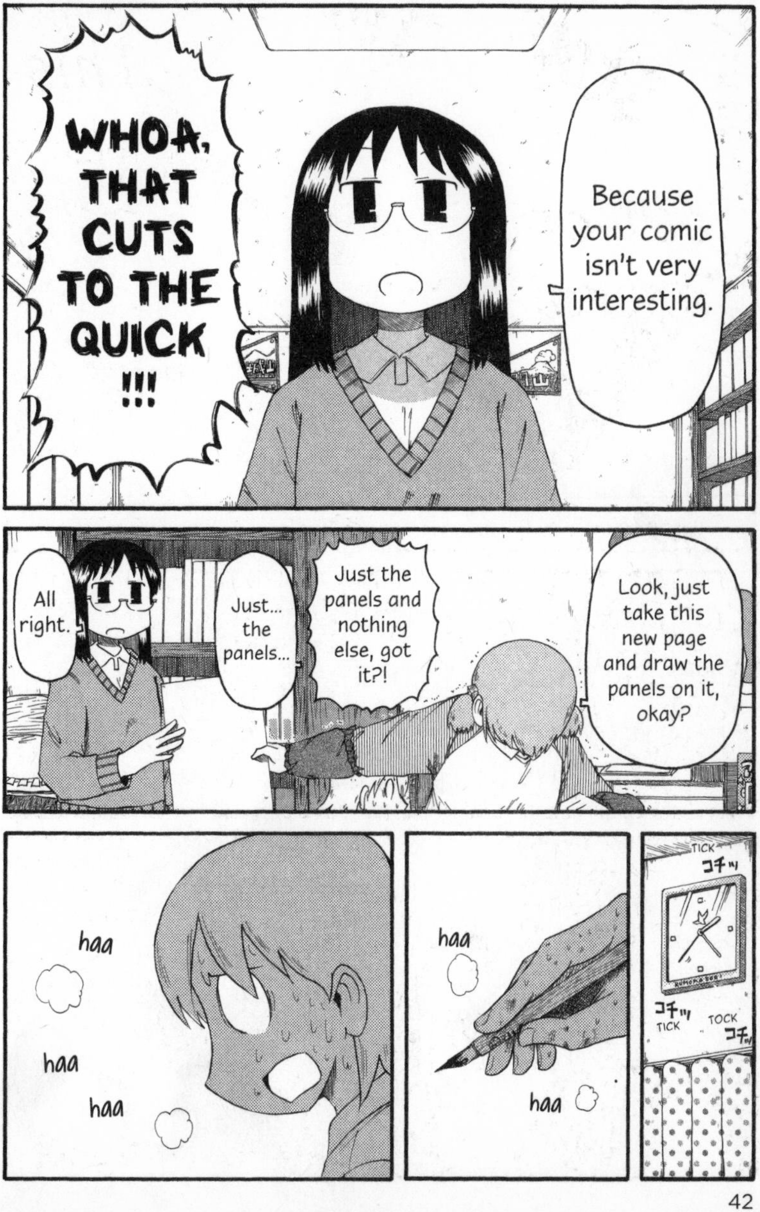
Because your comic isn't very interesting.
WHOA, THAT CUTS TO THE QUICK!!!
Look, just take this new page and draw the panels on it, okay?
Just the panels and nothing else, got it?!
Just... the panels...
All right.
TICK
コチッ
コチッ
TICK
TOCK
コチッ
haa
haa
haa
haa
haa

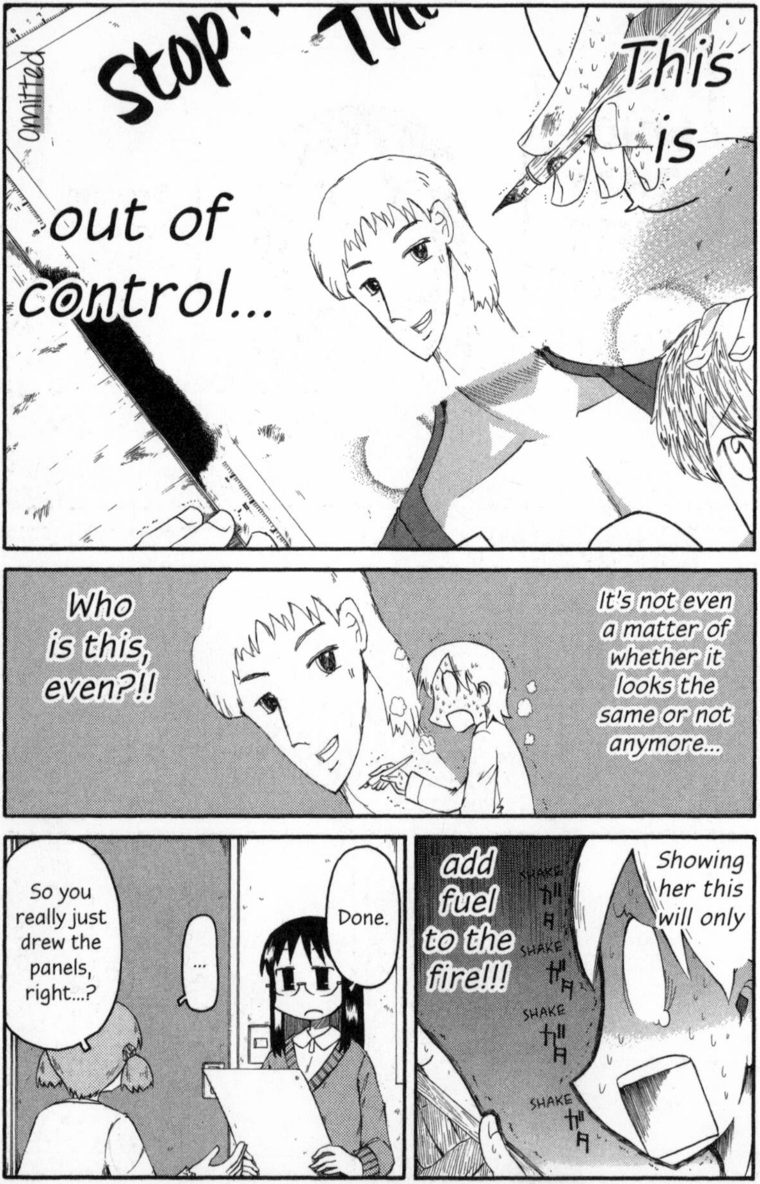
Stop!
omitted
This is
out of control...
It's not even a matter of whether it looks the same or not anymore...
Who is this, even?!!
Showing her this will only
add fuel to the fire!!!
SHAKE ガタ
SHAKE ガタ
SHAKE ガタ
SHAKE ガタ
Done.
...
So you really just drew the panels, right...?

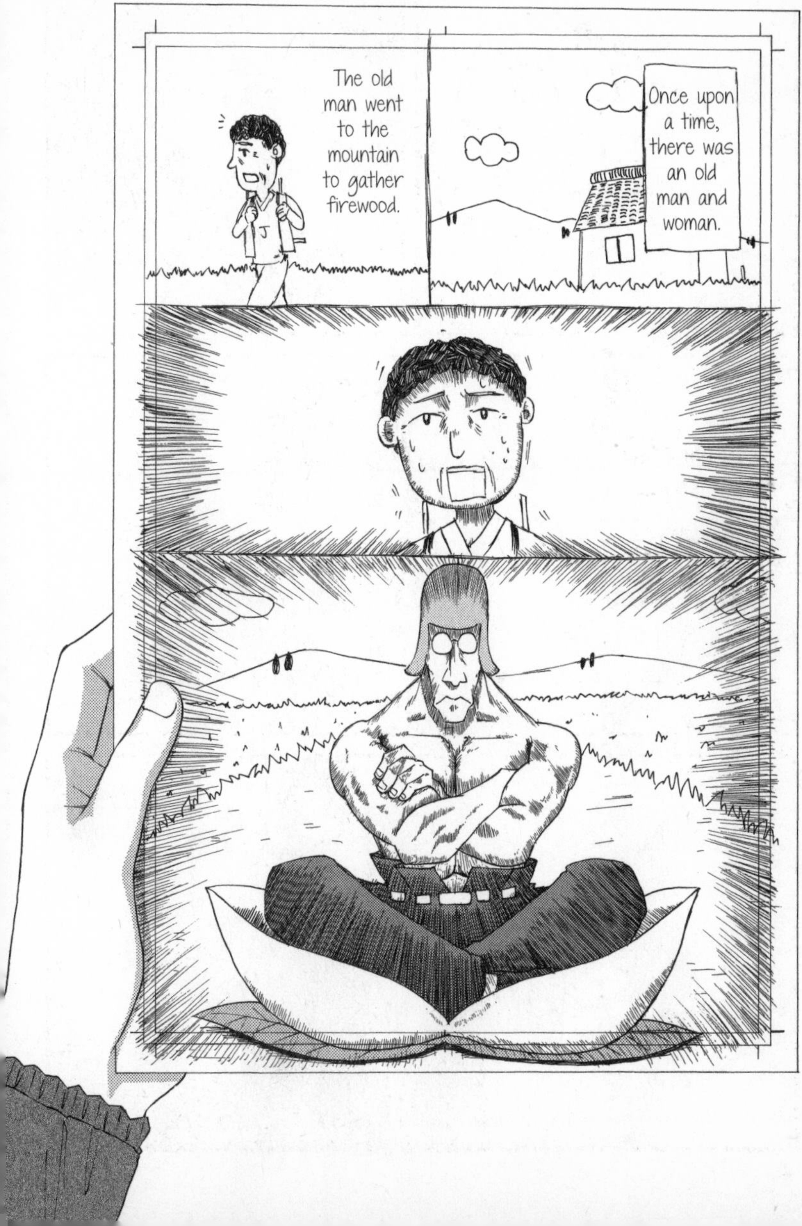
Once upon a time, there was an old man and woman.
The old man went to the mountain to gather firewood.

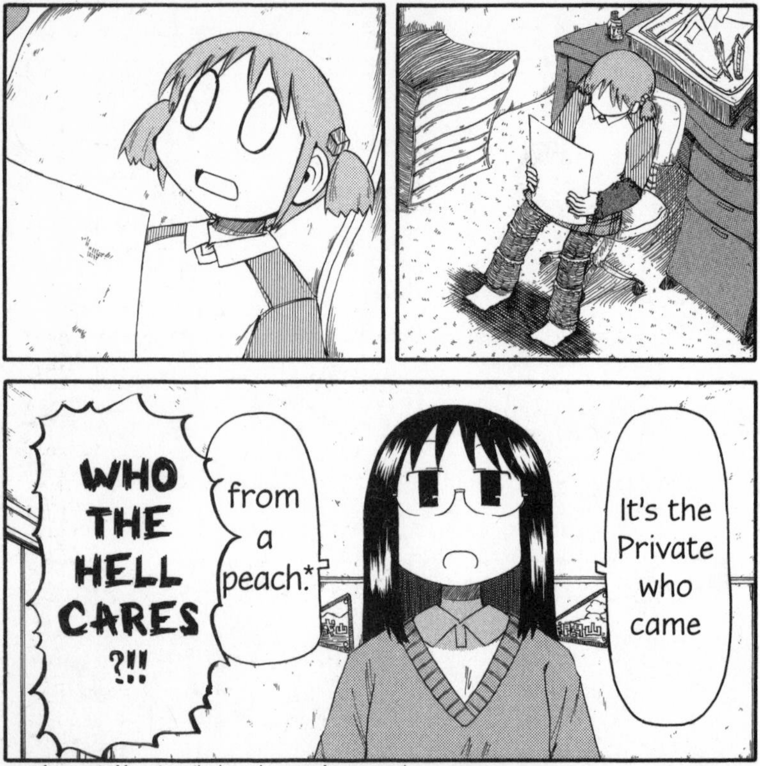
It's the Private who came
from a peach.*
WHO THE HELL CARES ?!!

* a reference to Momotaro, the boy who came from a peach.

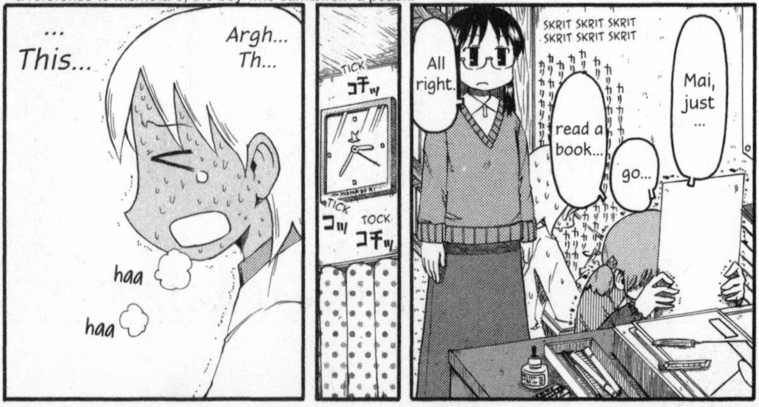
SKRIT SKRIT SKRIT SKRIT SKRIT SKRIT
Mai, just ...
go...
read a book...
All right.
TICK コチッ
TICK コッ
TOCK コチッ
Argh... Th...
... This...
haa
haa

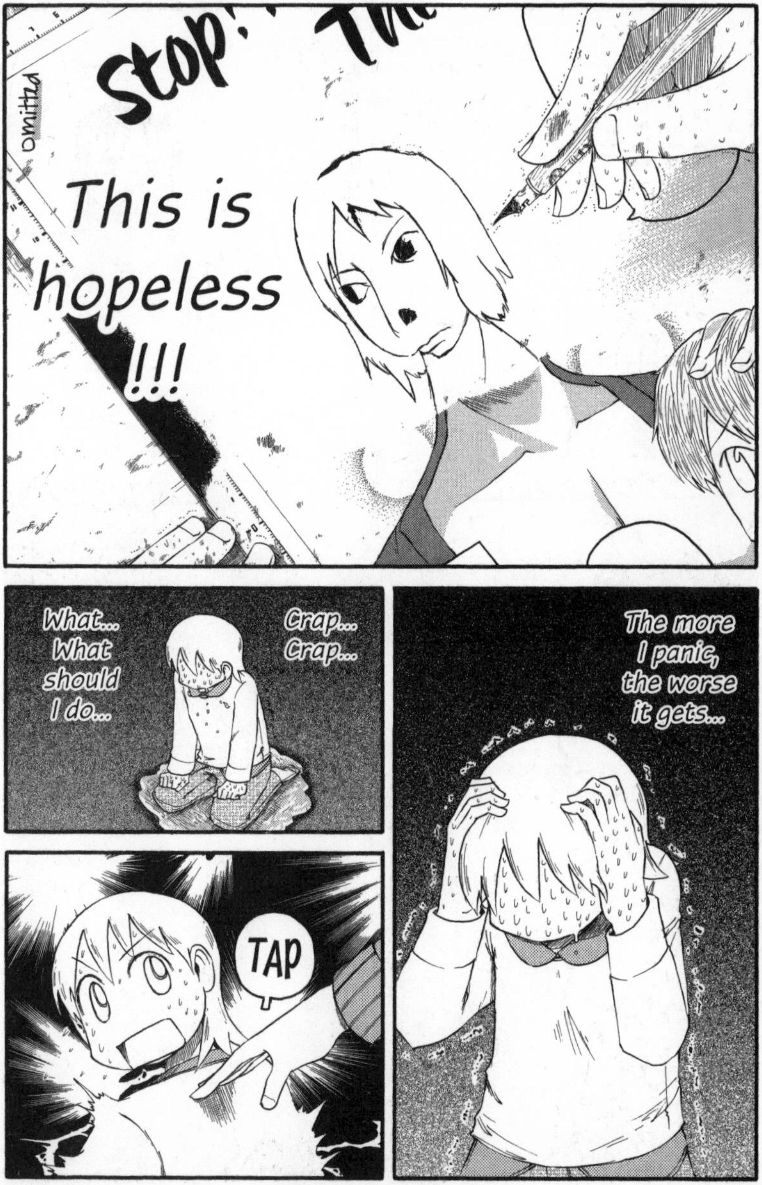
Stop!
omitted
This is hopeless !!!
The more I panic, the worse it gets...
Crap... Crap...
What... What should I do...
TAP

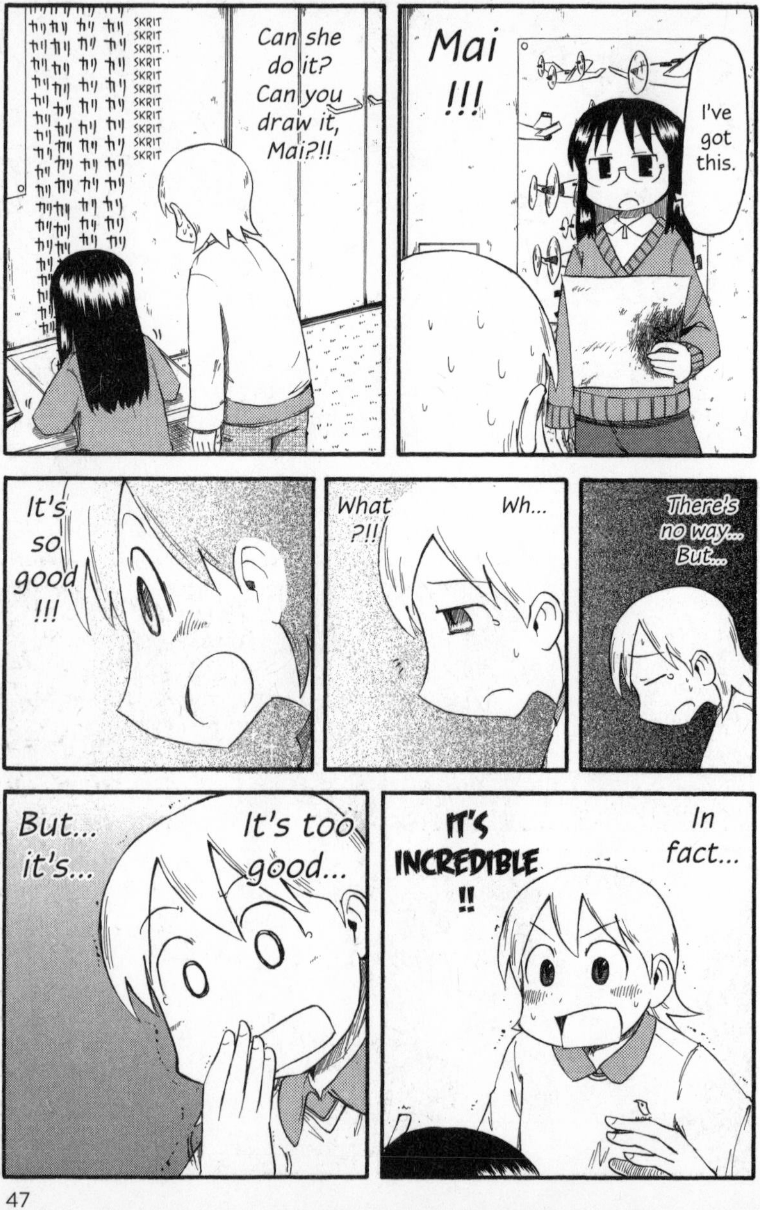
Mai !!!
I've got this.
Can she do it? Can you draw it, Mai?!!
SKRIT SKRIT SKRIT. SKRIT SKRIT SKRIT SKRIT SKRIT SKRIT SKRIT SKRIT
There's no way... But...
Wh...
What ?!!
It's so good !!!
In fact...
IT'S INCREDIBLE !!
It's too good...
But... it's...

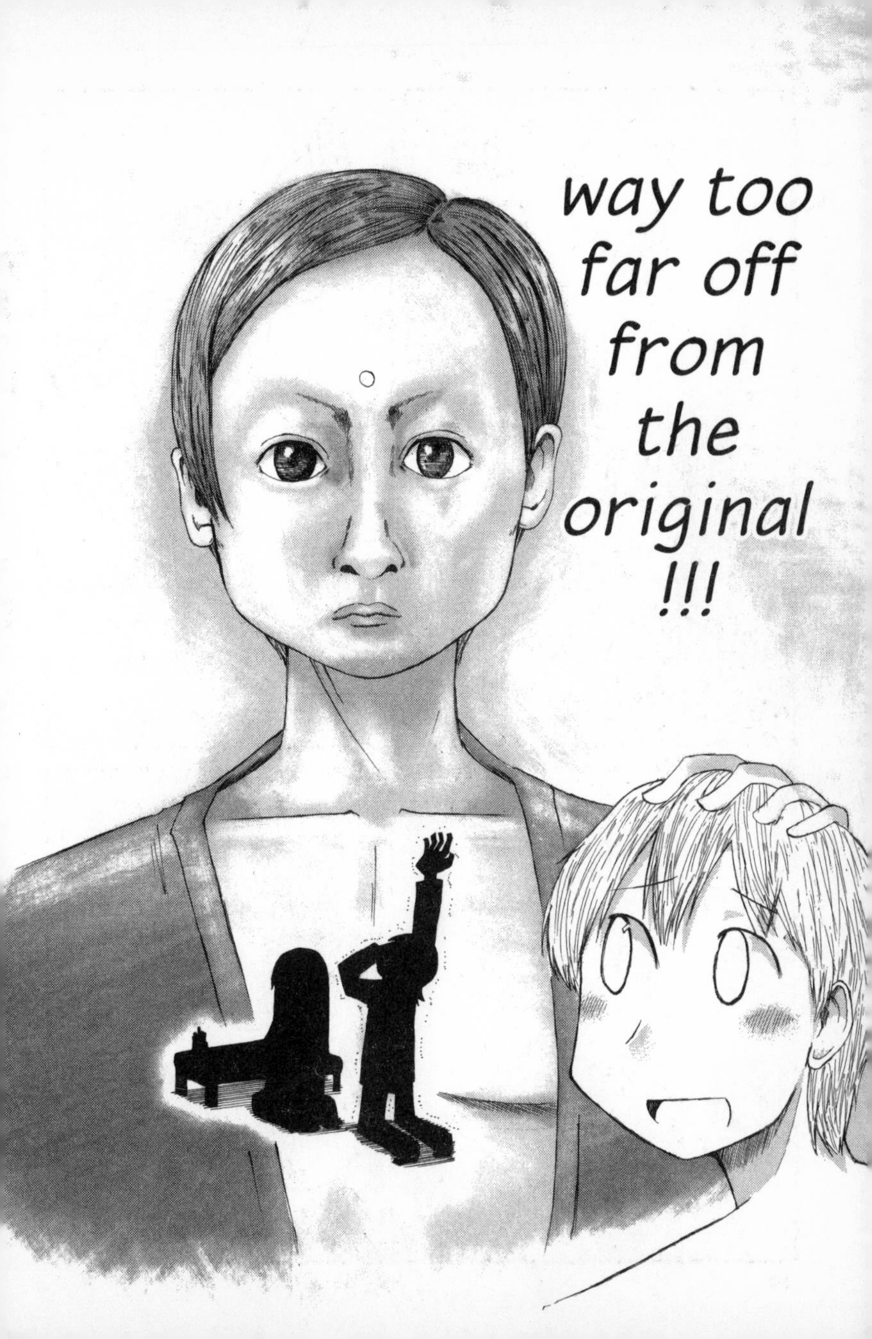
way too far off from the original !!!

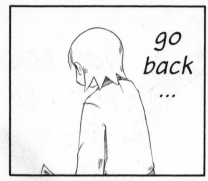

...
I'll just ...
go back ...
Back to when I didn't know left from right...
SQIK キュッ
SQIK キュッ
when everything still felt brand new.
Then I can show her!
Just the way
I am !!

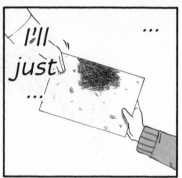

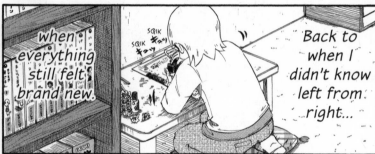

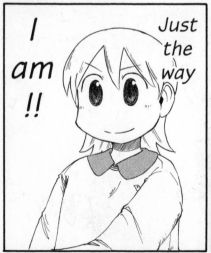

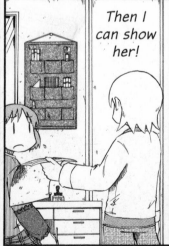

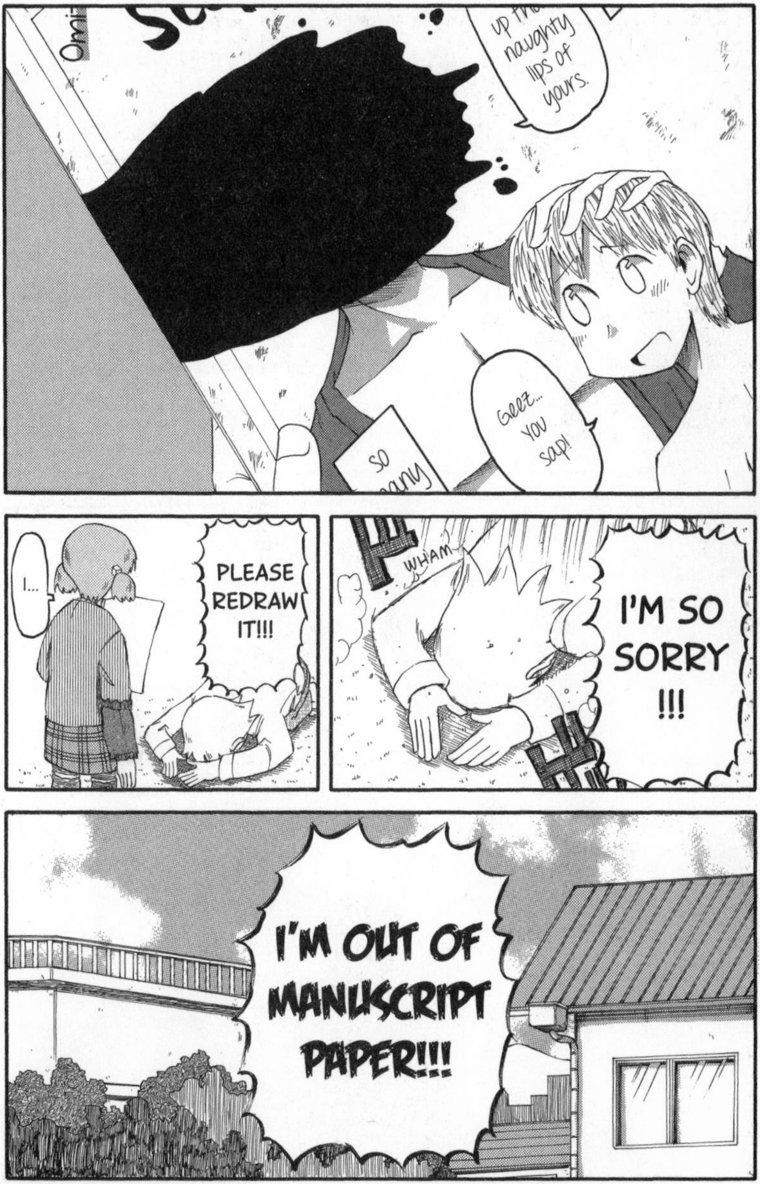

up the naughty lips of yours.
Geez... You sap!
So many
WHAM
I'M SO SORRY !!!
PLEASE REDRAW IT!!!
I...
I'M OUT OF MANUSCRIPT PAPER!!!

chapter 76: end

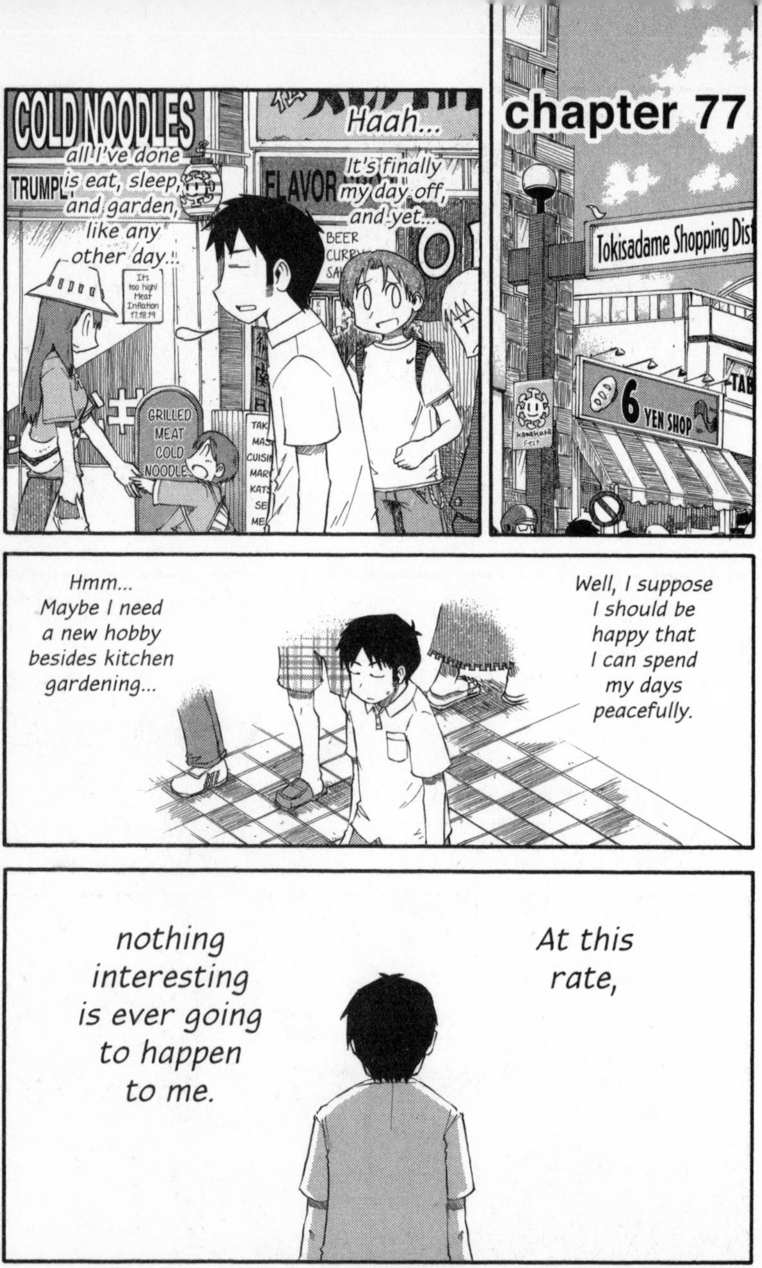
chapter 77
Tokisadame Shopping Dist
6 YEN SHOP
Haah...
It's finally my day off, and yet...
all I've done is eat, sleep, and garden, like any other day..!
COLD NOODLES
FLAVOR
BEER
It's too high! Meat Inflation 17.18.19
GRILLED MEAT COLD NOODLES
Well, I suppose I should be happy that I can spend my days peacefully.
Hmm... Maybe I need a new hobby besides kitchen gardening...
At this rate,
nothing interesting is ever going to happen to me.

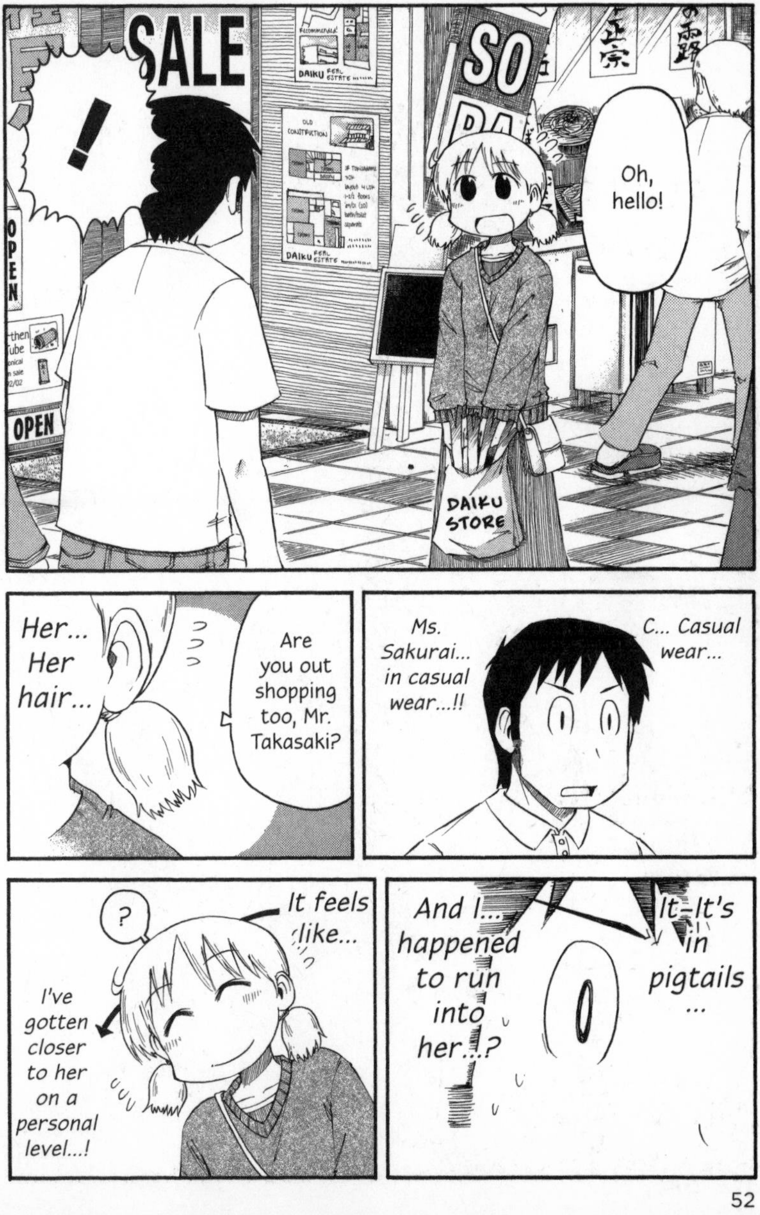
Oh, hello!
SO
SALE
!
DAIKU REAL ESTATE
OLD CONSTRUCTION
DAIKU REAL ESTATE
OPEN
OPEN
DAIKU STORE
C... Casual wear...
Ms. Sakurai... in casual wear...!!
Are you out shopping too, Mr. Takasaki?
Her... Her hair...
It-It's in pigtails ...
And I... happened to run into her...?
It feels like...
?
I've gotten closer to her on a personal level...!

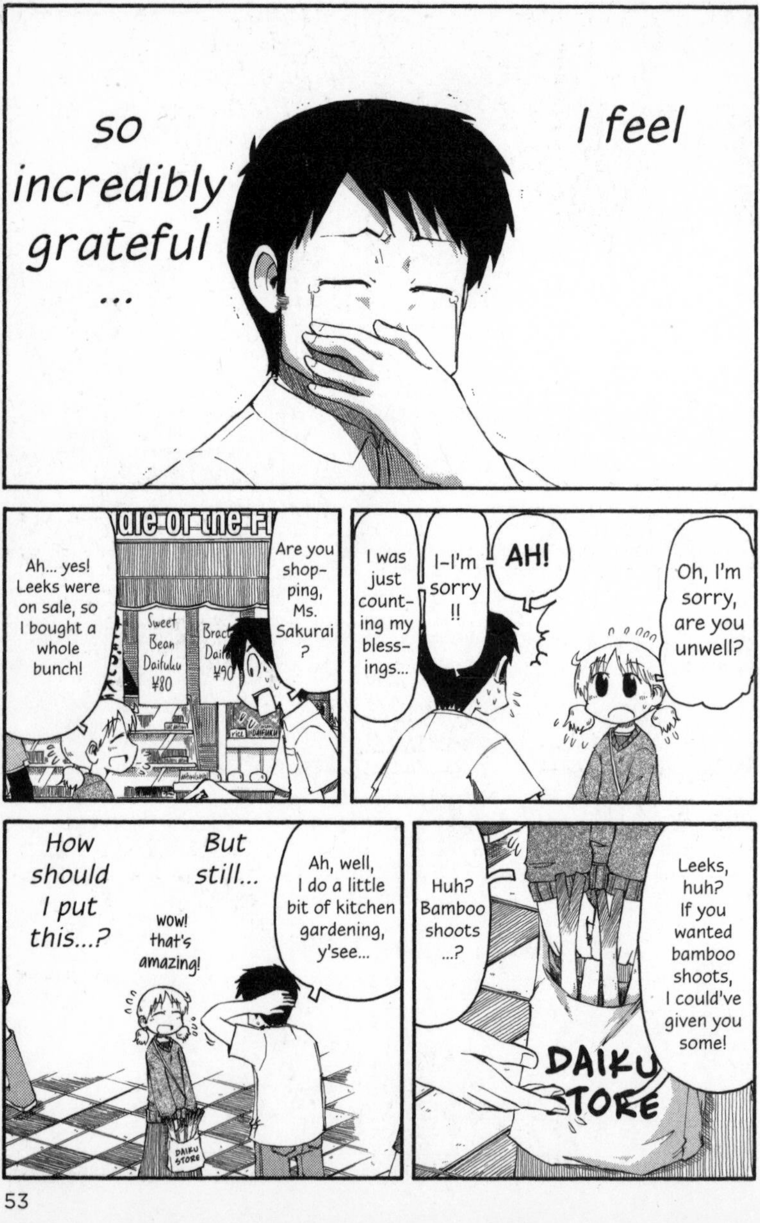
I feel
so incredibly grateful ...
Oh, I'm sorry, are you unwell?
AH!
I-I'm sorry !!
I was just counting my blessings...
Are you shopping, Ms. Sakurai?
Sweet Bean Daifuku ¥80
Ah... yes! Leeks were on sale, so I bought a whole bunch!
Leeks, huh? If you wanted bamboo shoots, I could've given you some!
Huh? Bamboo shoots ...?
DAIKU STORE
Ah, well, I do a little bit of kitchen gardening, y'see...
WOW! that's amazing!
But still...
How should I put this...?
DAIKU STORE

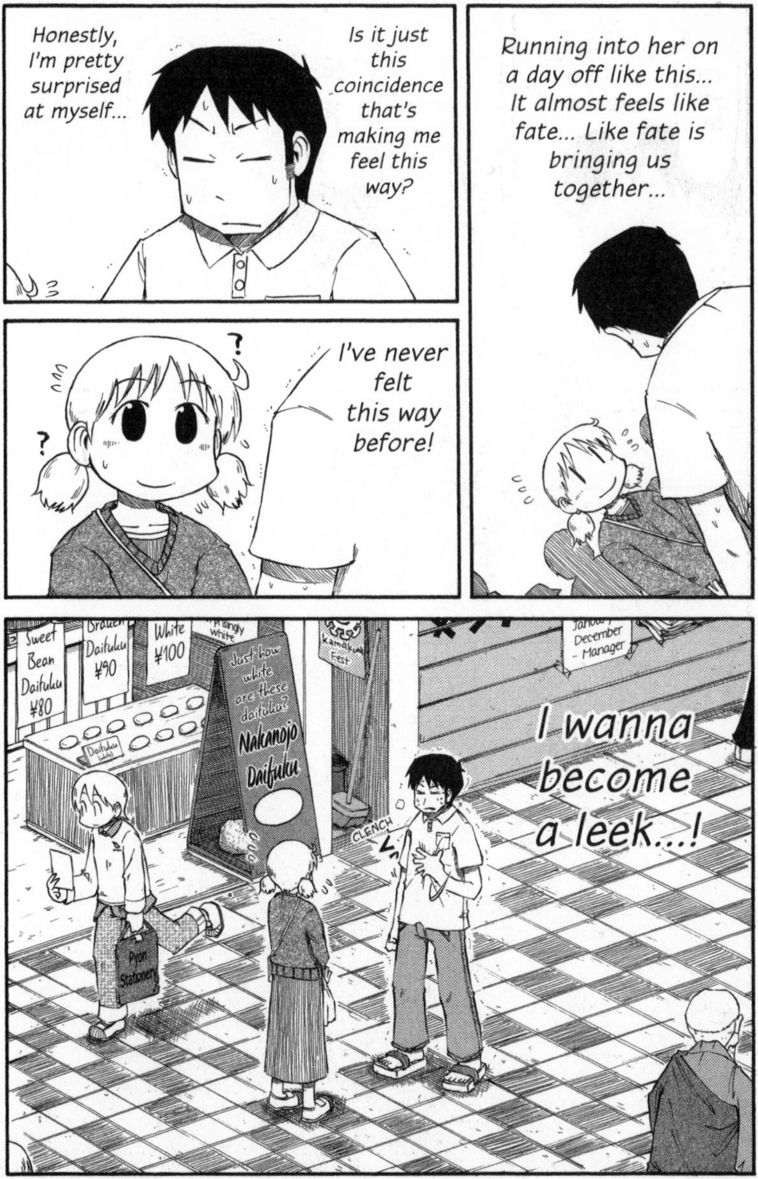
Running into her on a day off like this... It almost feels like fate... Like fate is bringing us together...
Is it just this coincidence that's making me feel this way?
Honestly, I'm pretty surprised at myself...
?
?
I've never felt this way before!
December - Manager
White ¥100
Sweet Bean Daifuku ¥80
Just how white are these daifuku? Nakanojo Daifuku
I wanna become a leek...!
CLENCH
Pyon Stationery

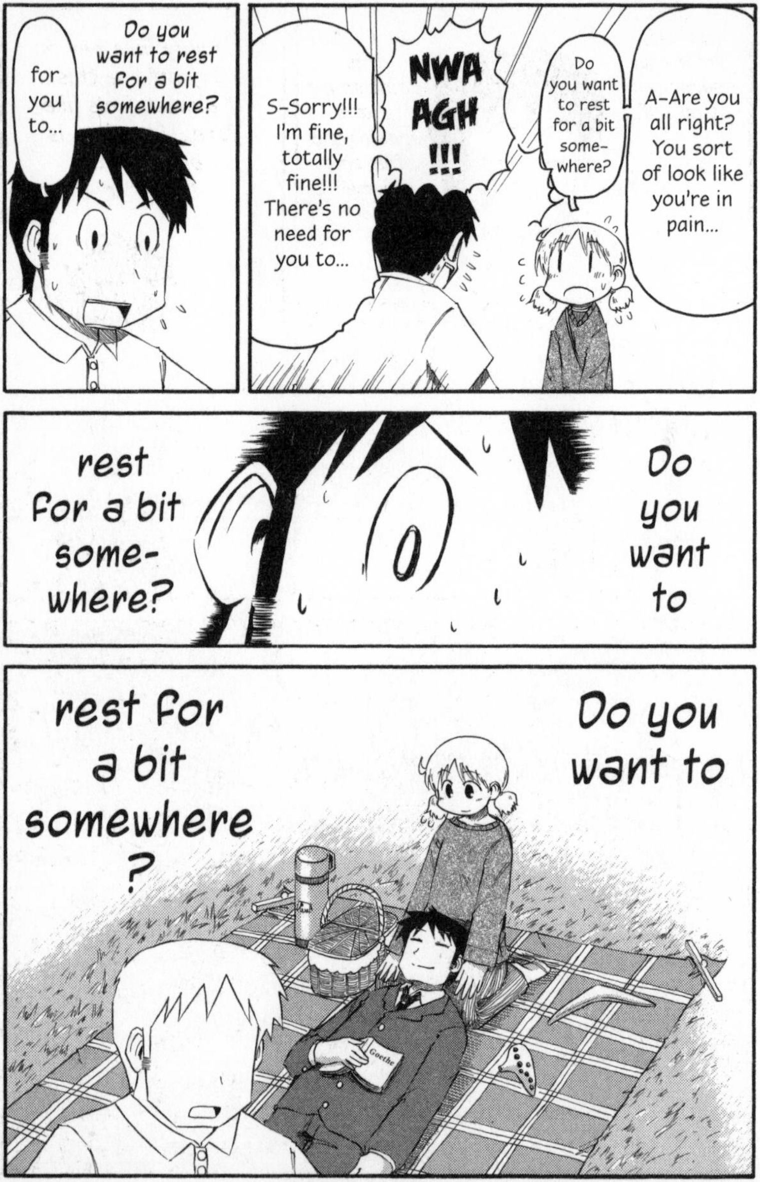
A-Are you all right? You sort of look like you're in pain...
Do you want to rest for a bit some-where?
NWAAGH!!!
S-Sorry!!! I'm fine, totally fine!!! There's no need for you to...
Do you want to rest for a bit somewhere?
for you to...
Do you want to
rest for a bit some-where?
Do you want to
rest for a bit somewhere ?
Goethe

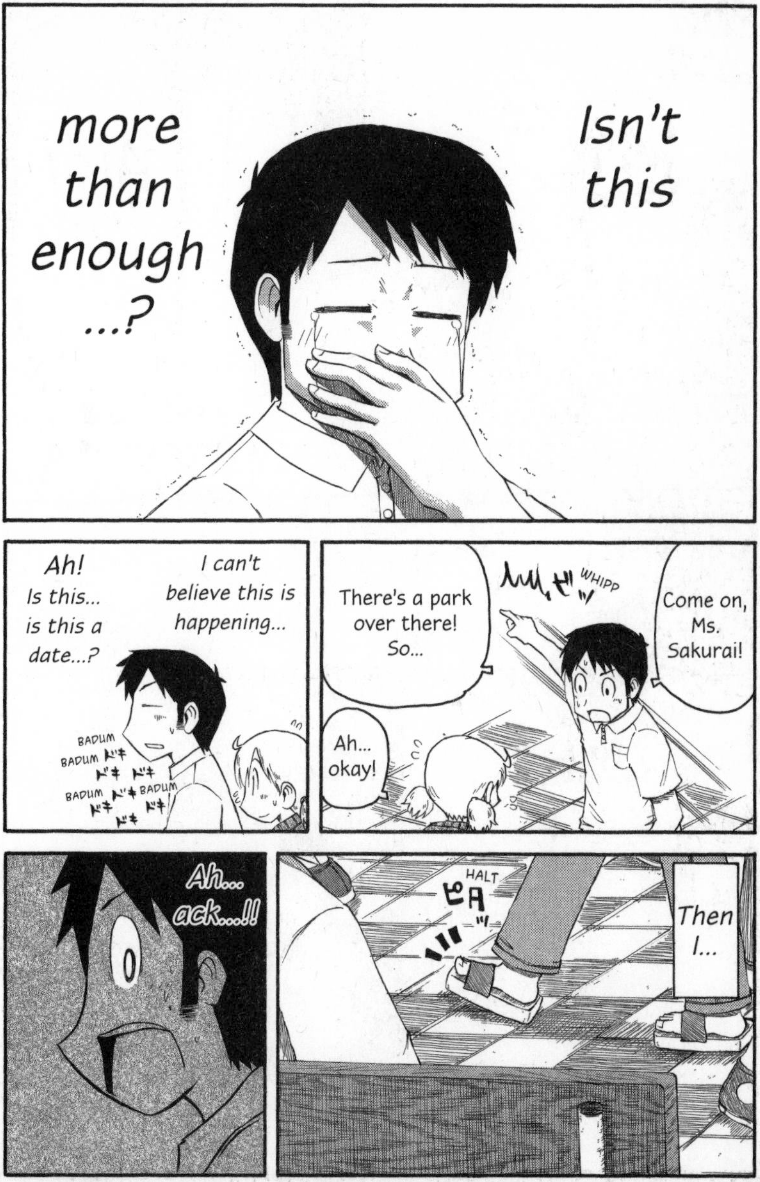
Isn't this
more than enough ...?
Come on, Ms. Sakurai!
WHIPP
There's a park over there! So...
Ah... okay!
I can't believe this is happening...
Ah! Is this... is this a date...?
BADUM BADUM BADUM BADUM
ドキ ドキ ドキ ドキ ドキ ドキ ドキ
Then I...
HALT
Ah... ack...!!

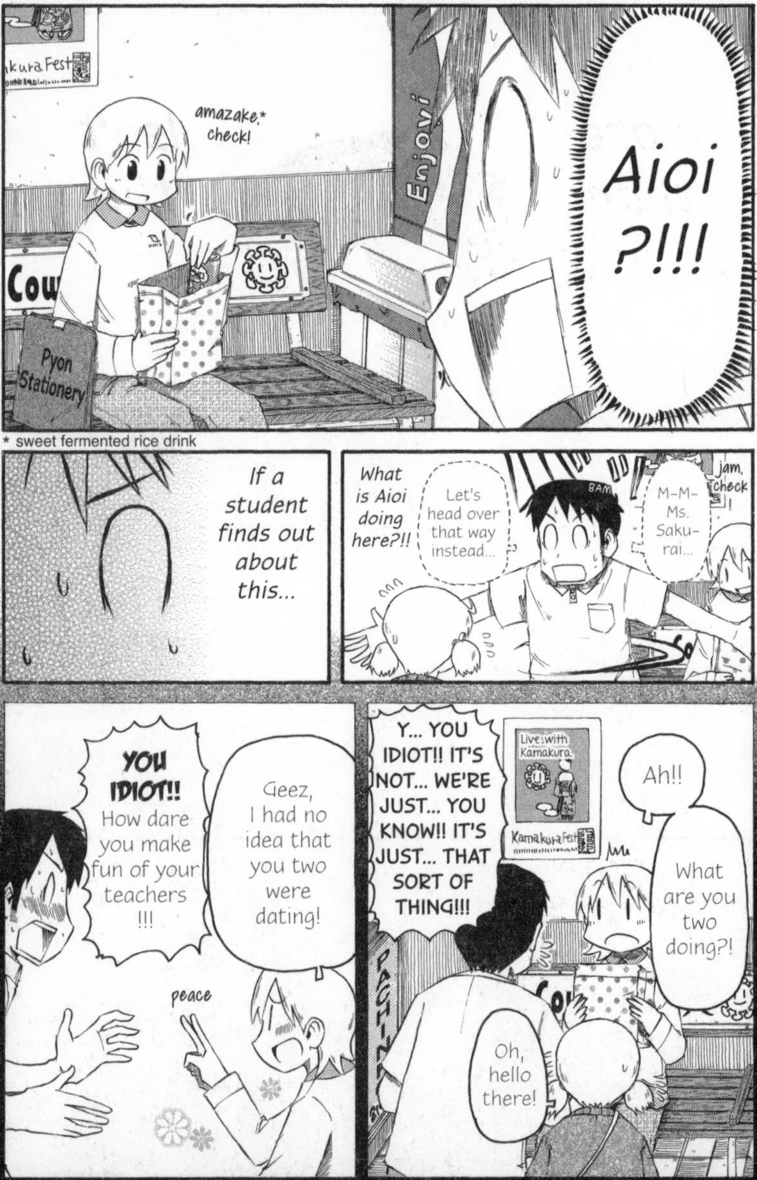
Aioi ?!!!
Enjoy!
kura Fest
amazake,* check!
Pyon Stationery
jam, check!
M-M-Ms. Sakurai...
BAM
Let's head over that way instead...
What is Aioi doing here?!!
If a student finds out about this...
Ah!!
Y... YOU IDIOT!! IT'S NOT... WE'RE JUST... YOU KNOW!! IT'S JUST... THAT SORT OF THING!!!
Live with Kamakura
Kamakura Fest
What are you two doing?!
Oh, hello there!
Geez, I had no idea that you two were dating!
YOU IDIOT!! How dare you make fun of your teachers!!!
peace

* sweet fermented rice drink

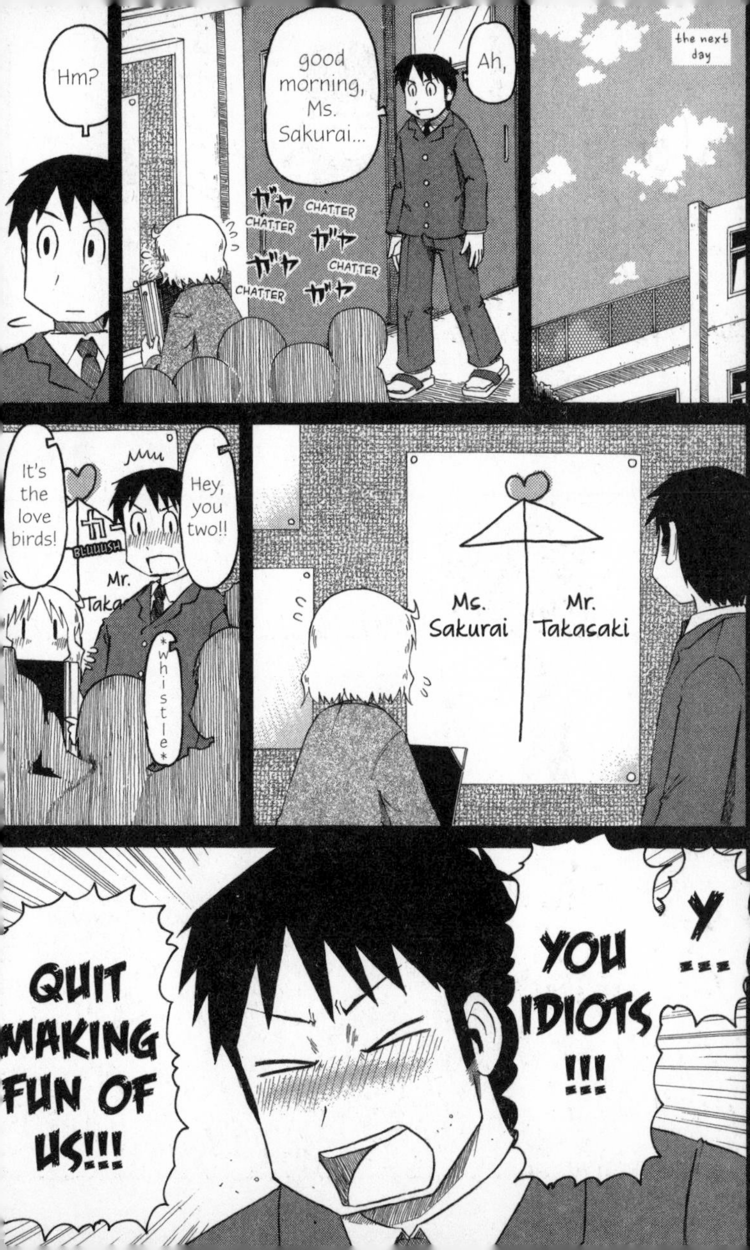
the next day
Ah,
good morning, Ms. Sakurai...
ガヤ CHATTER
ガヤ CHATTER
ガヤ CHATTER
ガヤ CHATTER
Hm?
Mr. Takasaki
Ms. Sakurai
Hey, you two!!
It's the love birds!
BLUUUSH
whistle
Y... YOU IDIOTS!!!
QUIT MAKING FUN OF US!!!

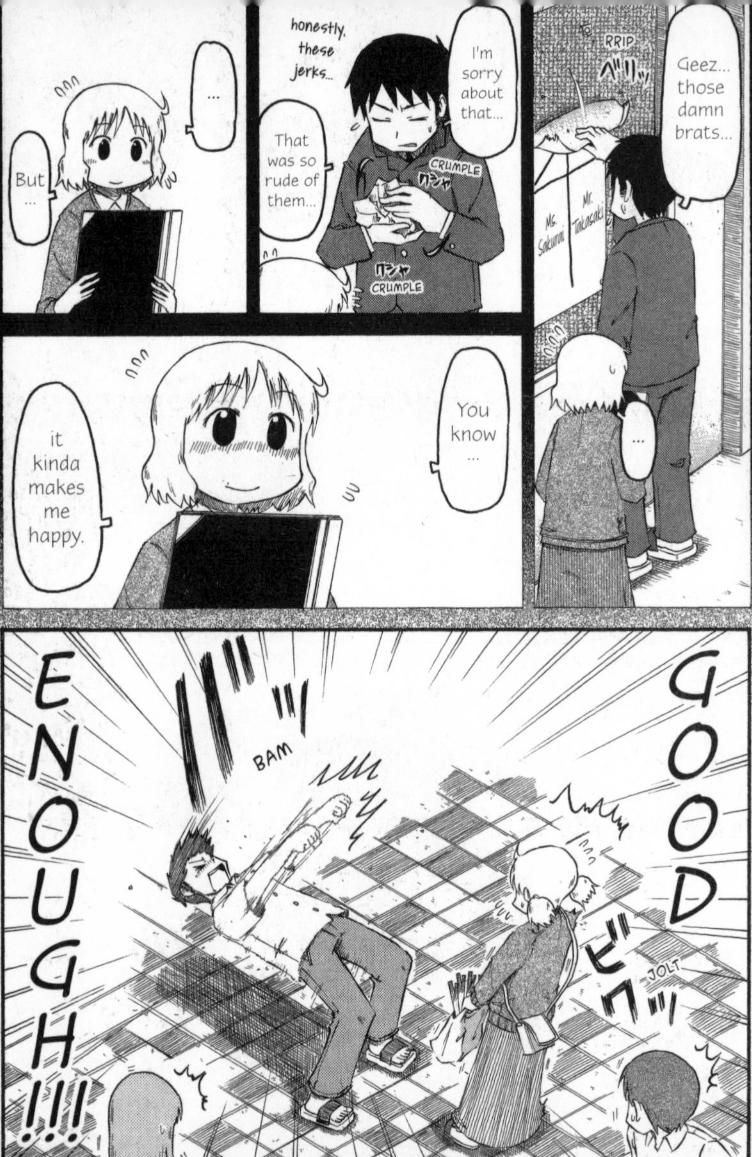
RRIP
ベリッ
Geez... those damn brats...
Mr. Takasaki
Ms. Sakurai
...
I'm sorry about that...
honestly, these jerks...
CRUMPLE
クシャ
That was so rude of them...
クシャ
CRUMPLE
...
But ...
You know ...
it kinda makes me happy.
GOOD ENOUGH!!!
BAM
JOLT
ビクッ

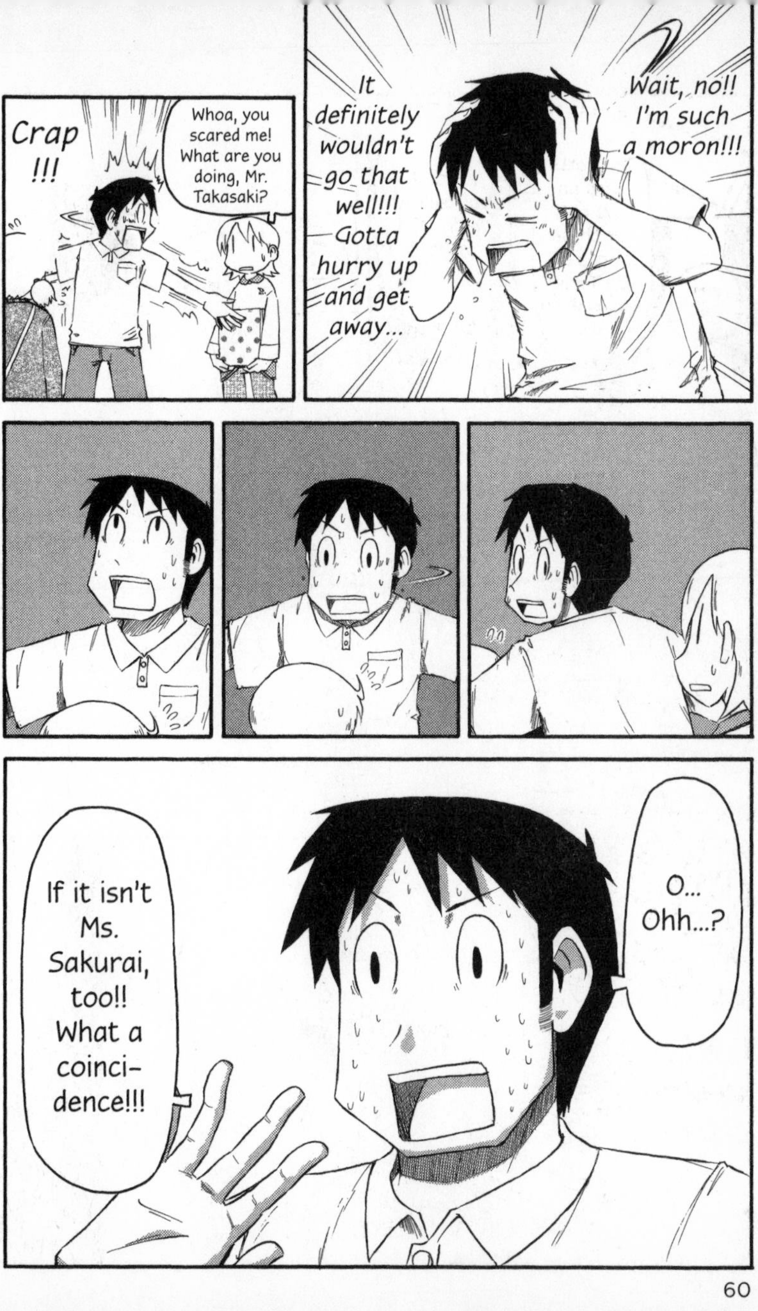
Wait, no!! I'm such a moron!!!
It definitely wouldn't go that well!!! Gotta hurry up and get away...
Whoa, you scared me! What are you doing, Mr. Takasaki?
Crap!!!
O... Ohh...?
If it isn't Ms. Sakurai, too!! What a coinci-dence!!!

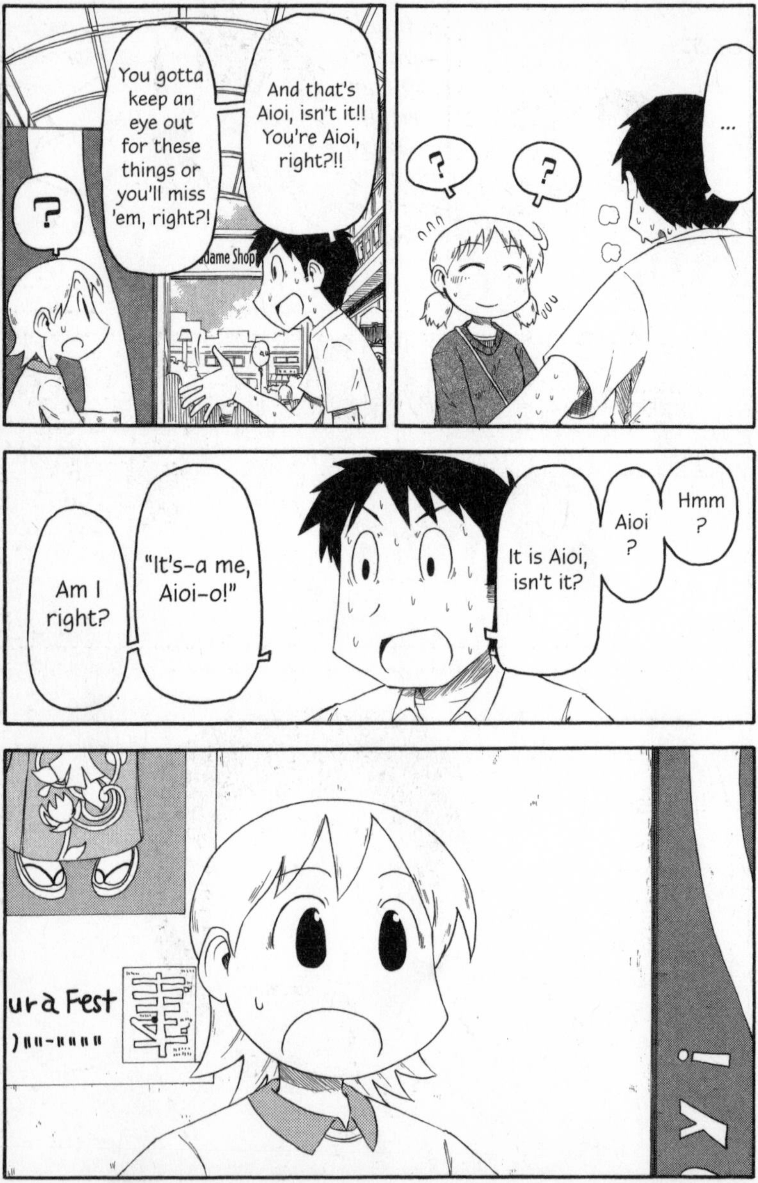
...
?
?
And that's Aioi, isn't it!! You're Aioi, right?!!
You gotta keep an eye out for these things or you'll miss 'em, right?!
?
Hmm ?
Aioi ?
It is Aioi, isn't it?
"It's-a me, Aioi-o!"
Am I right?
ura Fest

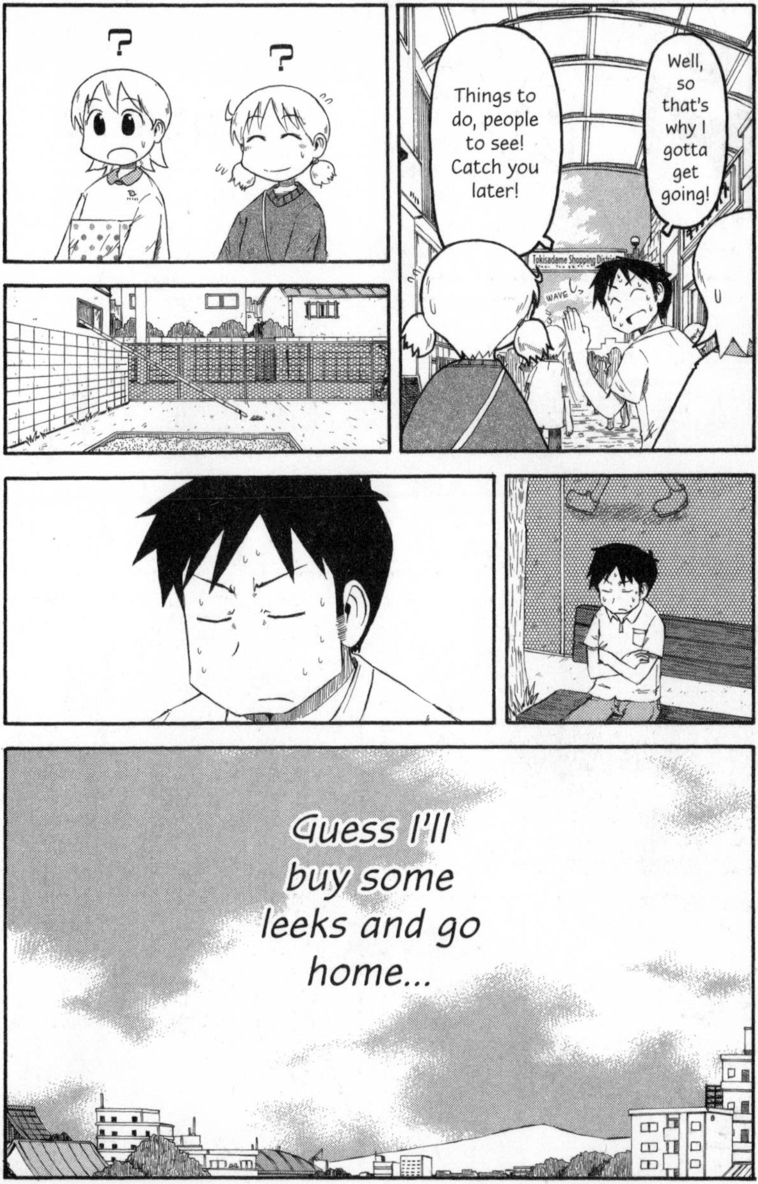
Well, so that's why I gotta get going!
Things to do, people to see! Catch you later!
Tokisadame Shopping District
WAVE
?
?
Guess I'll buy some leeks and go home...

chapter 77: end

chapter 78

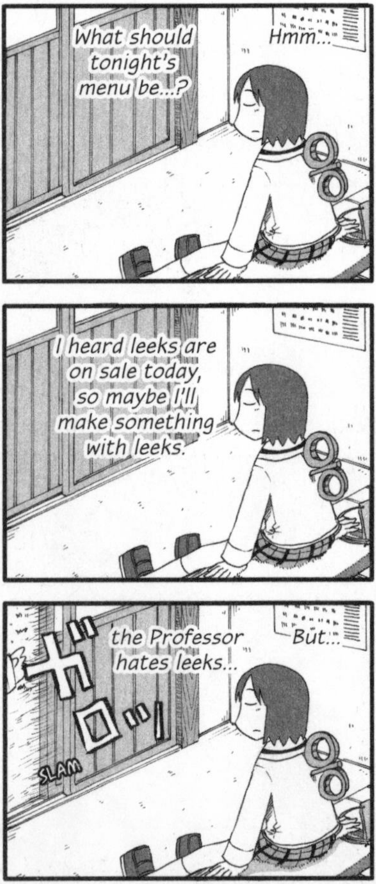
Hmm...
What should tonight's menu be...?
I heard leeks are on sale today, so maybe I'll make something with leeks.
But...
the Professor hates leeks...
SLAM

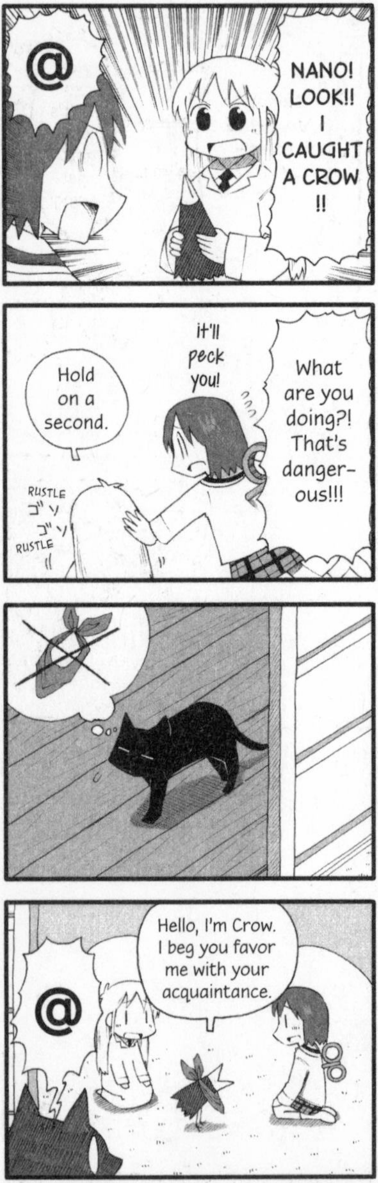
NANO! LOOK!! I CAUGHT A CROW !!
What are you doing?! That's danger-ous!!!
it'll peck you!
Hold on a second.
RUSTLE
ゴソ
ゴソ
RUSTLE
Hello, I'm Crow. I beg you favor me with your acquaintance.

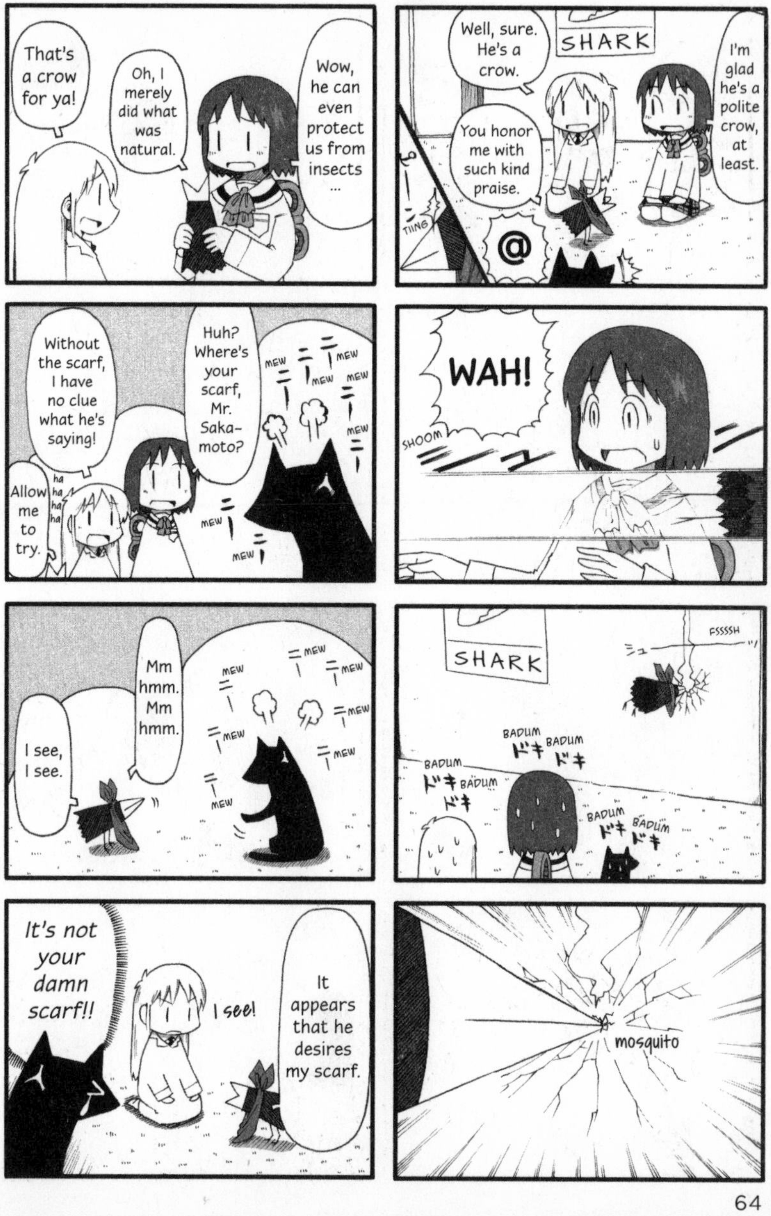
SHARK
I'm glad he's a polite crow, at least.
Well, sure. He's a crow.
You honor me with such kind praise.
TIING
@
Wow, he can even protect us from insects ...
Oh, I merely did what was natural.
That's a crow for ya!
WAH!
SHOOM
MEW MEW MEW MEW MEW MEW
Huh? Where's your scarf, Mr. Sakamoto?
Without the scarf, I have no clue what he's saying!
MEW MEW
ha ha ha ha
Allow me to try.
SHARK
FSSSSH
BADUM ドキ BADUM ドキ
BADUM ドキ BADUM ドキ
BADUM ドキ BADUM ドキ
MEW MEW MEW MEW MEW MEW
Mm hmm. Mm hmm.
I see, I see.
mosquito
It appears that he desires my scarf.
I see!
It's not your damn scarf!!

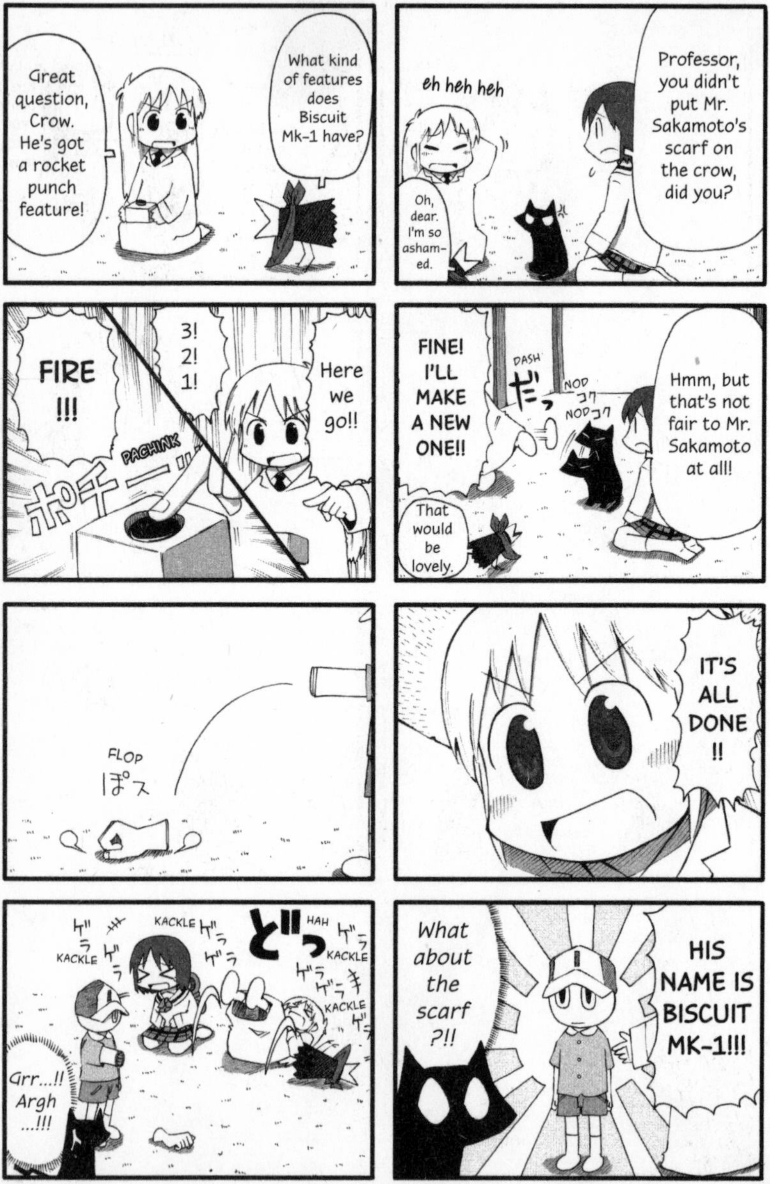

Professor, you didn't put Mr. Sakamoto's scarf on the crow, did you?
eh heh heh
Oh, dear. I'm so asham-ed.
Hmm, but that's not fair to Mr. Sakamoto at all!
NOD コク
NOD コク
DASH
だっ
FINE! I'LL MAKE A NEW ONE!!
That would be lovely.
IT'S ALL DONE !!
HIS NAME IS BISCUIT MK-1!!!
What about the scarf ?!!
What kind of features does Biscuit Mk-1 have?
Great question, Crow. He's got a rocket punch feature!
Here we go!!
3! 2! 1!
FIRE !!!
PACHINK
ポチーッ
FLOP
ぽス
HAH
どっ
KACKLE
ゲラゲラ
KACKLE
ゲラゲラ
KACKLE
Grr...!! Argh ...!!!

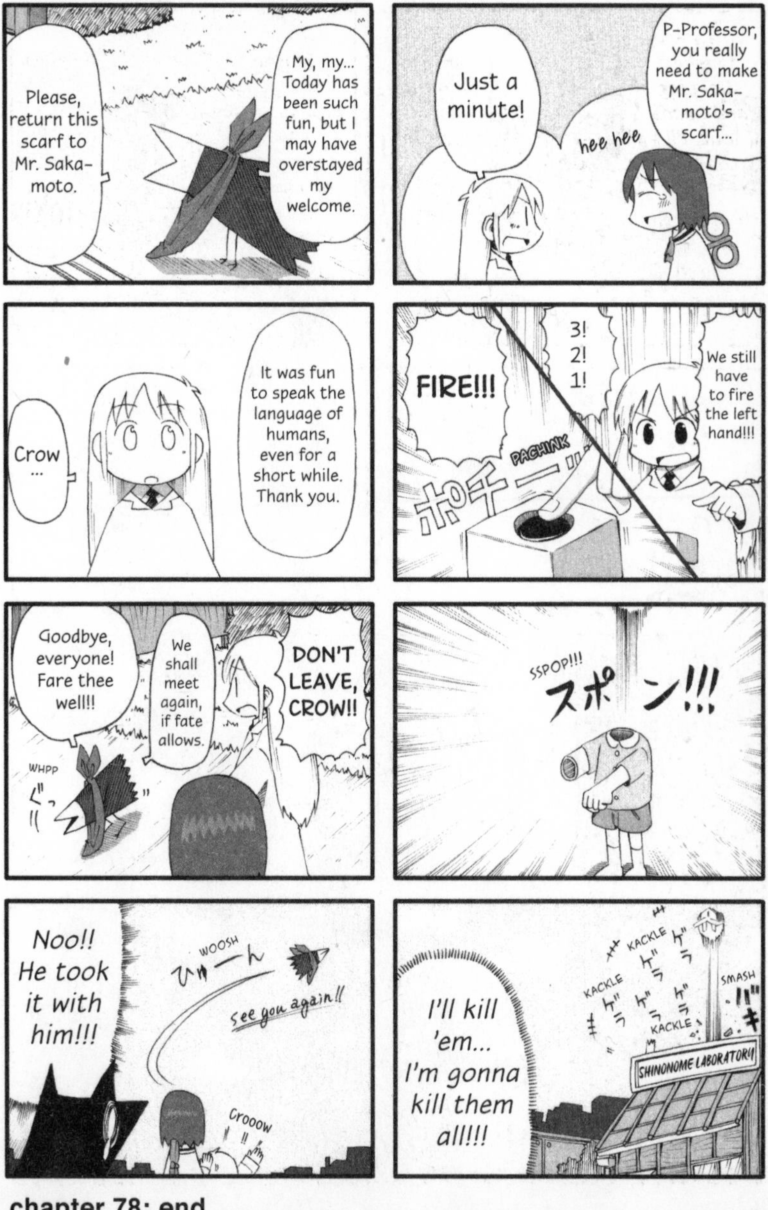
P-Professor, you really need to make Mr. Saka-moto's scarf...
hee hee
Just a minute!
My, my... Today has been such fun, but I may have overstayed my welcome.
Please, return this scarf to Mr. Saka-moto.
We still have to fire the left hand!!!
3! 2! 1!
FIRE!!!
PACHINK
ポチーッ
It was fun to speak the language of humans, even for a short while. Thank you.
Crow ...
SSPOP!!!
スポン!!!
DON'T LEAVE, CROW!!
We shall meet again, if fate allows.
Goodbye, everyone! Fare thee well!!
WHPP
ぐっ
KACKLE
KACKLE
KACKLE
SMASH
バキ
I'll kill 'em... I'm gonna kill them all!!!
SHINONOME LABORATORY
WOOSH
ひゅーん
see you again!!
Noo!! He took it with him!!!
Grooow

chapter 78: end

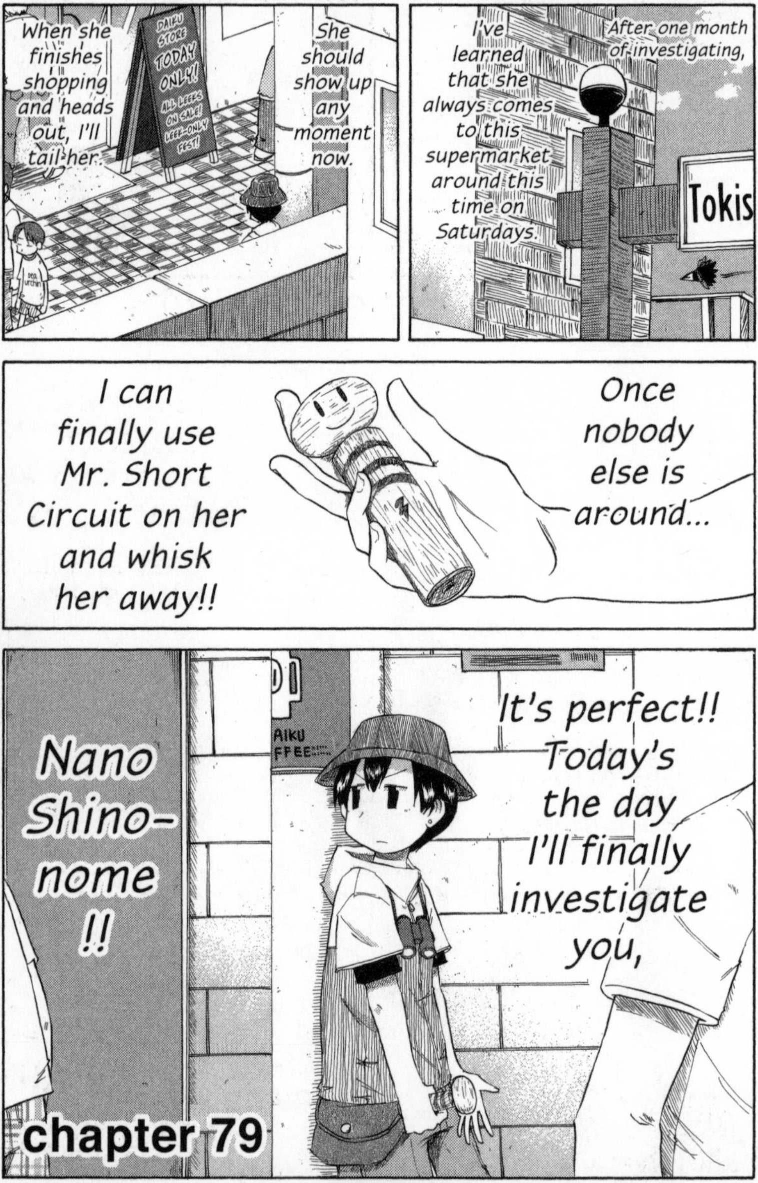
After one month of investigating,
I've learned that she always comes to this supermarket around this time on Saturdays.
Tokis
She should show up any moment now.
When she finishes shopping and heads out, I'll tail her.
DAIKU STORE TODAY ONLY! ALL LEEKS ON SALE! LEEK-ONLY FEST!
sea urchin
Once nobody else is around...
I can finally use Mr. Short Circuit on her and whisk her away!!
It's perfect!! Today's the day I'll finally investigate you,
Nano Shino-nome !!
AIKU FFEE
chapter 79

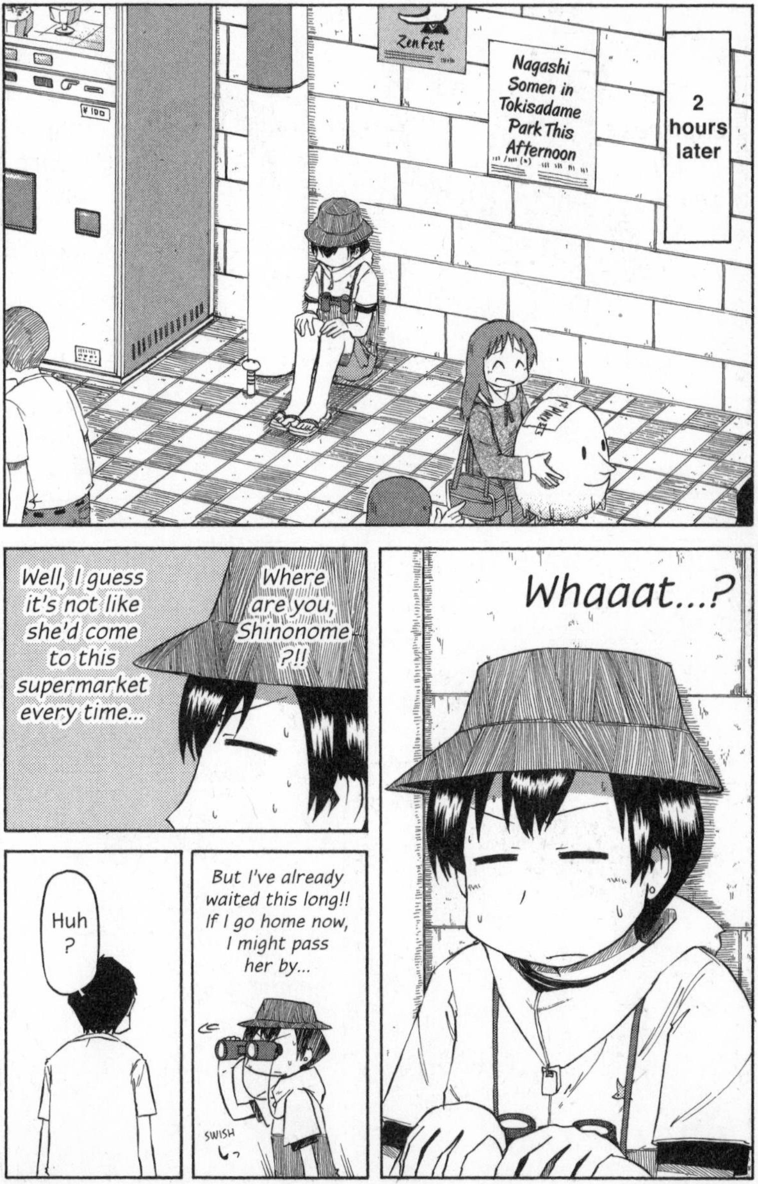
Zen Fest
Nagashi Somen in Tokisadame Park This Afternoon
2 hours later
Whaaat...?
Where are you, Shinonome ?!!
Well, I guess it's not like she'd come to this supermarket every time...
But I've already waited this long!! If I go home now, I might pass her by...
SWISH
Huh ?

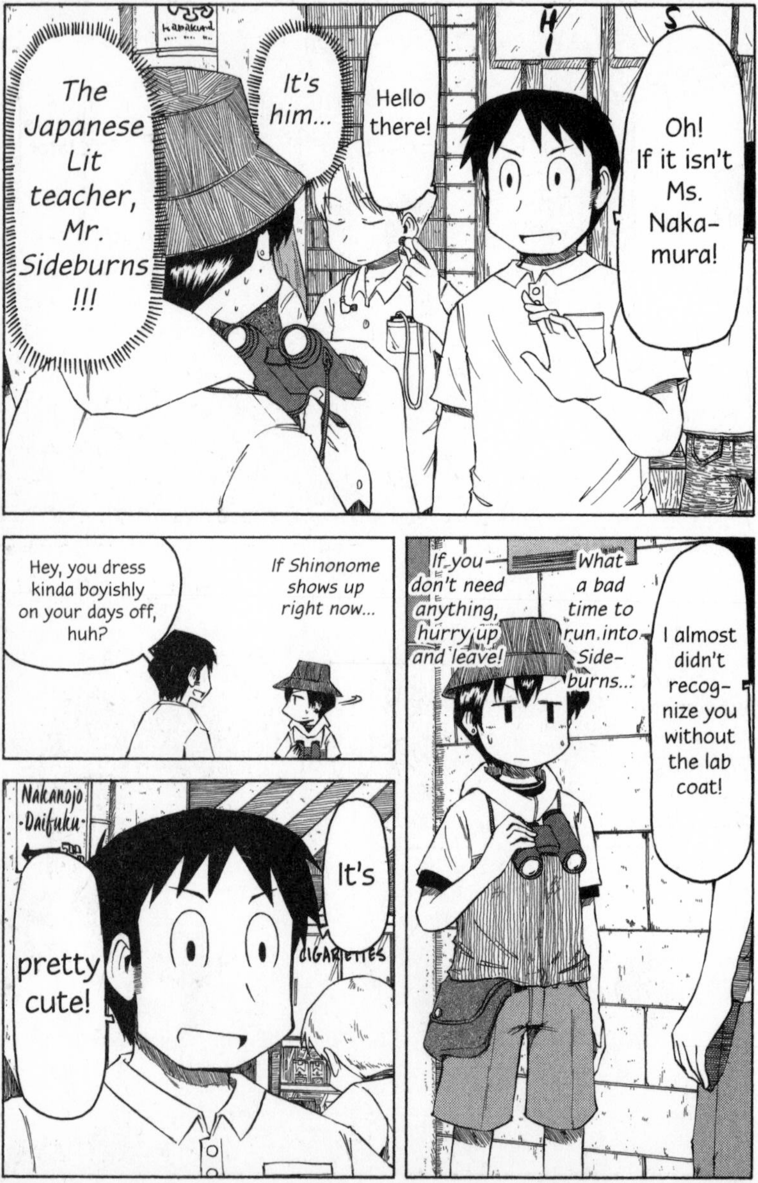

Oh! If it isn't Ms. Naka-mura!
Hello there!
It's him...
The Japanese Lit teacher, Mr. Sideburns!!!
I almost didn't recog-nize you without the lab coat!
What a bad time to run into Side-burns...
If you don't need anything, hurry up and leave!
If Shinonome shows up right now...
Hey, you dress kinda boyishly on your days off, huh?
It's
pretty cute!
Nakanojo Daifuku
CIGARETTES

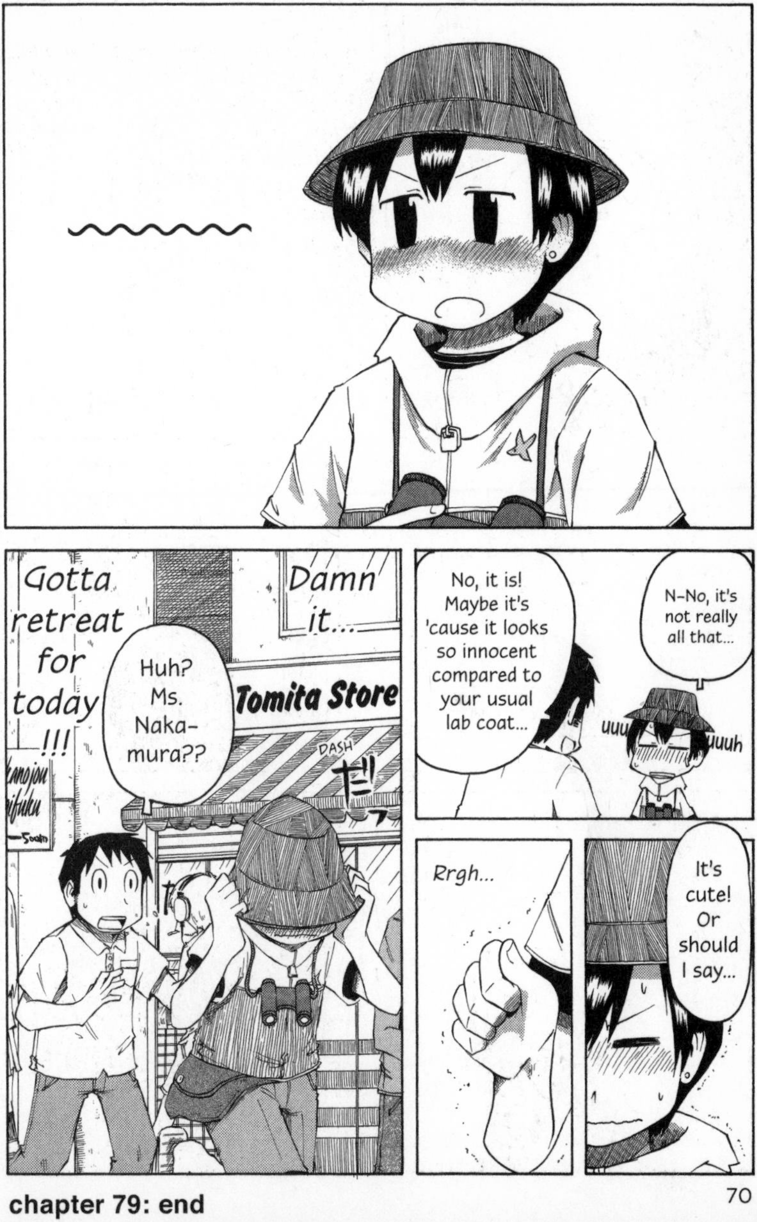
N-No, it's not really all that...
uuu uuuh
No, it is! Maybe it's 'cause it looks so innocent compared to your usual lab coat...
It's cute! Or should I say...
Rrgh...
Damn it...
Tomita Store
Huh? Ms. Naka-mura??
DASH
Gotta retreat for today!!!

chapter 79: end

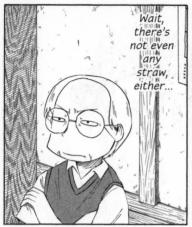

Wait, there's not even any straw, either...

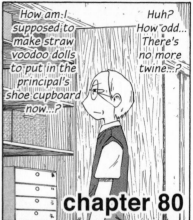

How am I supposed to make straw voodoo dolls to put in the principal's shoe cupboard now...?

Huh? How odd... There's no more twine...?

chapter 80

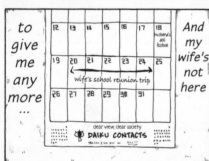

to give me any more...

And my wife's not here

	12	13	14	15	16	17	18 husband's doll festival
19	20	21	22	23	24	25
			wife's school reunion trip		
26	27	28	29	30	31	

clear view, clear society
DAIKU CONTACTS

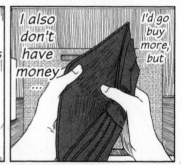

I also don't have money...

I'd go buy more, but

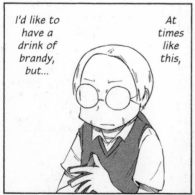

I'd like to have a drink of brandy, but...

At times like this,

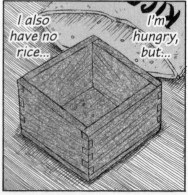

I also have no rice...

I'm hungry, but...

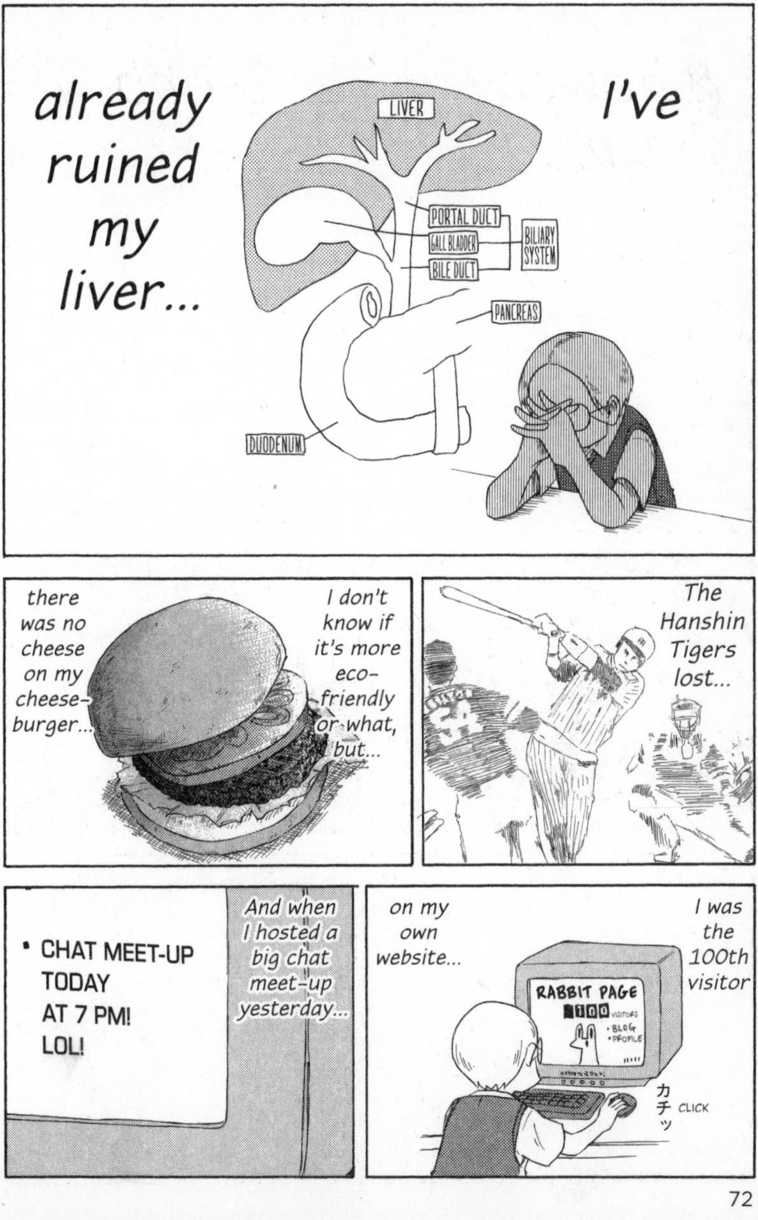
I've
already ruined my liver...
LIVER
PORTAL DUCT
GALL BLADDER
BILE DUCT
BILIARY SYSTEM
PANCREAS
DUODENUM
The Hanshin Tigers lost...
I don't know if it's more eco-friendly or what, but...
there was no cheese on my cheeseburger...
I was the 100th visitor
on my own website...
RABBIT PAGE
100 VISITORS
• BLOG
• PROFILE
カチッ CLICK
And when I hosted a big chat meet-up yesterday...
• CHAT MEET-UP TODAY AT 7 PM! LOL!

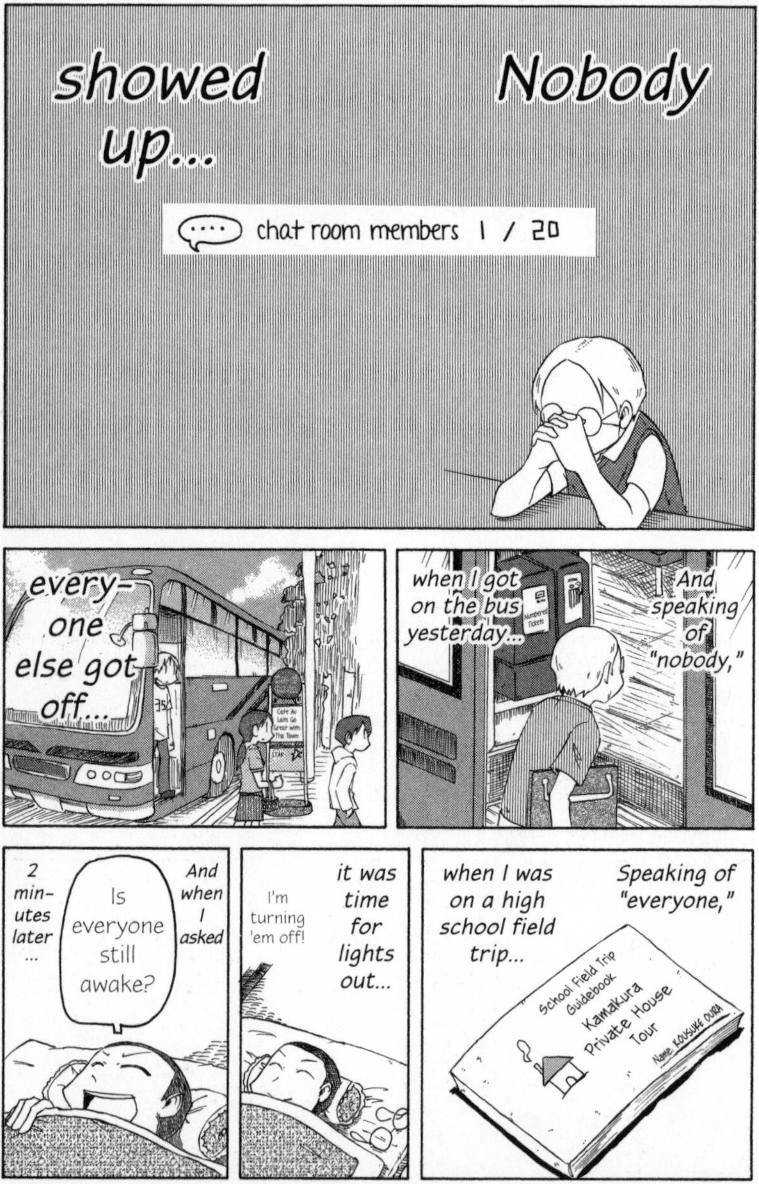
Nobody
showed up...
chat room members 1 / 20
And speaking of "nobody,"
when I got on the bus yesterday...
Numbered Tickets
every-one else got off...
Cafe Au Laits Go Great with The Town
Speaking of "everyone,"
when I was on a high school field trip...
School Field Trip Guidebook
Kamakura Private House Tour
Name: KOUSUKE OURA
it was time for lights out...
I'm turning 'em off!
And when I asked
Is everyone still awake?
2 min-utes later...

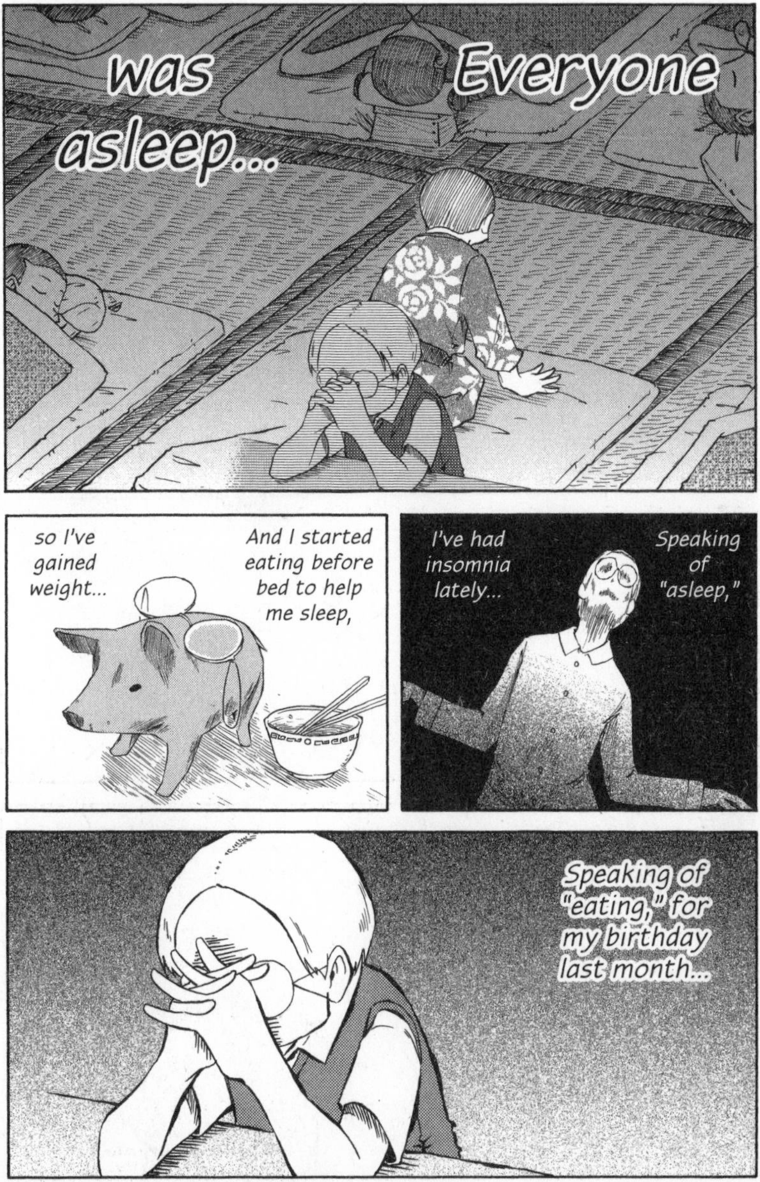
Everyone was asleep...
Speaking of "asleep,"
I've had insomnia lately...
And I started eating before bed to help me sleep,
so I've gained weight...
Speaking of "eating," for my birthday last month...

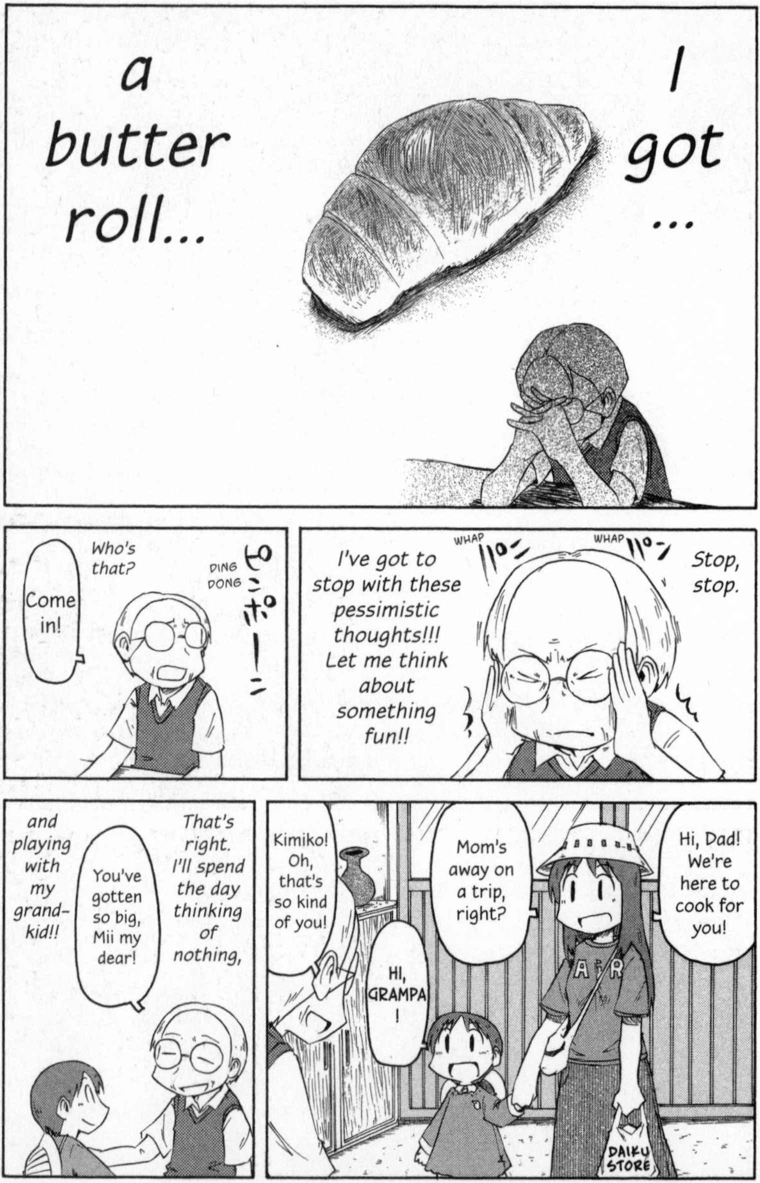
I got ...
a butter roll...
Stop, stop.
WHAP
WHAP
I've got to stop with these pessimistic thoughts!!! Let me think about something fun!!
ピンポーン
DING DONG
Who's that?
Come in!
Hi, Dad! We're here to cook for you!
Mom's away on a trip, right?
Kimiko! Oh, that's so kind of you!
HI, GRAMPA!
DAIKU STORE
That's right. I'll spend the day thinking of nothing,
You've gotten so big, Mii my dear!
and playing with my grand-kid!!

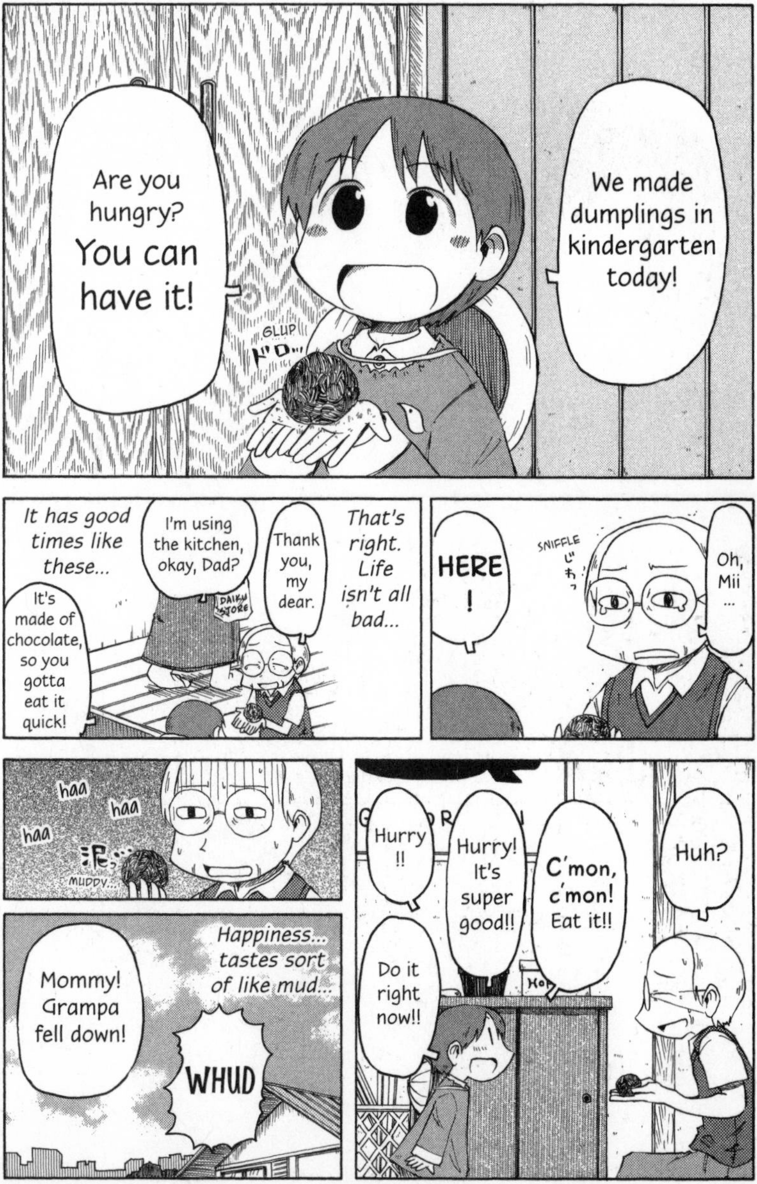
We made dumplings in kindergarten today!
Are you hungry? You can have it!
GLUP
ドロ…
Oh, Mii ...
SNIFFLE
じわっ
HERE!
That's right. Life isn't all bad...
Thank you, my dear.
I'm using the kitchen, okay, Dad?
DAIKU STORE
It has good times like these...
It's made of chocolate, so you gotta eat it quick!
Huh?
C'mon, c'mon! Eat it!!
Hurry! It's super good!!
Hurry !!
Do it right now!!
haa
haa
haa
泥…
MUDDY...
Happiness... tastes sort of like mud...
Mommy! Grampa fell down!
WHUD

chapter 80: end

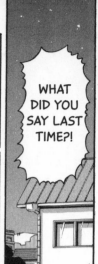

WHAT DID YOU SAY LAST TIME?!
Oh !!
But this time ...
THERE IS NO "THIS TIME" !!

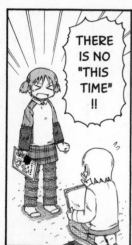

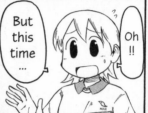

chapter 81

Stop!! Kiss Thief!
To-night he will steal
I'll seal up those naughty lips of yours.
Geez... you sap!
so many...!
Daisuke Naganohara

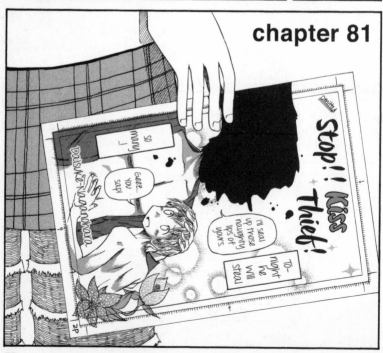

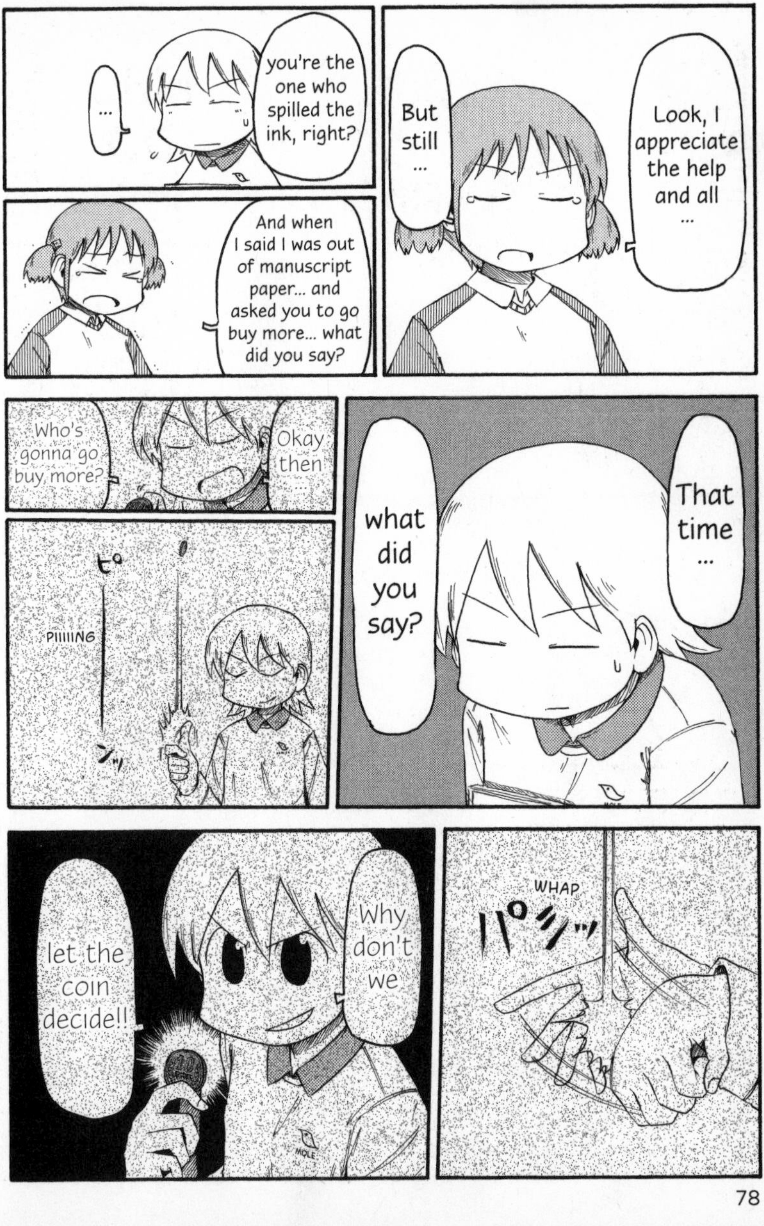
Look, I appreciate the help and all ...
But still ...
you're the one who spilled the ink, right?
...
And when I said I was out of manuscript paper... and asked you to go buy more... what did you say?
That time ...
what did you say?
Okay then ...
Who's gonna go buy more?
PIIIING
WHAP
Why don't we
let the coin decide!!

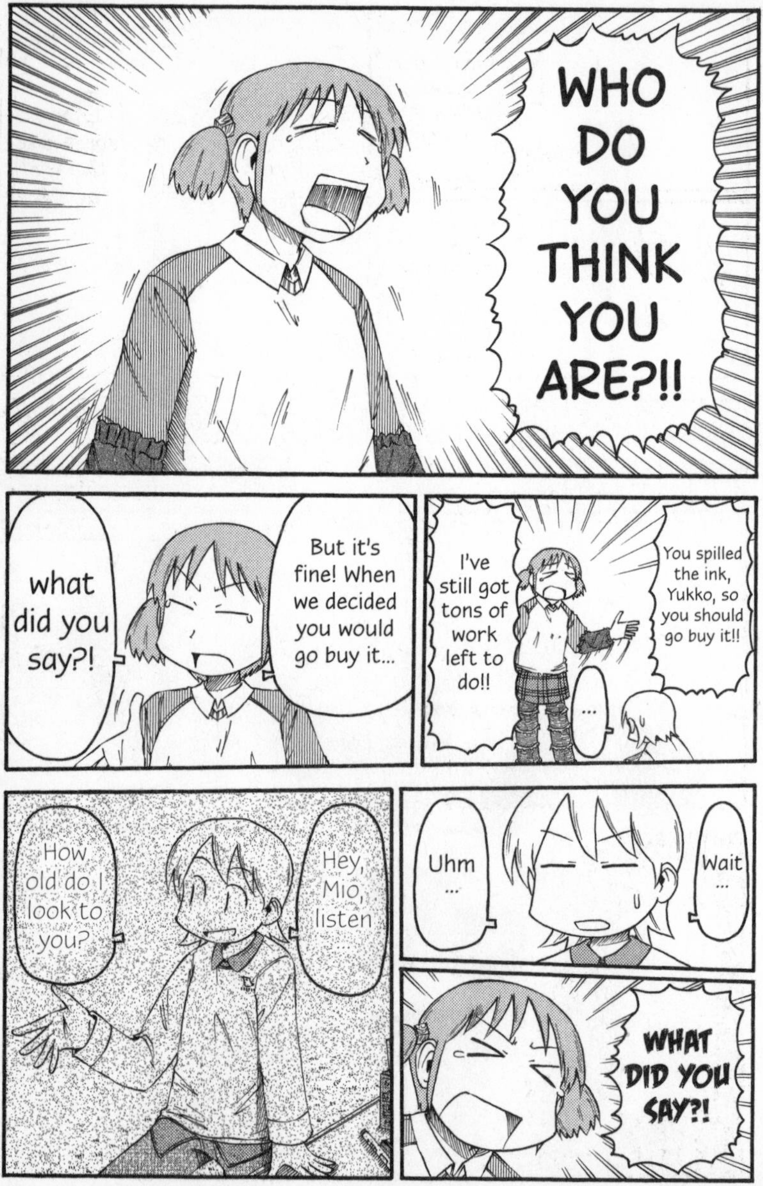

WHO DO YOU THINK YOU ARE?!!
You spilled the ink, Yukko, so you should go buy it!!
I've still got tons of work left to do!!
...
But it's fine! When we decided you would go buy it...
what did you say?!
Wait...
Uhm...
WHAT DID YOU SAY?!
Hey, Mio, listen...
How old do I look to you?

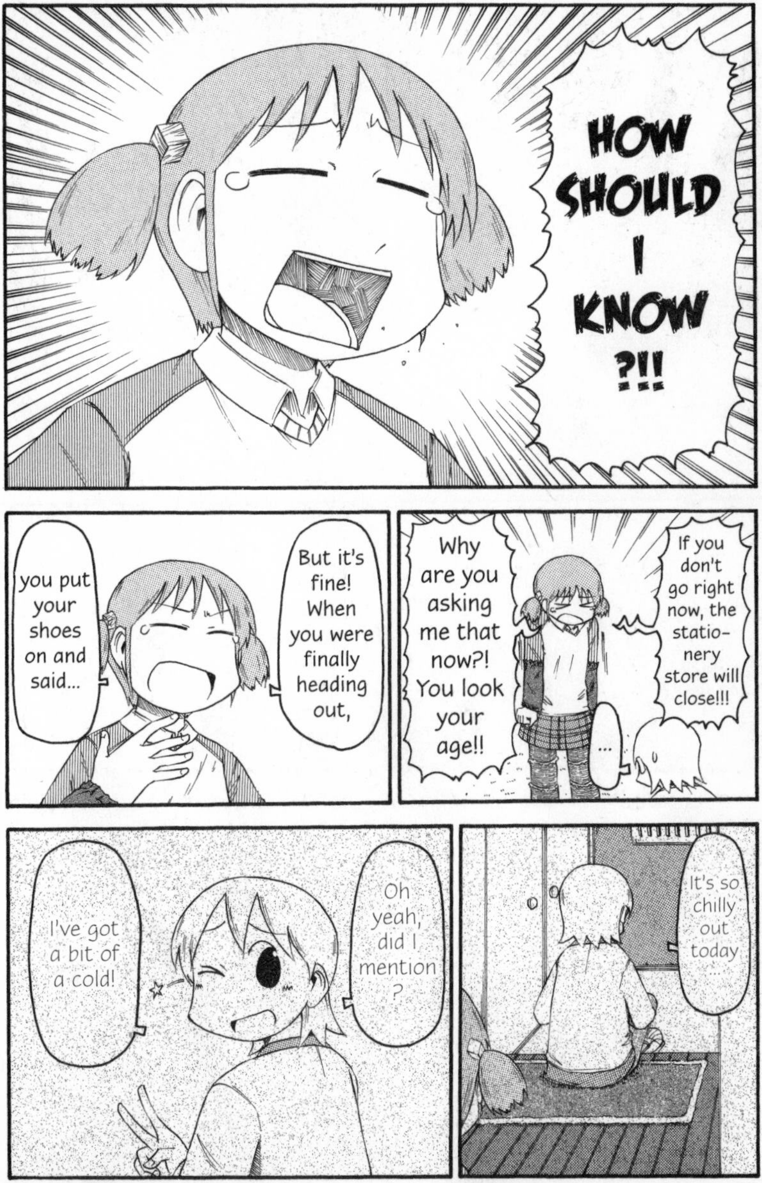
HOW SHOULD I KNOW ?!!
If you don't go right now, the statio-nery store will close!!!
Why are you asking me that now?! You look your age!!
...
But it's fine! When you were finally heading out,
you put your shoes on and said...
It's so chilly out today...
Oh yeah, did I mention?
I've got a bit of a cold!

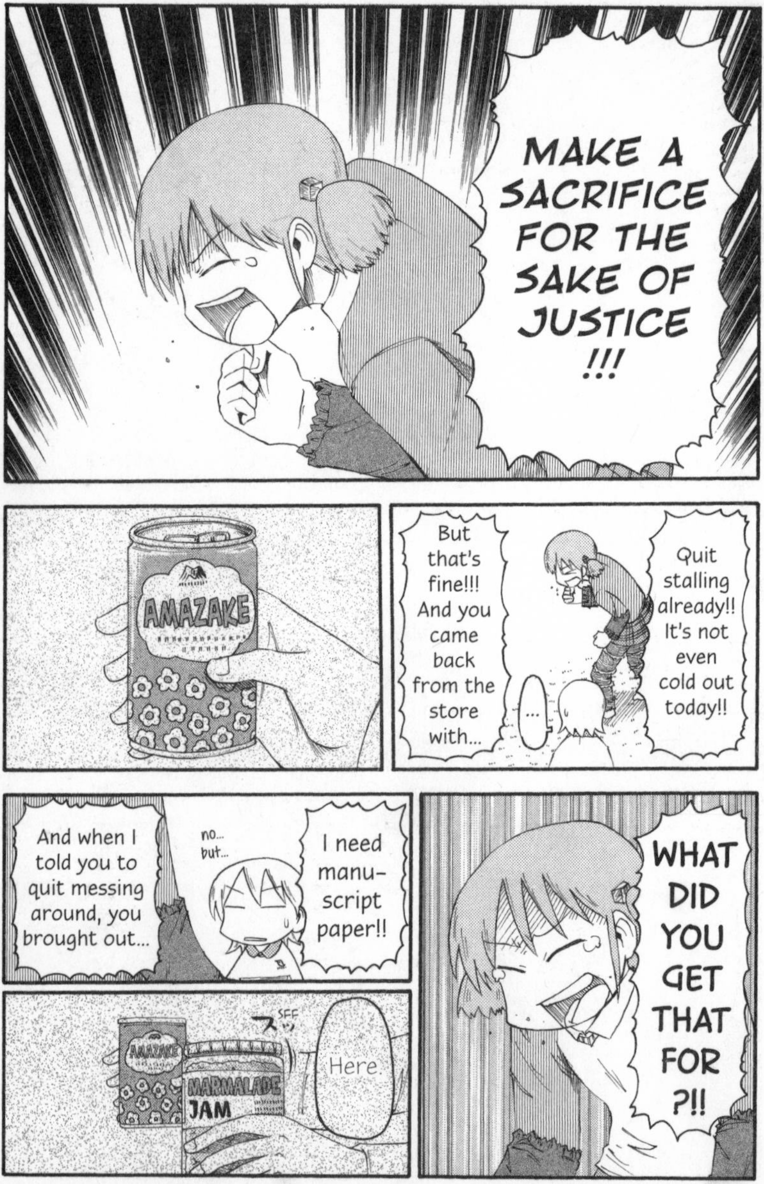
MAKE A SACRIFICE FOR THE SAKE OF JUSTICE !!!
Quit stalling already!! It's not even cold out today!!
...
But that's fine!!! And you came back from the store with...
AMAZAKE
WHAT DID YOU GET THAT FOR ?!!
I need manu-script paper!!
no... but...
And when I told you to quit messing around, you brought out...
SFF
Here.
MARMALADE JAM
AMAZAKE

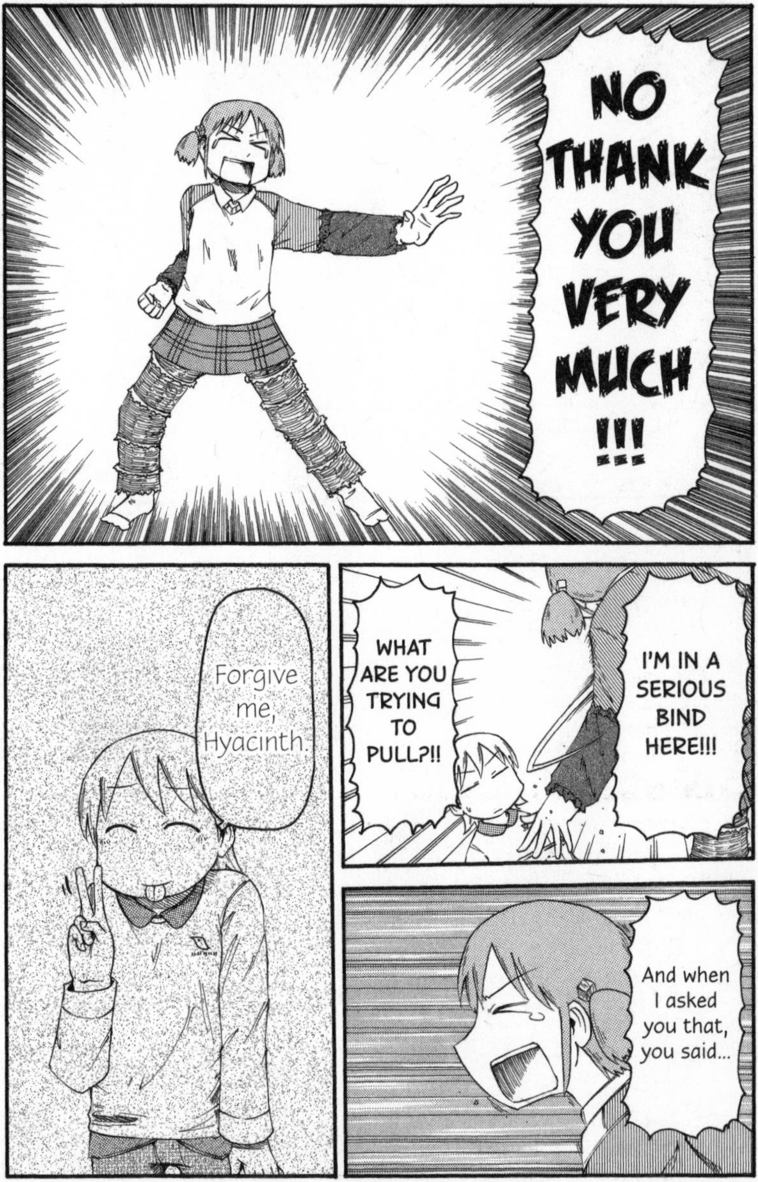
NO THANK YOU VERY MUCH!!!
I'M IN A SERIOUS BIND HERE!!!
WHAT ARE YOU TRYING TO PULL?!!
And when I asked you that, you said...
Forgive me, Hyacinth.

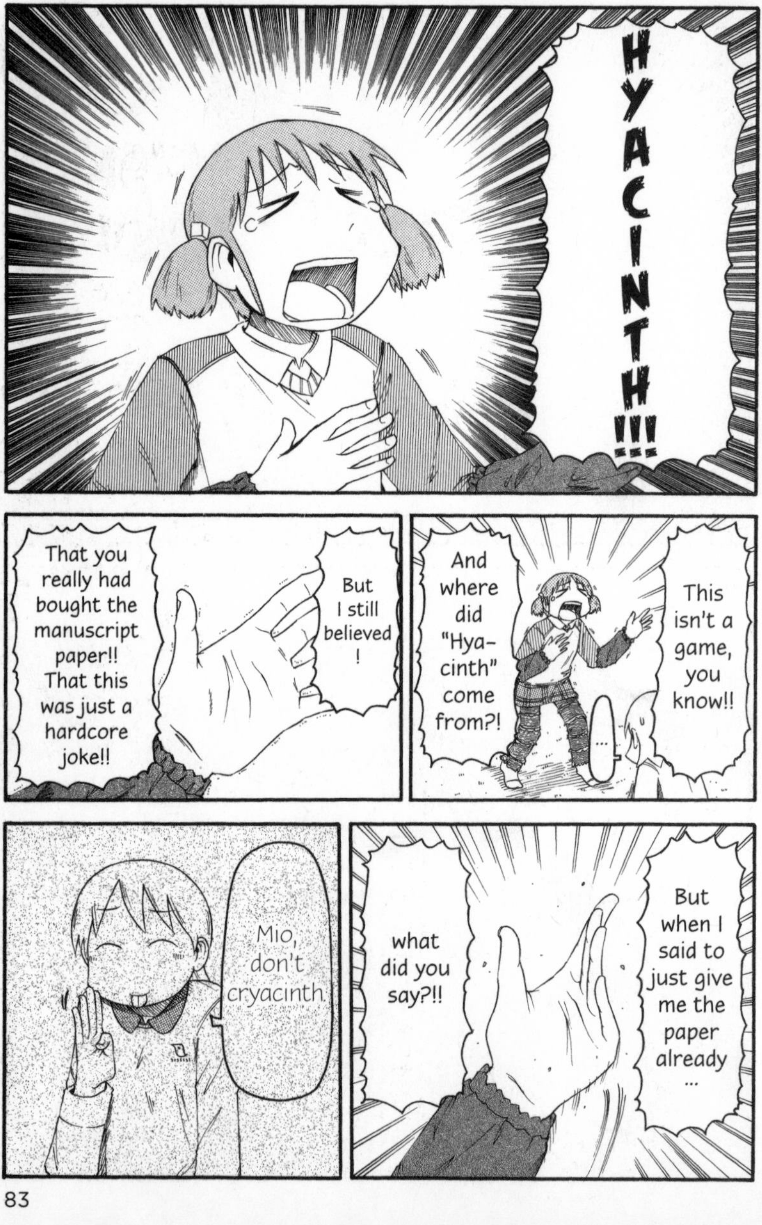
HYACINTH!!!
This isn't a game, you know!!
And where did "Hyacinth" come from?!
...
But I still believed!
That you really had bought the manuscript paper!! That this was just a hardcore joke!!
But when I said to just give me the paper already...
what did you say?!!
Mio, don't cryacinth.

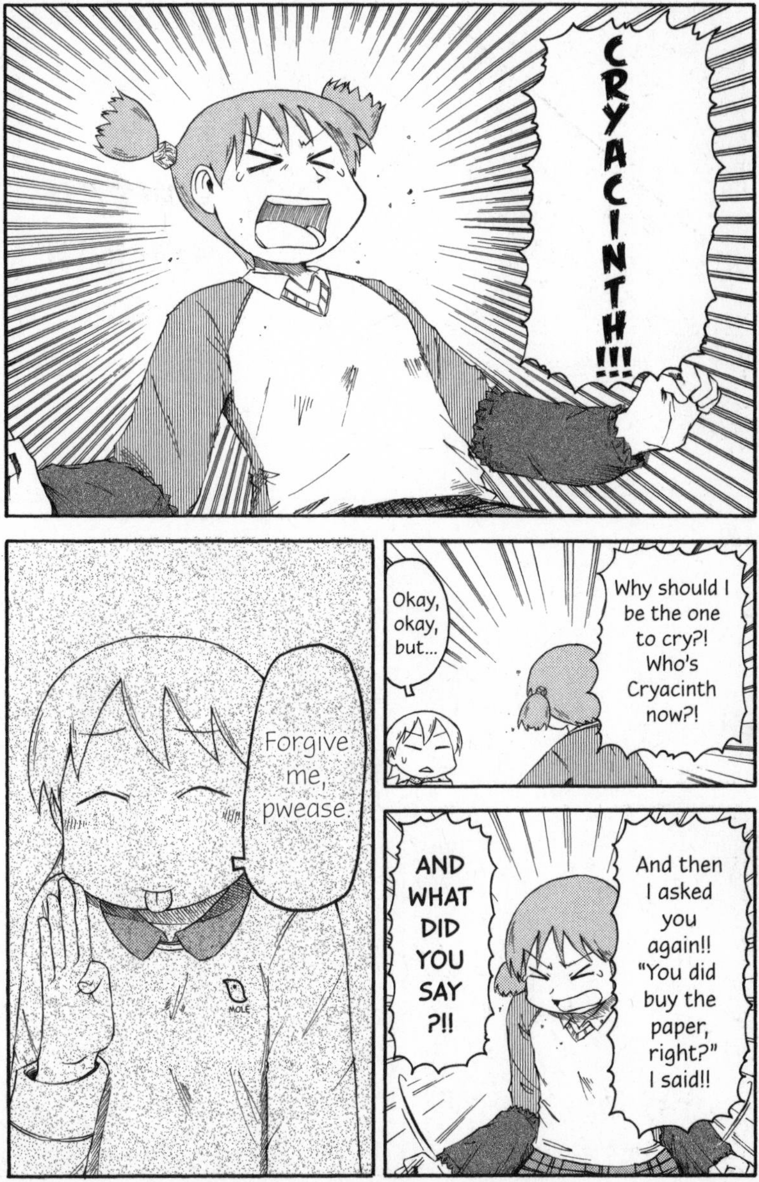
CRYACINTH!!!
Why should I be the one to cry?! Who's Cryacinth now?!
Okay, okay, but...
And then I asked you again!! "You did buy the paper, right?" I said!!
AND WHAT DID YOU SAY ?!!
Forgive me, pwease.

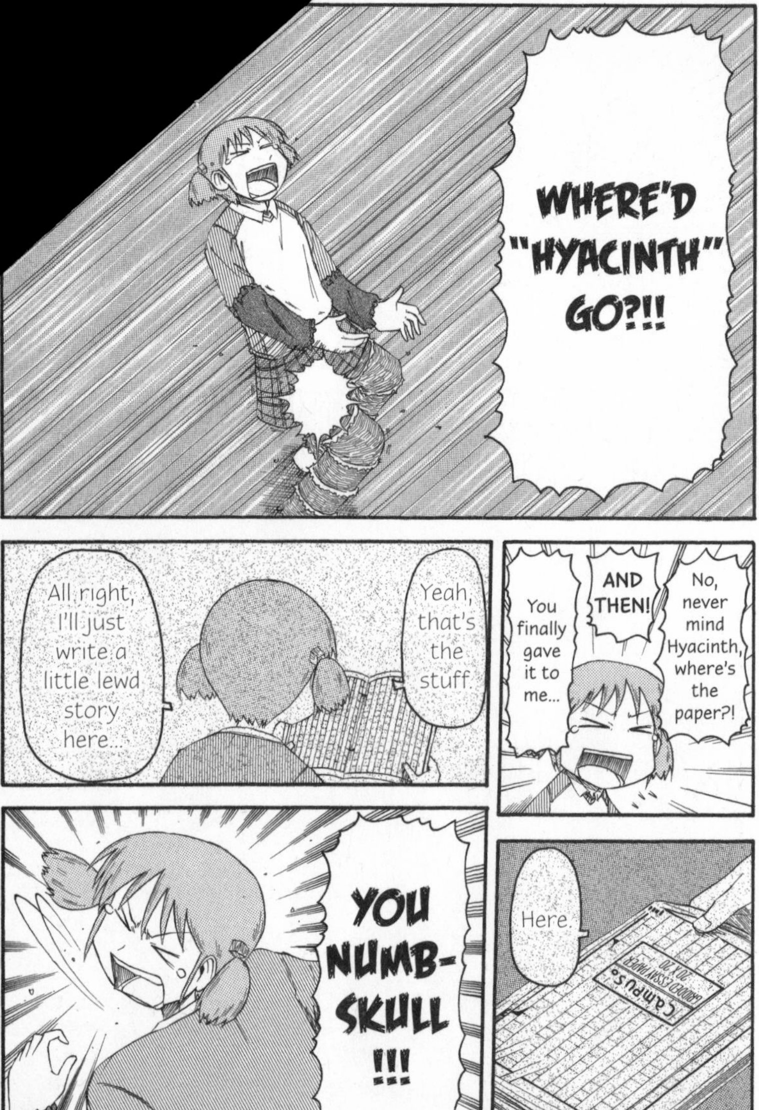
WHERE'D "HYACINTH" GO?!!
No, never mind Hyacinth, where's the paper?!
AND THEN!
You finally gave it to me...
Yeah, that's the stuff.
All right, I'll just write a little lewd story here...
Here.
Campus
GRIDDED ESSAY PAPER
YOU NUMB-SKULL!!!

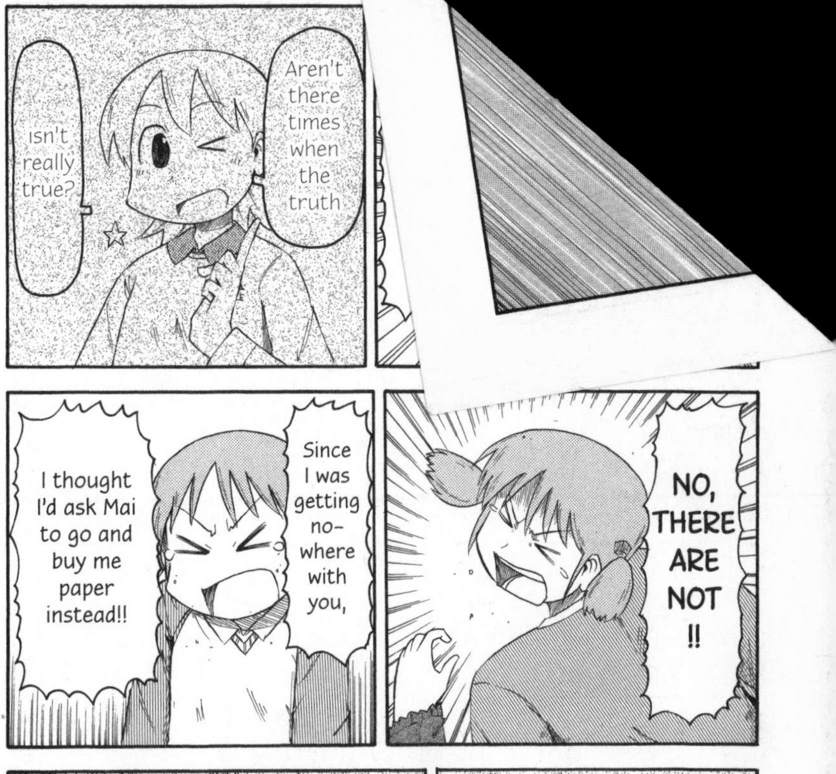
Aren't there times when the truth
isn't really true?
NO, THERE ARE NOT!!
Since I was getting no-where with you,
I thought I'd ask Mai to go and buy me paper instead!!
Mai, would you mind buying it for me?
PROPELLER
I'm going home

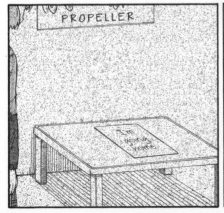

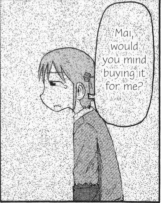

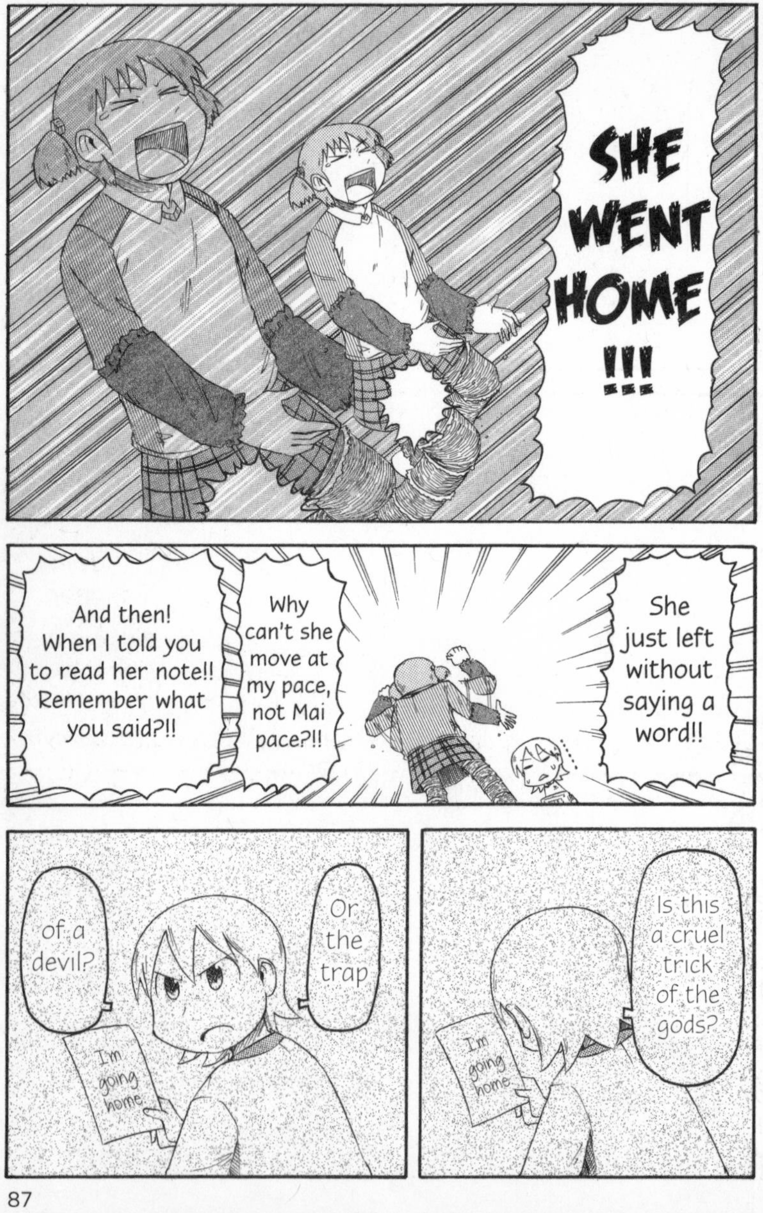
SHE WENT HOME !!!
She just left without saying a word!!
Why can't she move at my pace, not Mai pace?!!
And then! When I told you to read her note!! Remember what you said?!!
Is this a cruel trick of the gods?
I'm going home
Or the trap
of a devil?
I'm going home

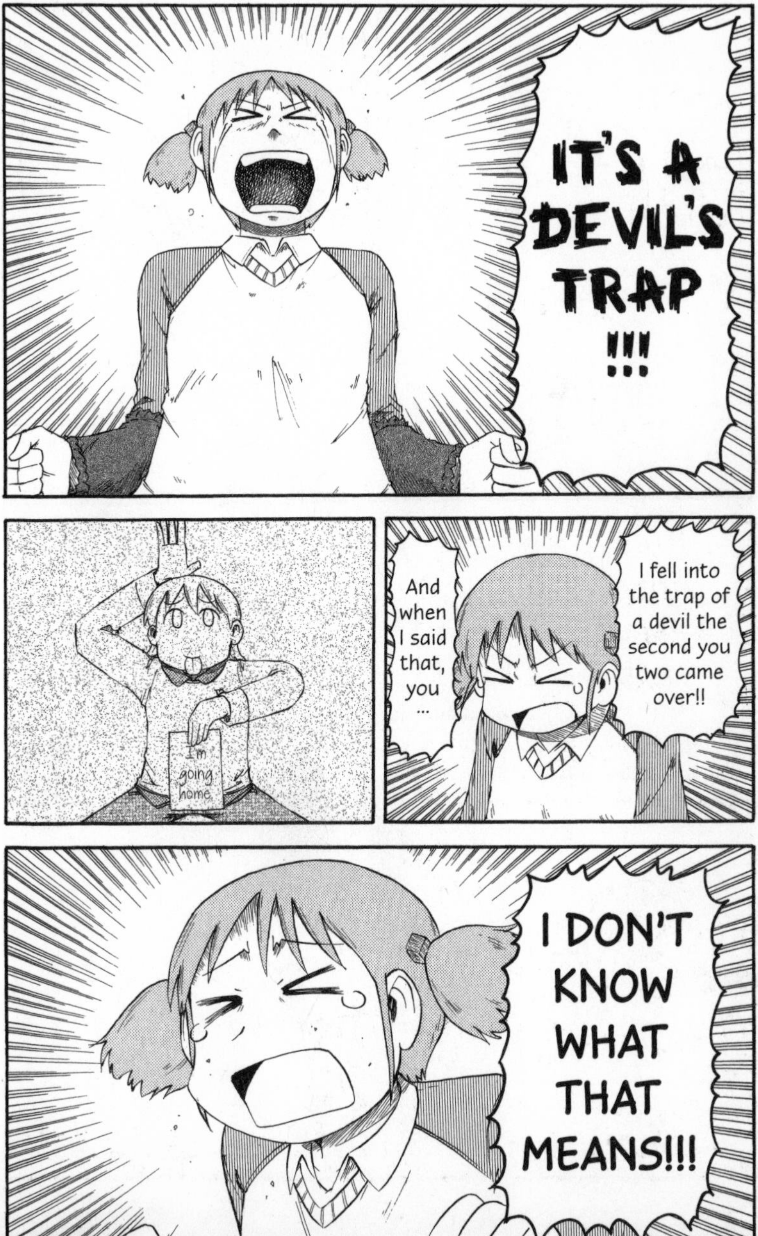
IT'S A DEVIL'S TRAP !!!
I fell into the trap of a devil the second you two came over!!
And when I said that, you ...
I'm going home
I DON'T KNOW WHAT THAT MEANS!!!

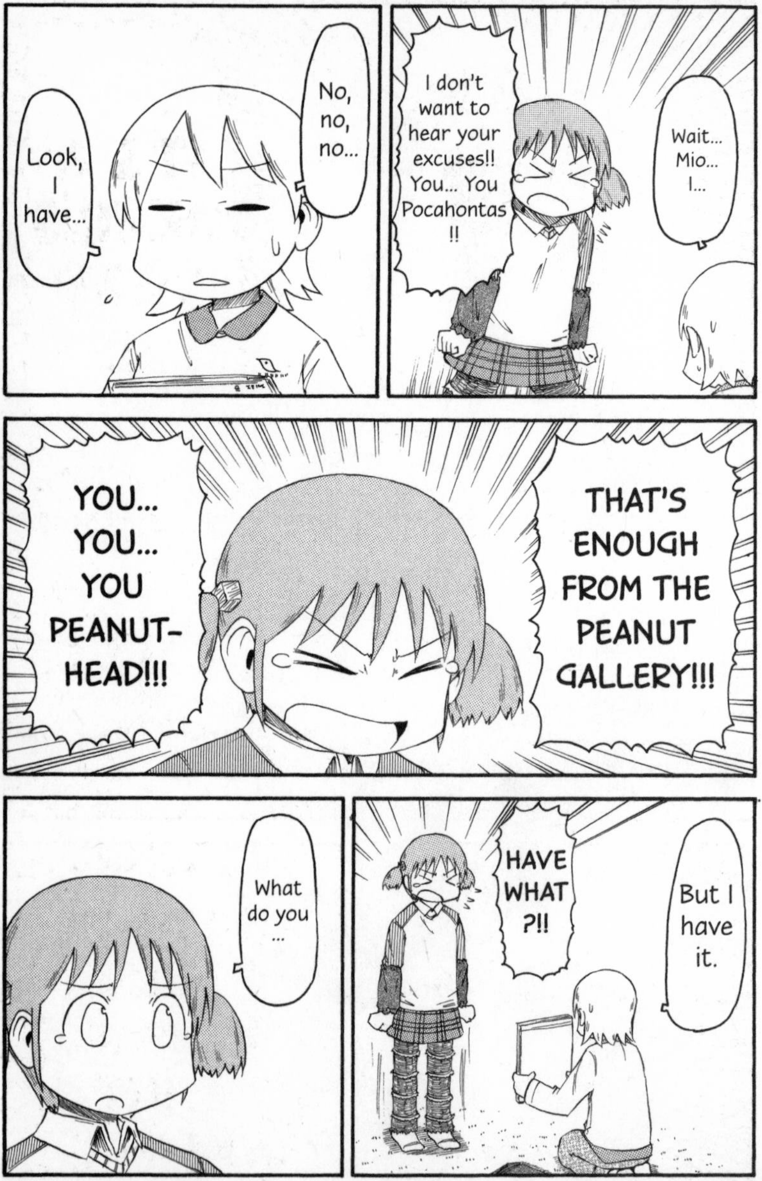
Wait... Mio... I...
I don't want to hear your excuses!! You... You Pocahontas!!
No, no, no...
Look, I have...
THAT'S ENOUGH FROM THE PEANUT GALLERY!!!
YOU... YOU... YOU PEANUT-HEAD!!!
But I have it.
HAVE WHAT?!!
What do you ...

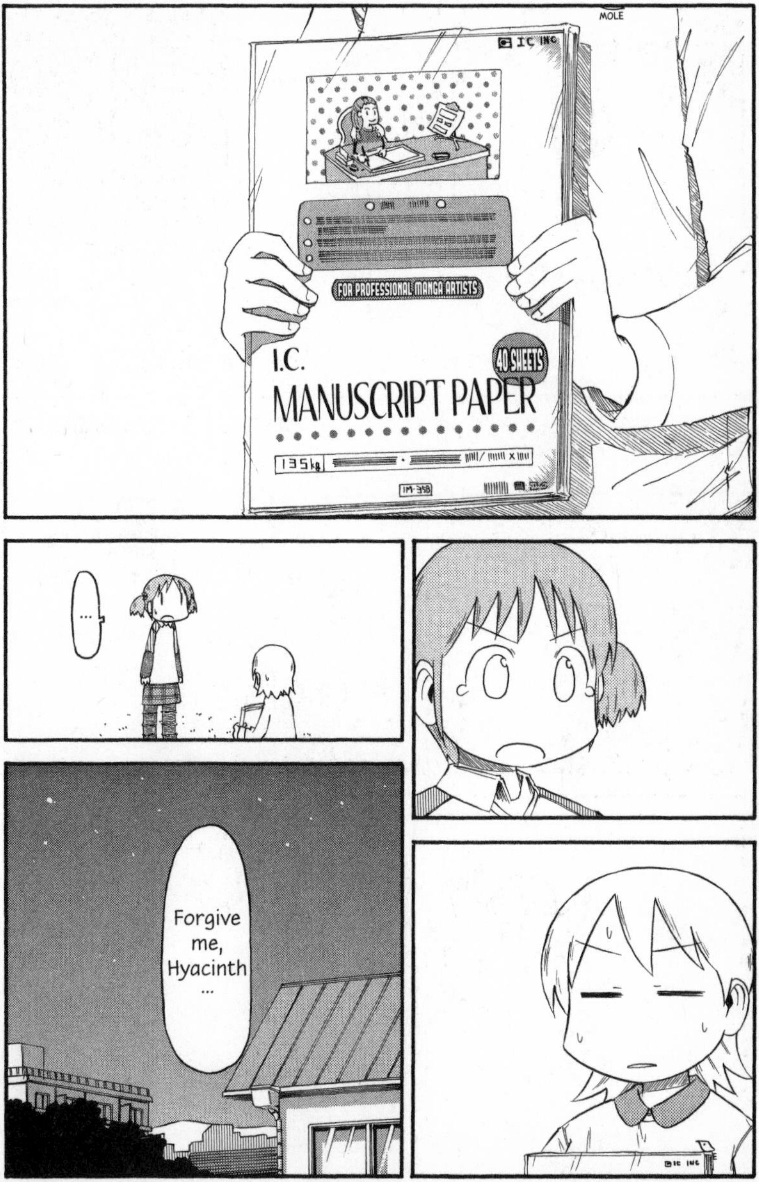
MOLE
IC INC
FOR PROFESSIONAL MANGA ARTISTS
40 SHEETS
I.C.
MANUSCRIPT PAPER
135kg
IM-358
…
IC INC
Forgive me, Hyacinth …

chapter 81: end

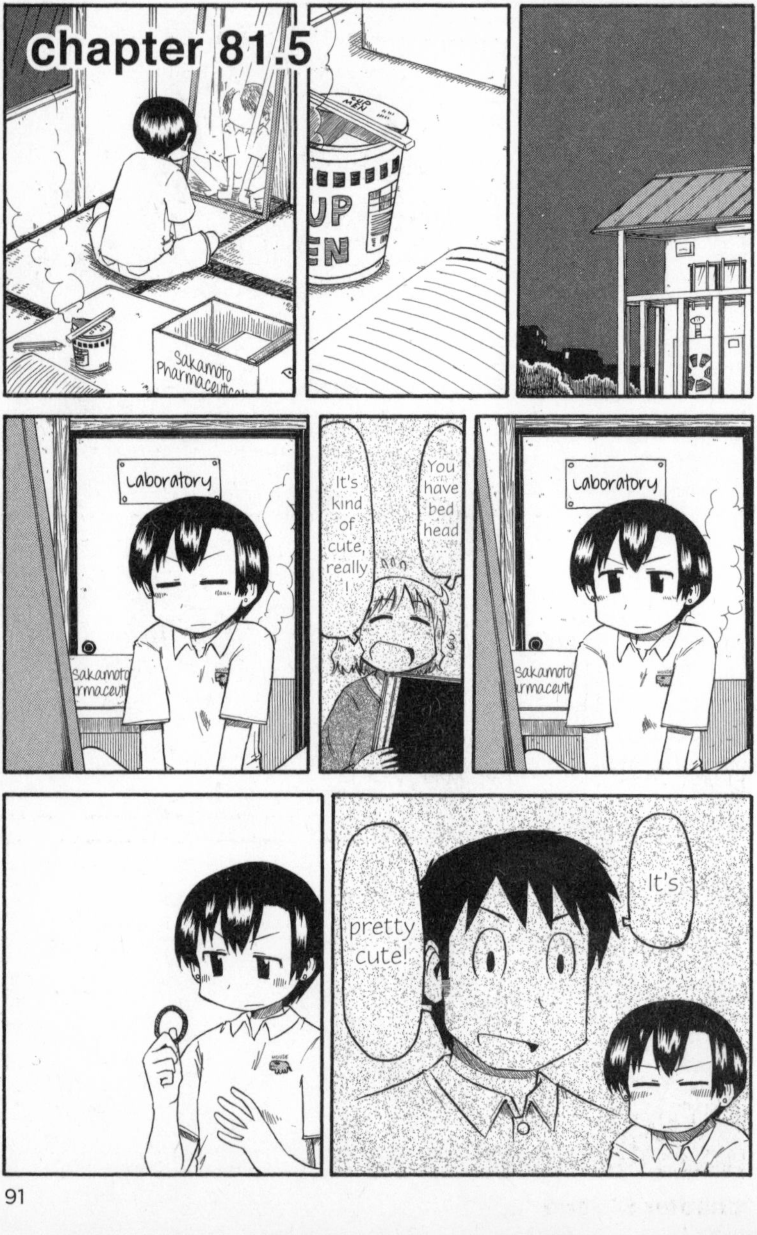
chapter 81.5
Laboratory
You have bed head...
It's kind of cute, really!
Laboratory
It's pretty cute!

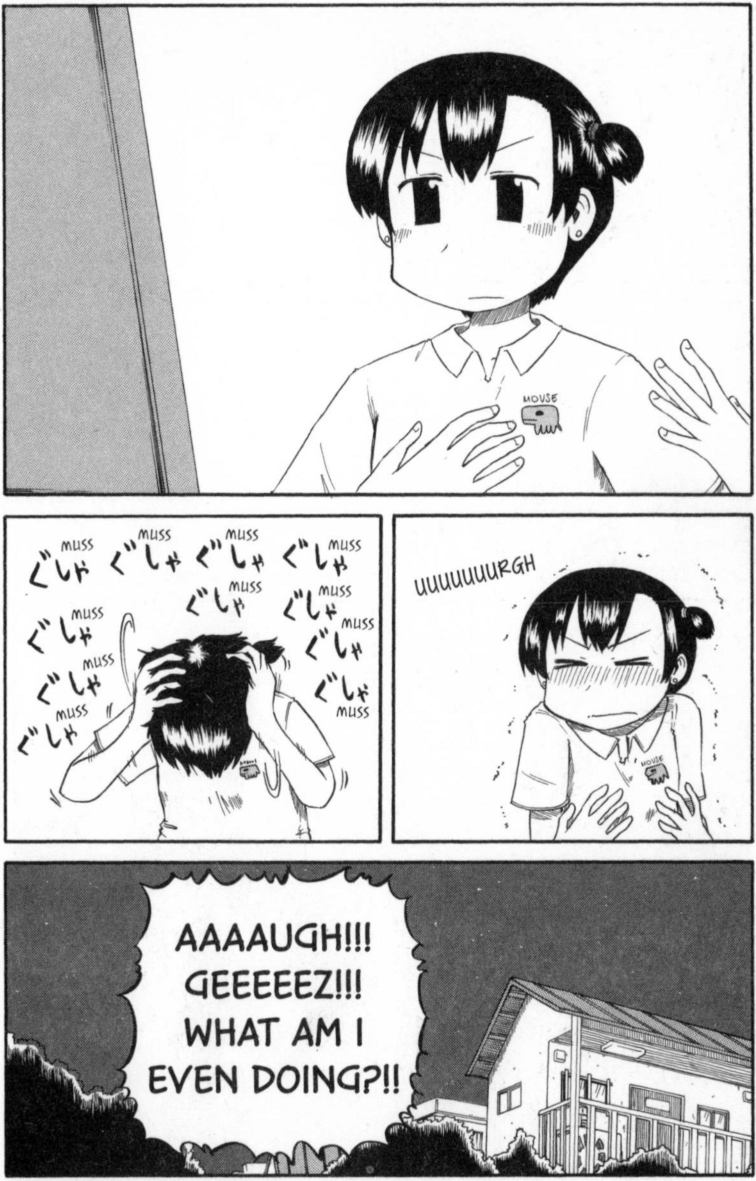
MOUSE
UUUUUUURGH
ぐしゃ muss
ぐしゃ muss
ぐしゃ muss
ぐしゃ muss
ぐしゃ muss
ぐしゃ muss
ぐしゃ muss
ぐしゃ muss
ぐしゃ muss
ぐしゃ muss
AAAAUGH!!! GEEEEEZ!!! WHAT AM I EVEN DOING?!!

chapter 81.5: end

ordinary shorts 7

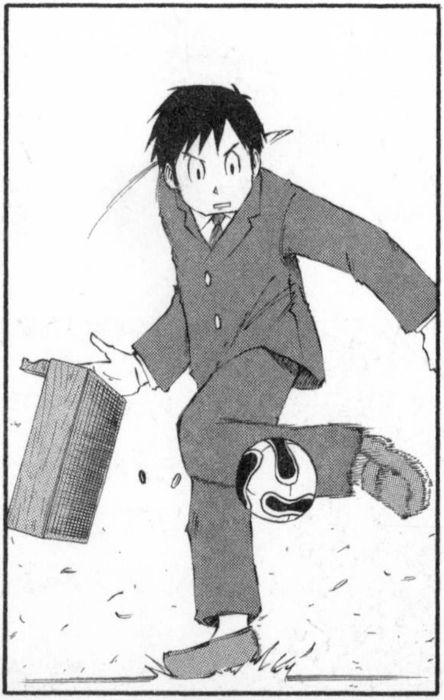

game 1

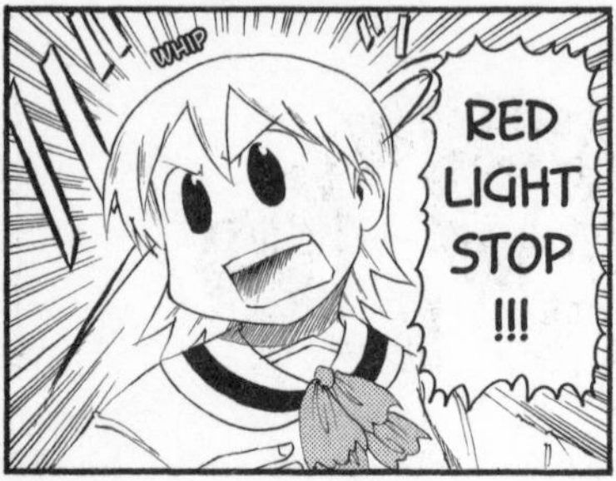
WHIP
RED LIGHT STOP !!!

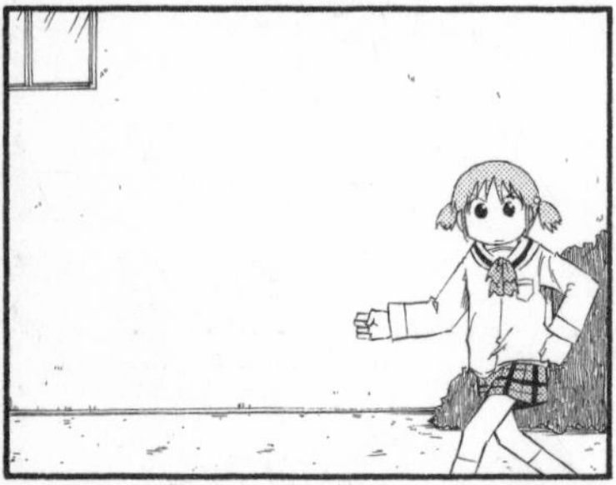

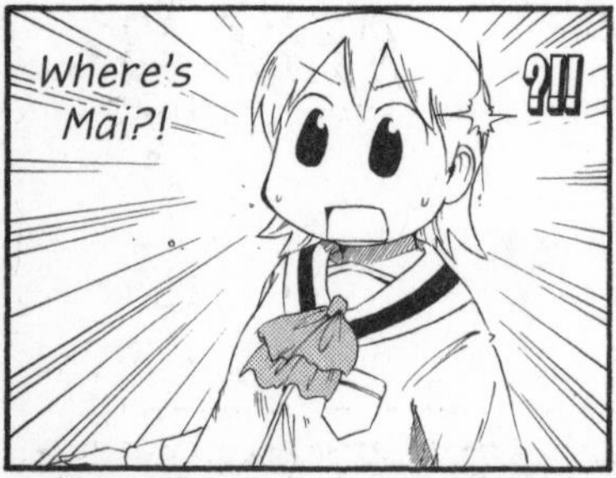
?!!
Where's Mai?!

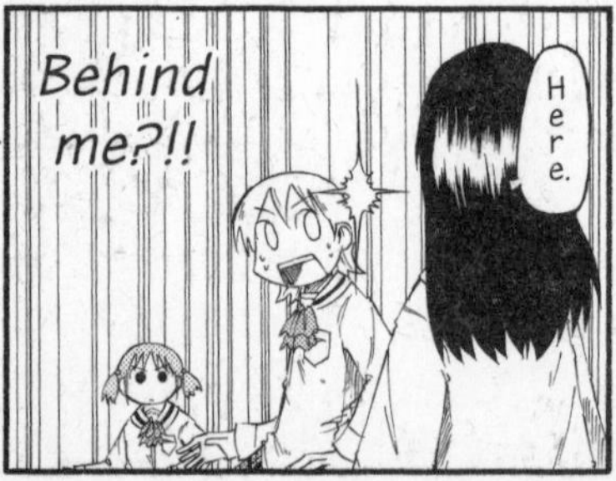
Here.
Behind me?!!

dictator

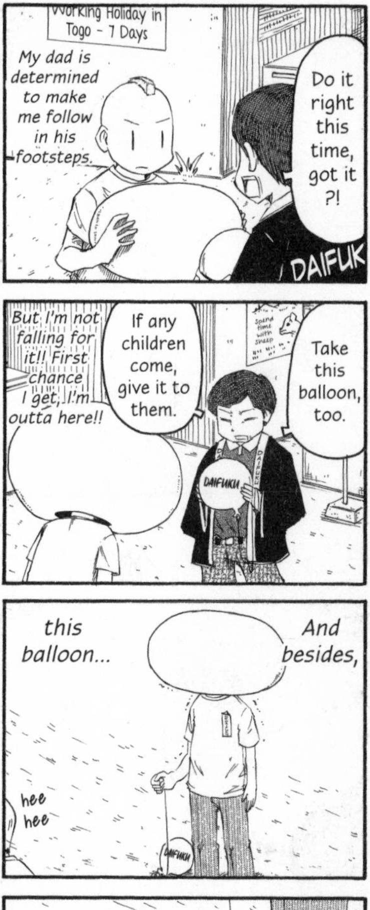
Working Holiday in Togo - 7 Days
Do it right this time, got it ?!
My dad is determined to make me follow in his footsteps.
DAIFUK
Take this balloon, too.
If any children come, give it to them.
But I'm not falling for it!! First chance I get, I'm outta here!!
Spend time with sheep
DAIFUKU
And besides,
this balloon...
hee hee
DAIFUKU
isn't even floating...
DAIFUKU

undone

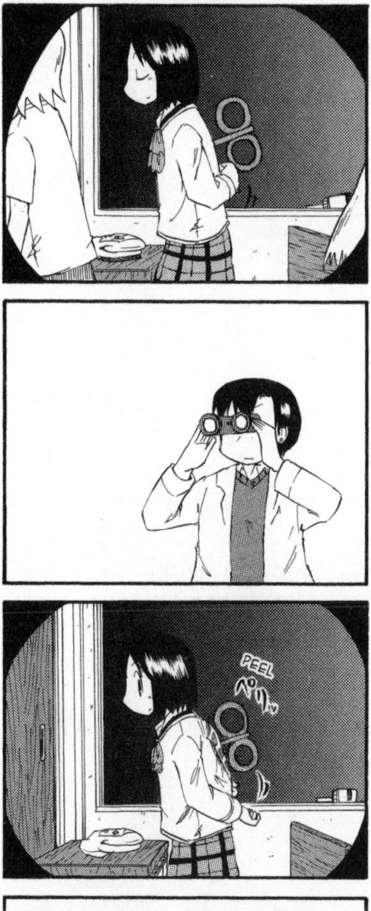
PEEL
ペリッ
Fascinating !!

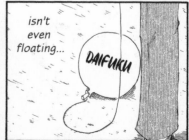

open

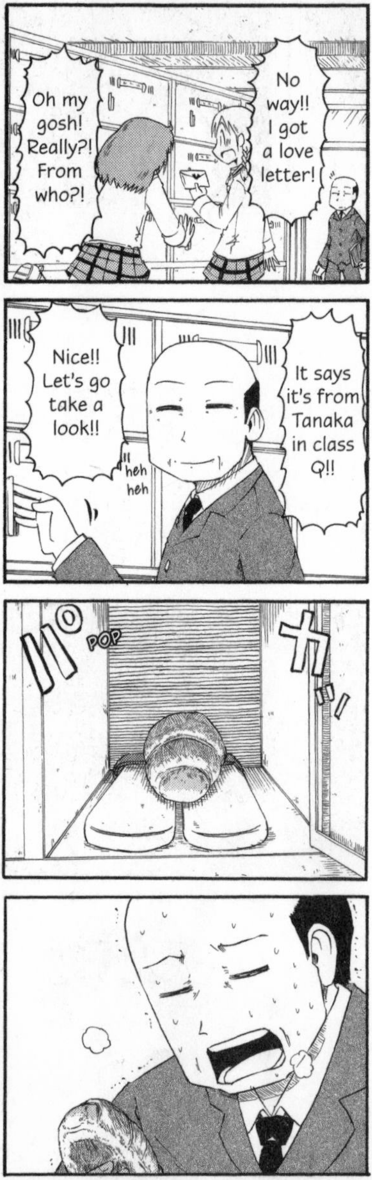
No way!! I got a love letter!
Oh my gosh! Really?! From who?!
It says it's from Tanaka in class Q!!
Nice!! Let's go take a look!!
heh heh
POP

jump

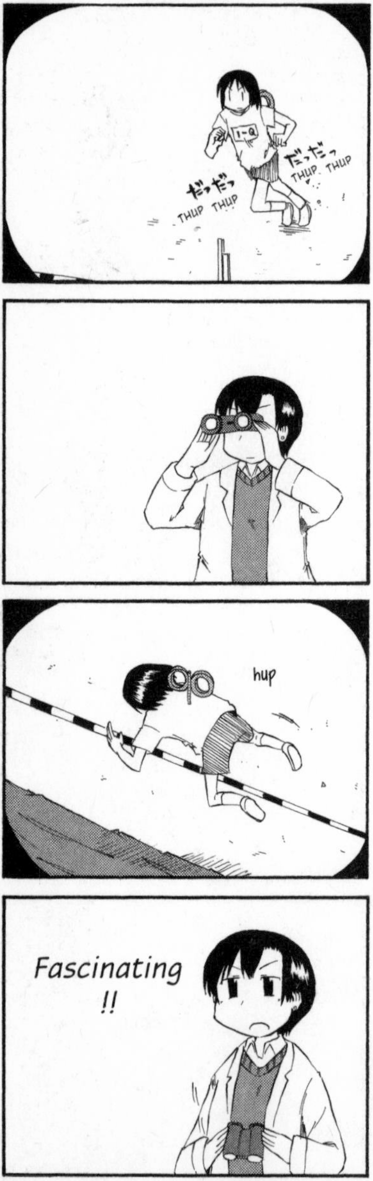
だっだっ THUP THUP
だっだっ THUP THUP
hup
Fascinating !!

sleep

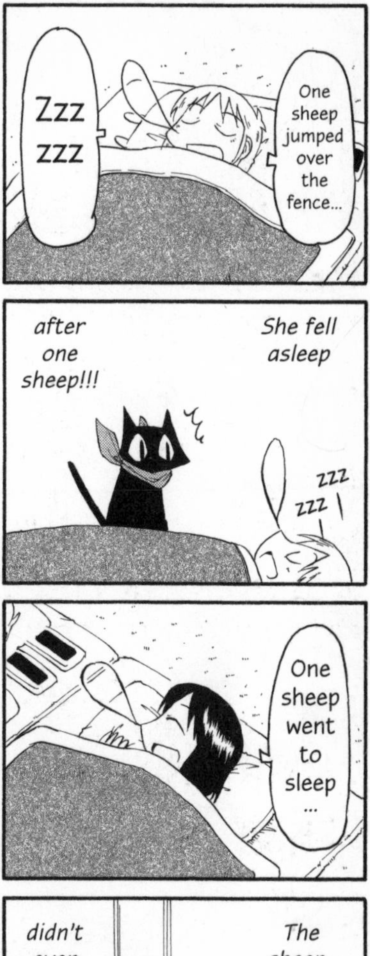
One sheep jumped over the fence...
Zzz zzz
She fell asleep
after one sheep!!!
zzz zzz
One sheep went to sleep ...
The sheep...
didn't even get to jump...
zzz
zzz

game 2

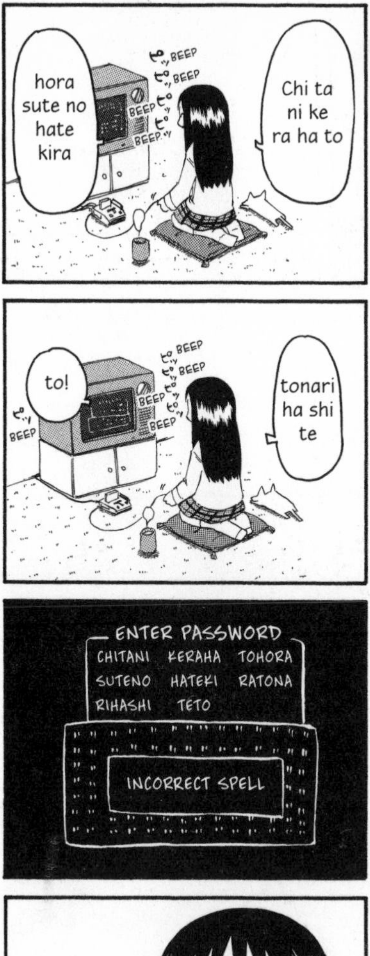
ピッ BEEP ピッ BEEP ピッ BEEP ピッ BEEP
Chi ta ni ke ra ha to
hora sute no hate kira
ピッ BEEP ピッ BEEP ピッ BEEP ピッ BEEP ピッ BEEP
tonari ha shi te
to!
ENTER PASSWORD
CHITANI KERAHA TOHORA
SUTENO HATEKI RATONA
RIHASHI TETO
INCORRECT SPELL

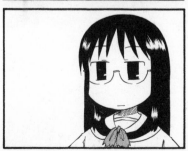

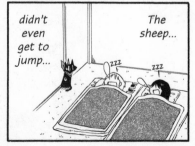

trap

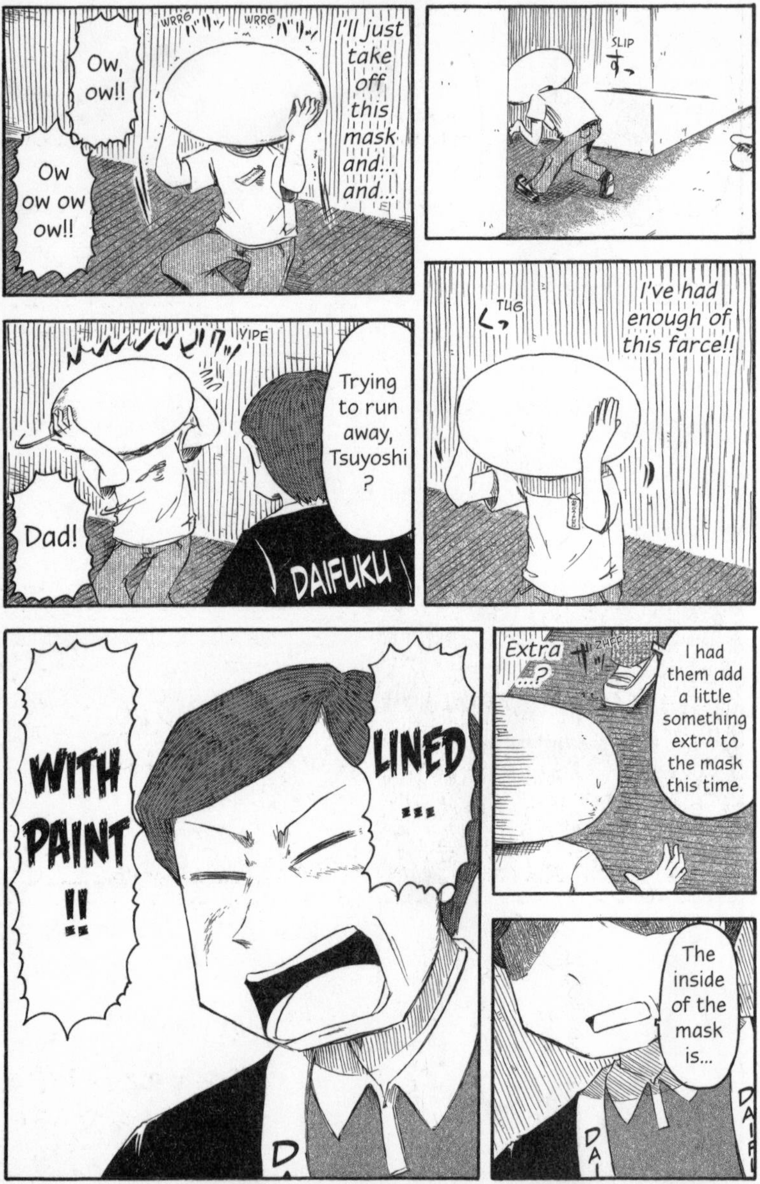

SLIP
I'll just take off this mask and... and...
WRRG
WRRG
Ow, ow!!
Ow ow ow ow!!
I've had enough of this farce!!
TUG
Trying to run away, Tsuyoshi?
YIPE
DAIFUKU
Dad!
I had them add a little something extra to the mask this time.
ZHFF
Extra...?
The inside of the mask is...
LINED...
WITH PAINT!!

escape to freedom

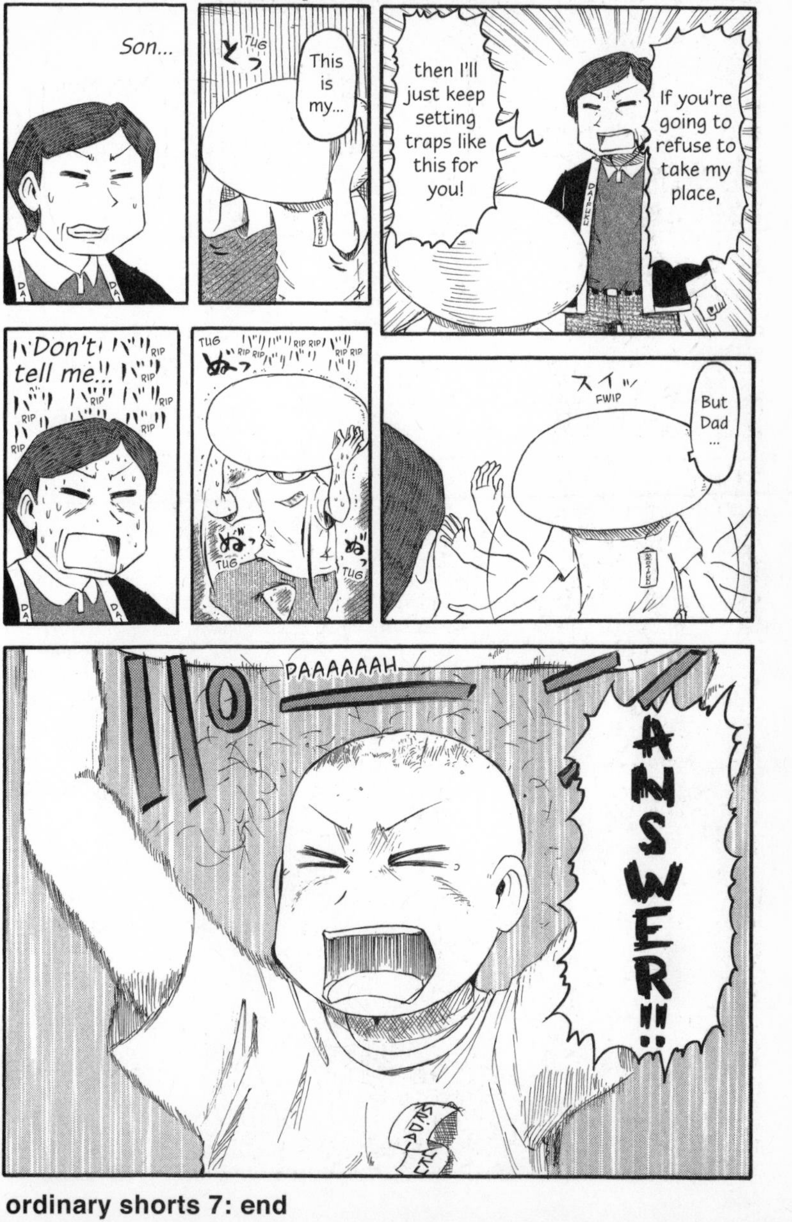
If you're going to refuse to take my place,
then I'll just keep setting traps like this for you!
とっ
TUG
This is my...
Son...
スイッ
FWIP
But Dad ...
TUG
ぬっ
RIP RIP
RIP RIP
RIP RIP
ぬっ
TUG
ぬっ
TUG
Don't tell me!!
RIP
RIP
RIP
RIP
RIP
RIP
PAAAAAAH
ANSWER!!

ordinary shorts 7: end

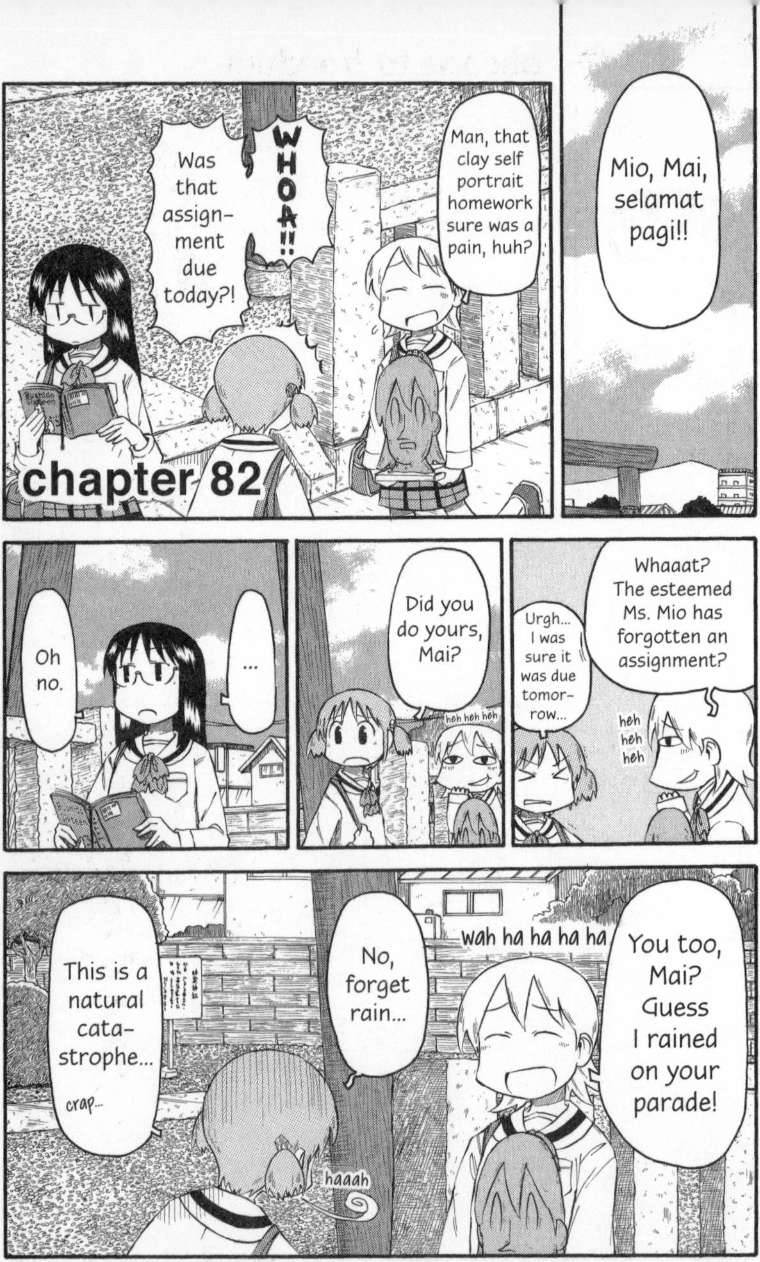
Mio, Mai, selamat pagi!!
Man, that clay self portrait homework sure was a pain, huh?
WHOA!!
Was that assignment due today?!
chapter 82
Whaaat? The esteemed Ms. Mio has forgotten an assignment?
heh heh heh
Urgh... I was sure it was due tomorrow...
Did you do yours, Mai?
heh heh heh
...
Oh no.
You too, Mai? Guess I rained on your parade!
wah ha ha ha ha
No, forget rain...
haaah
This is a natural catastrophe...
crap...

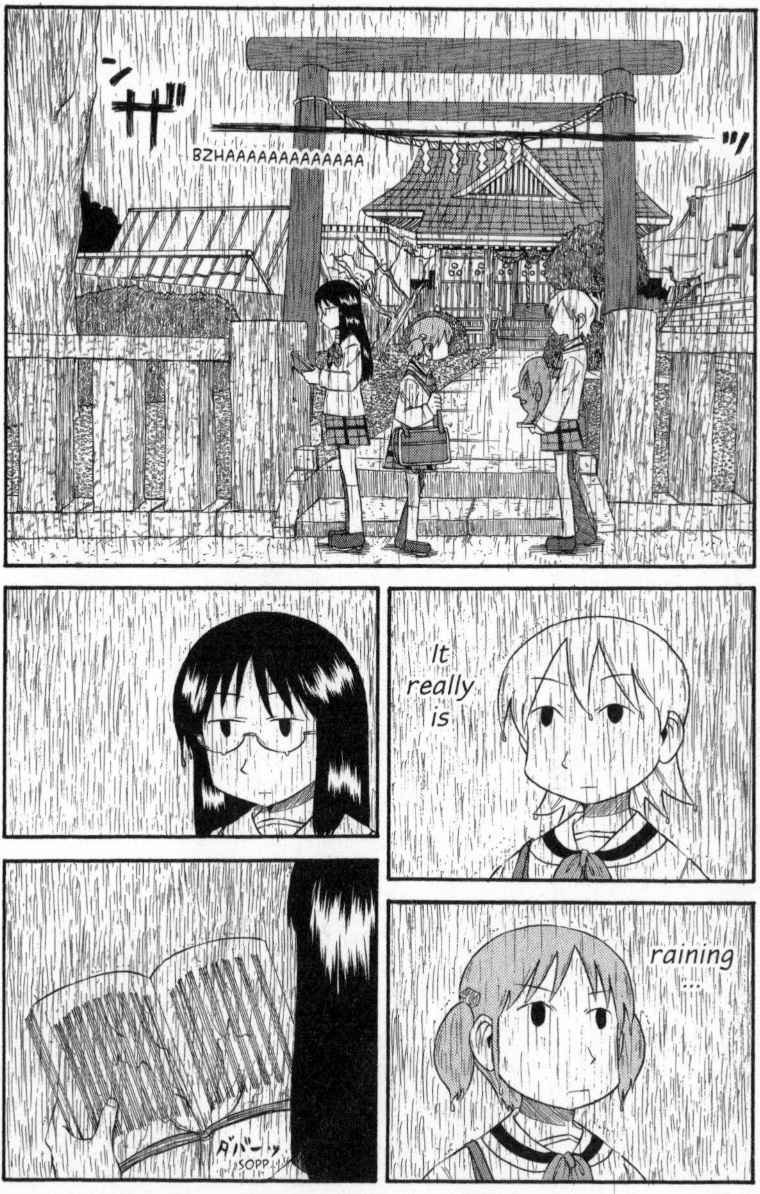
ザン
ッ
BZHAAAAAAAAAAAAAA
It really is
raining ...
ダバーッ
SOPP

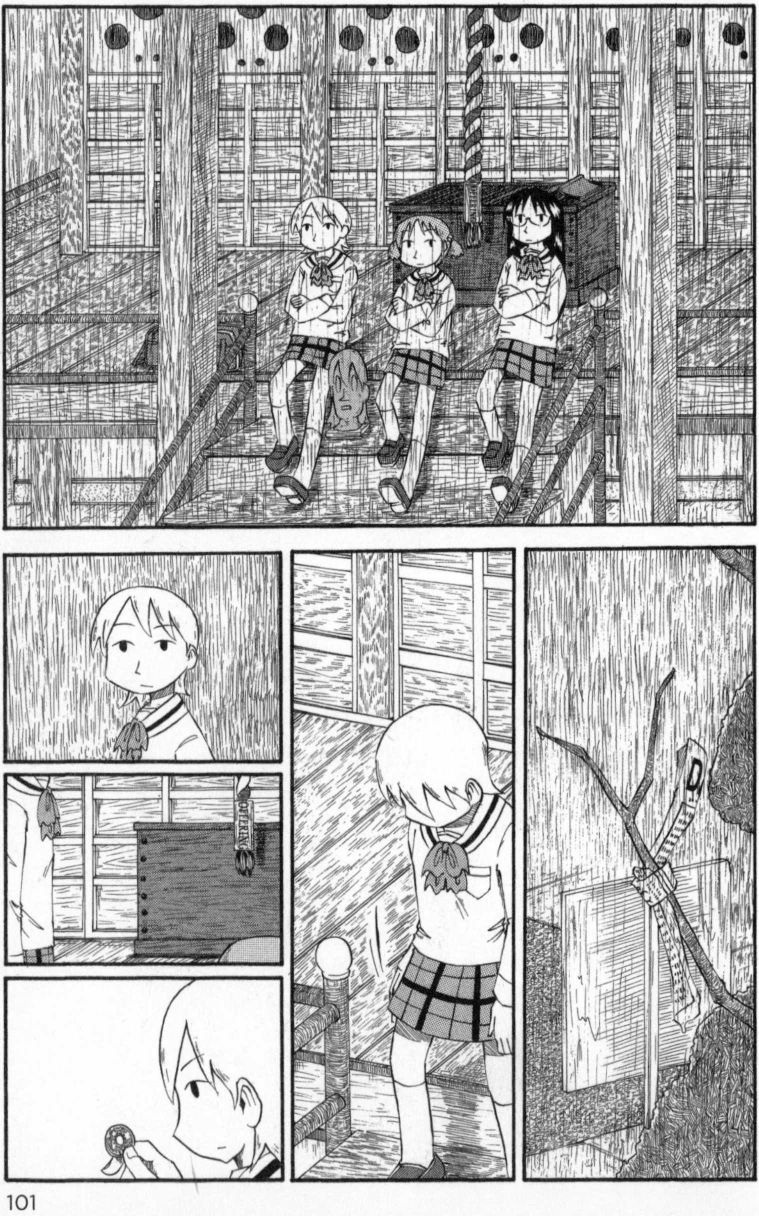
OFFERING

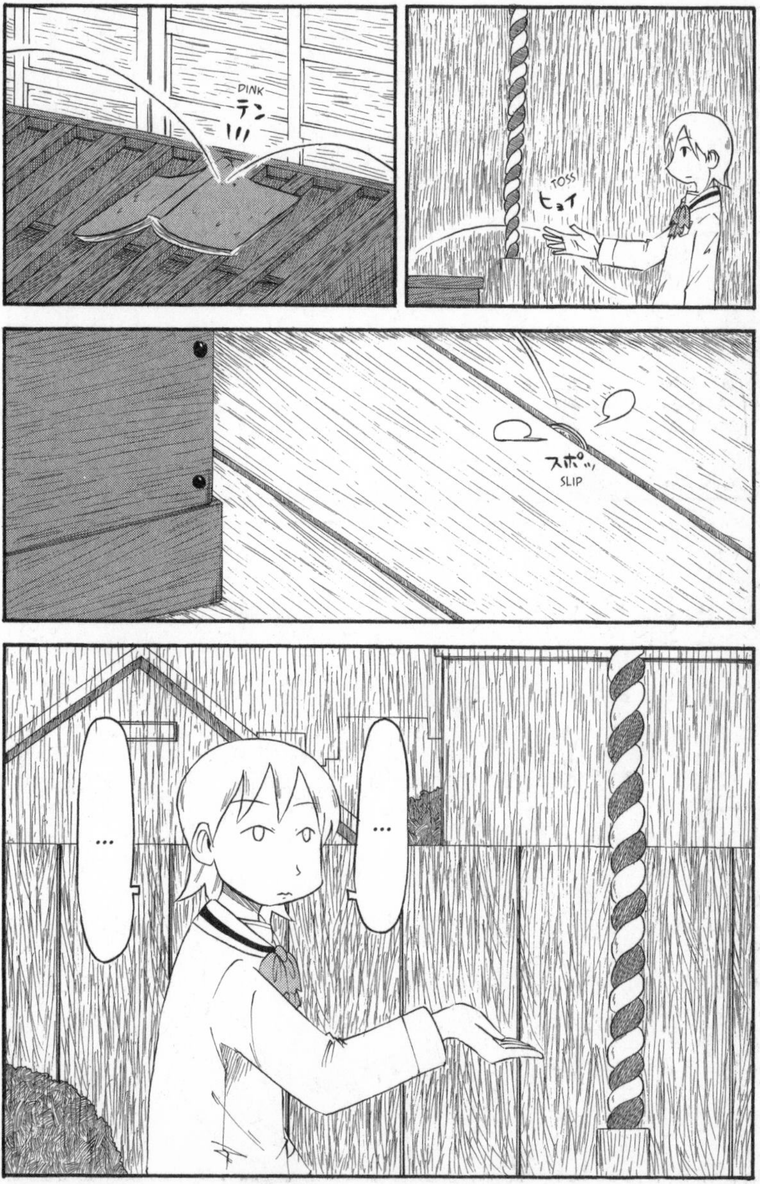
TOSS
ヒョイ
DINK
テン!!!
スポッ
SLIP
...
...

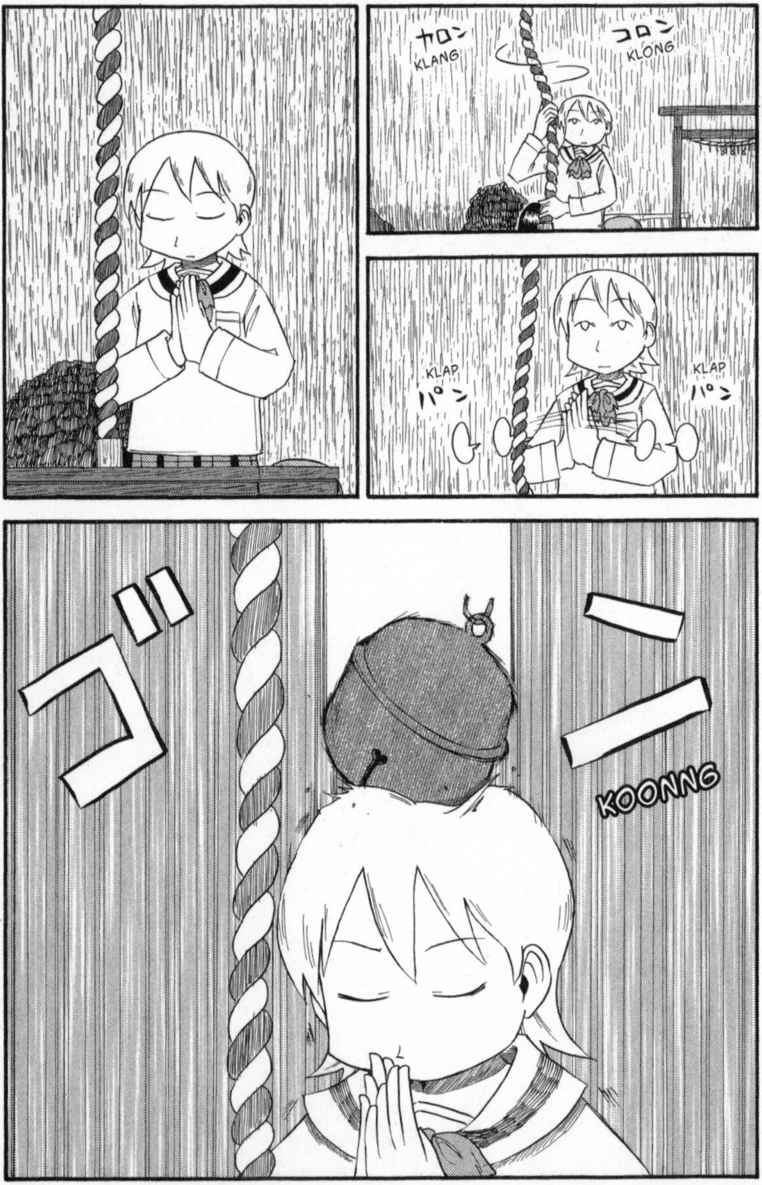

コロン
KLONG
カロン
KLANG
KLAP
パン
KLAP
パン
ゴーー
KOONNG

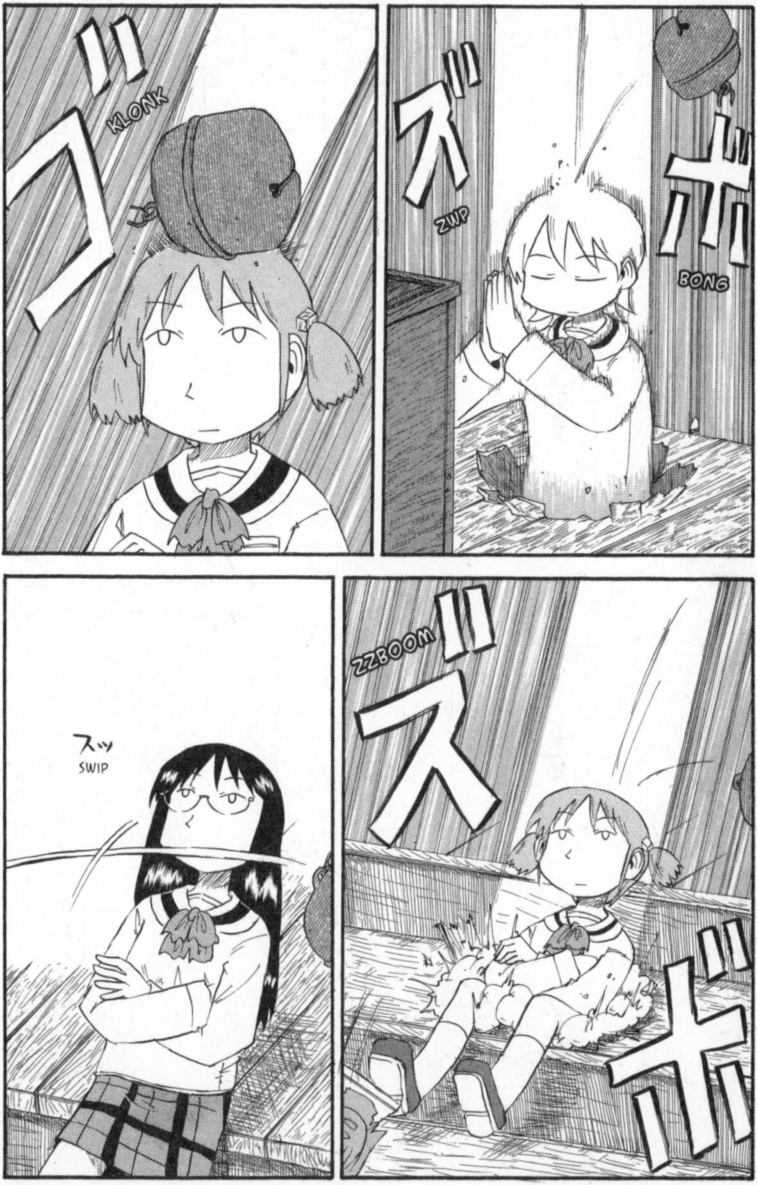
ズ
ZWP
ボ
BONG
ゴ
KLONK
ズ
ZZBOOM
ボ
スッ
SWIP

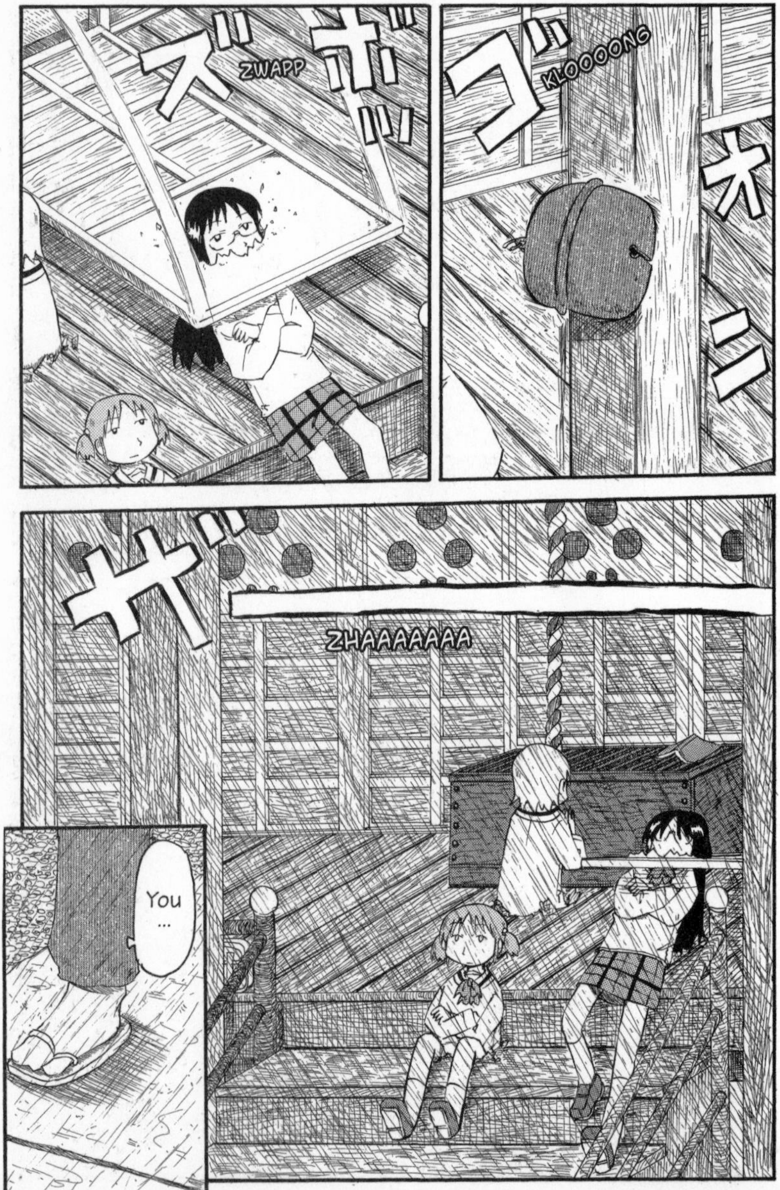
KLOOOONG
ZWAPP
ZHAAAAAAA
You ...

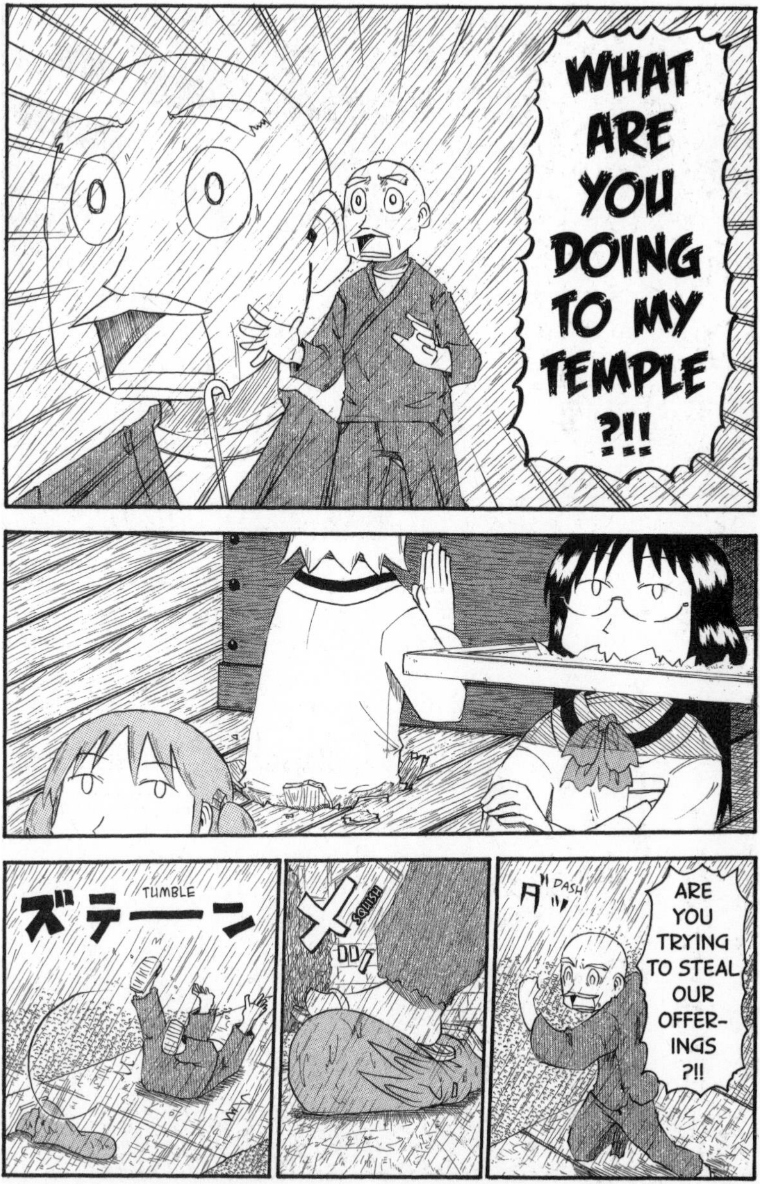
WHAT ARE YOU DOING TO MY TEMPLE ?!!
ダッ
DASH
ARE YOU TRYING TO STEAL OUR OFFER-INGS ?!!
SQUISH
ズテーン
TUMBLE

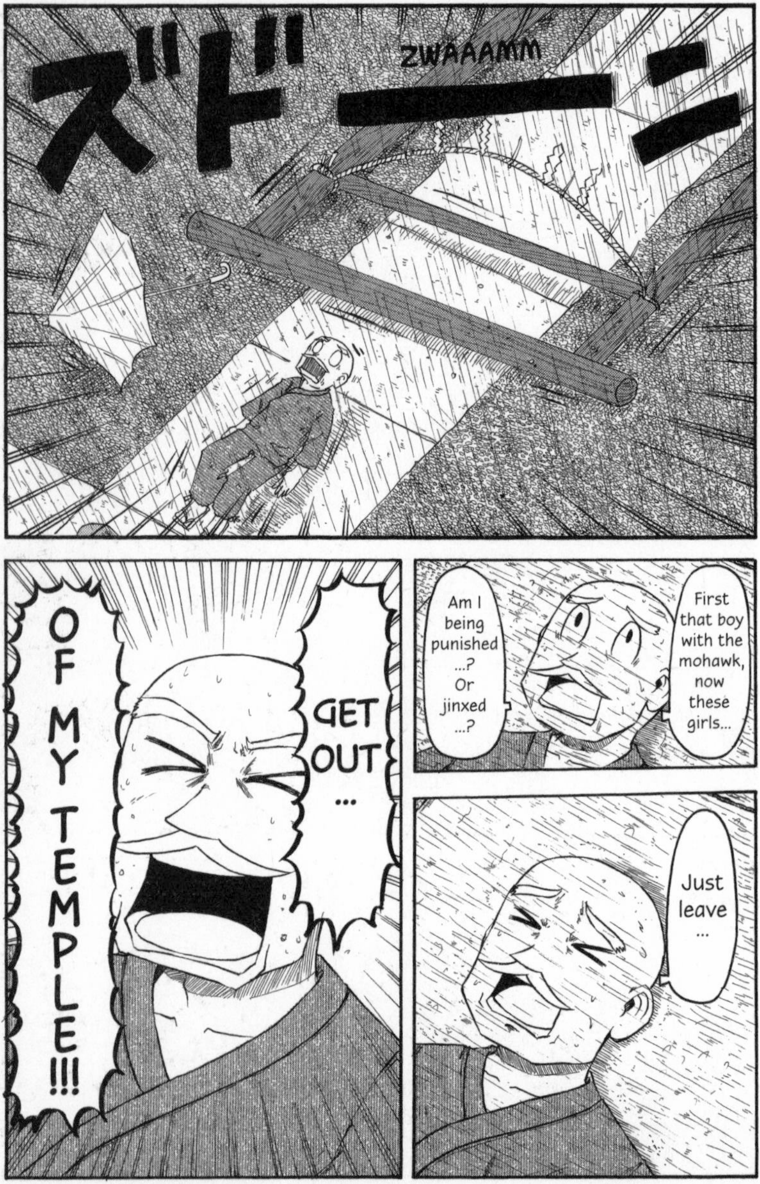
ズドーン
ZWAAAMM
First that boy with the mohawk, now these girls...
Am I being punished ...? Or jinxed ...?
Just leave ...
GET OUT ...
OF MY TEMPLE!!!

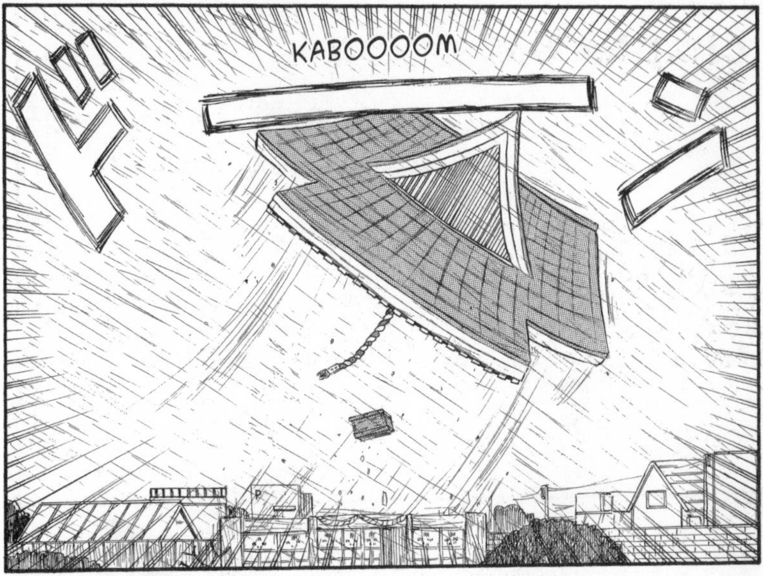
KABOOOOM

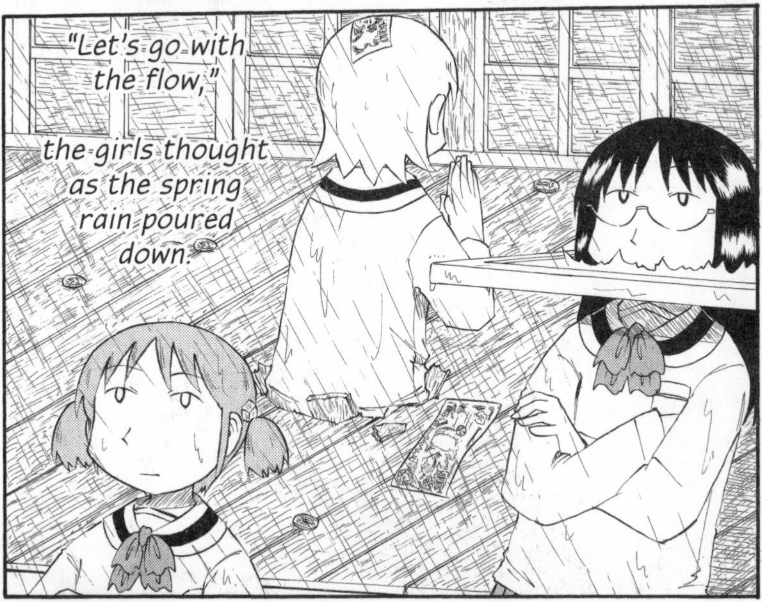
"Let's go with the flow,"
the girls thought as the spring rain poured down.

chapter 82: end

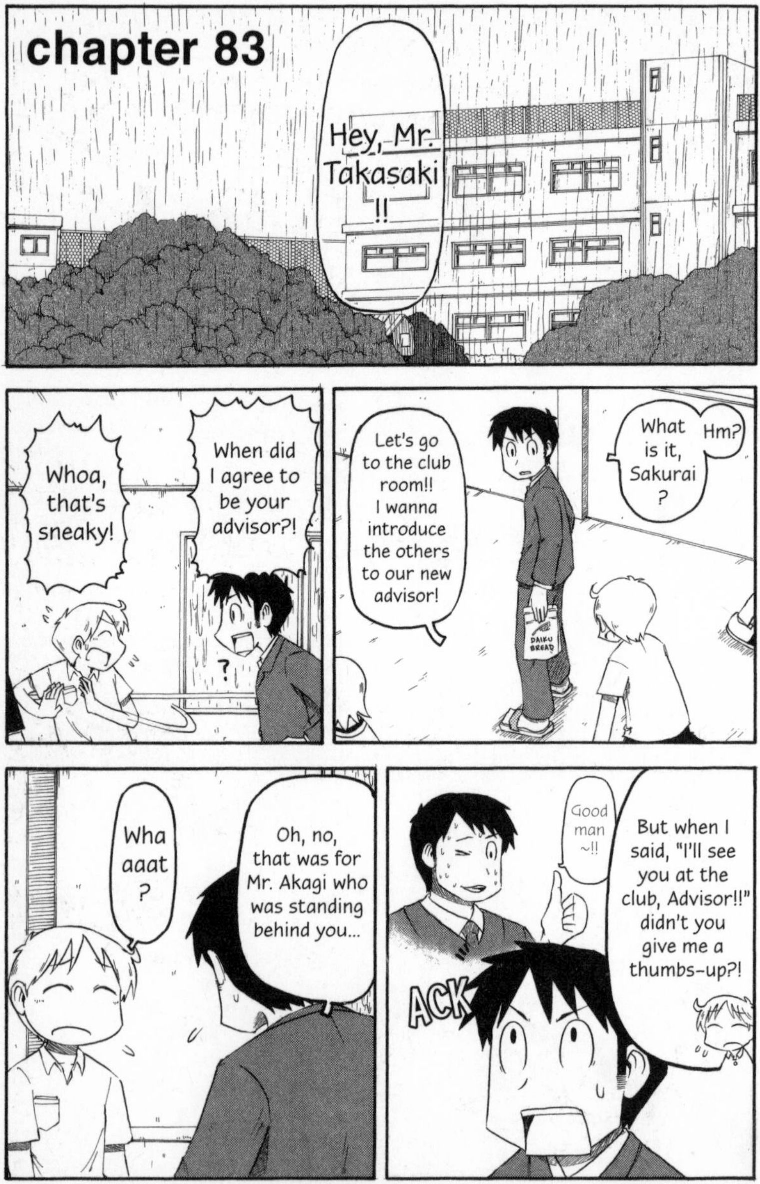
chapter 83
Hey, Mr. Takasaki !!
Hm?
What is it, Sakurai ?
Let's go to the club room!! I wanna introduce the others to our new advisor!
DAIKU BREAD
When did I agree to be your advisor?!
?
Whoa, that's sneaky!
But when I said, "I'll see you at the club, Advisor!!" didn't you give me a thumbs-up?!
Good man ~!!
ACK
Oh, no, that was for Mr. Akagi who was standing behind you...
Wha aaat ?

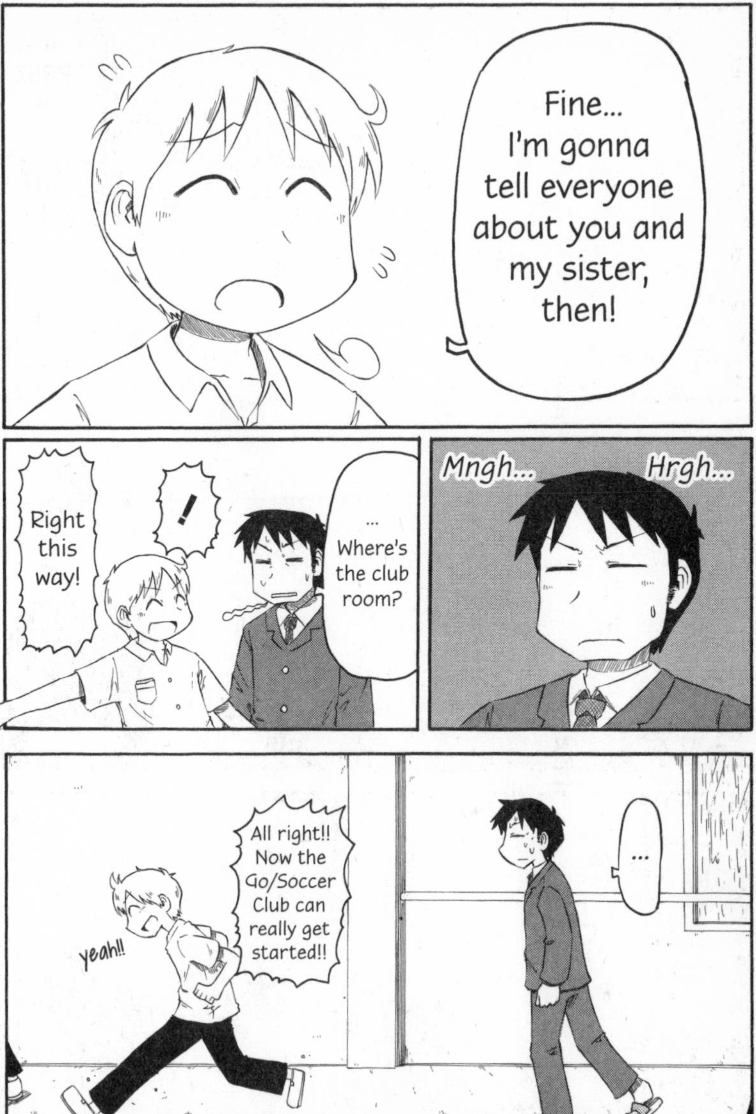
Fine... I'm gonna tell everyone about you and my sister, then!
Mngh...
Hrgh...
... Where's the club room?
!
Right this way!
...
All right!! Now the Go/Soccer Club can really get started!!
yeah!!

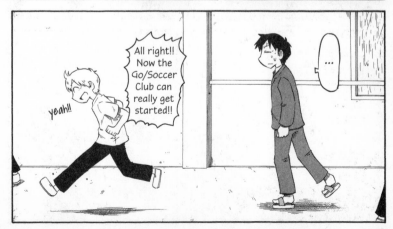

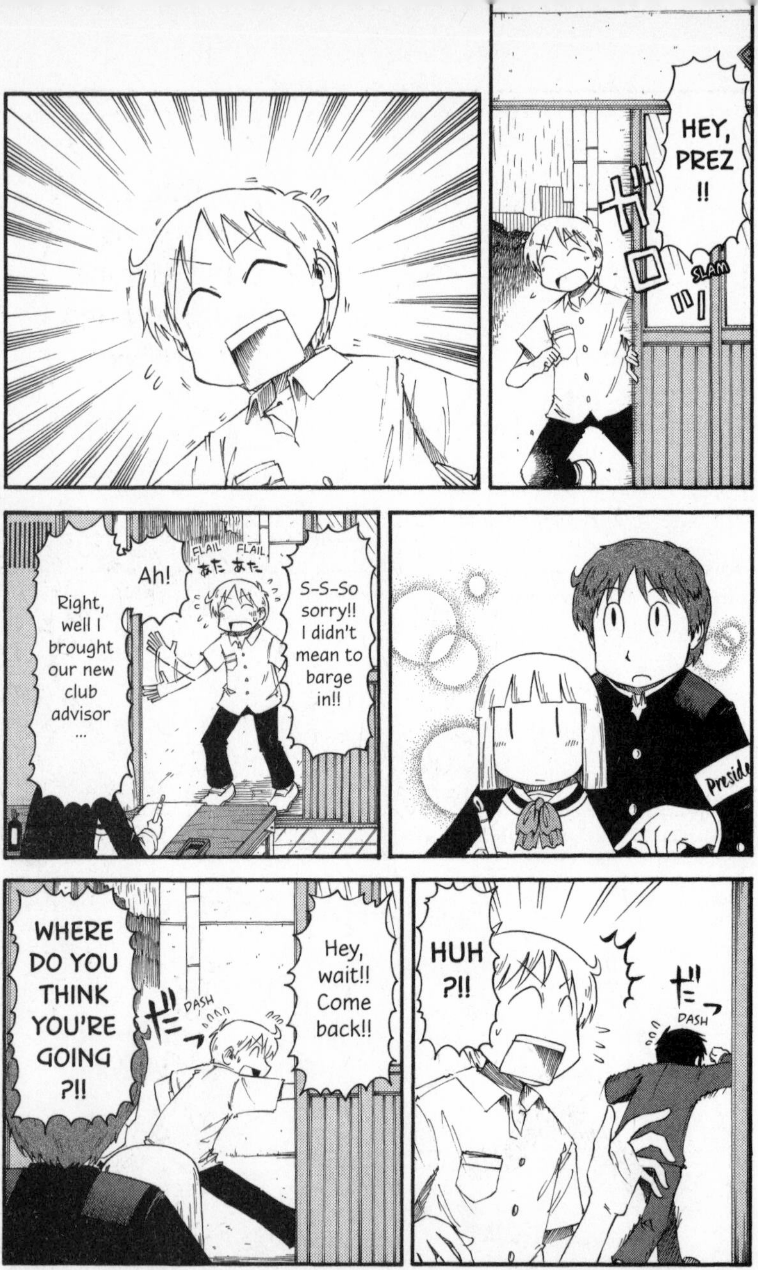
HEY, PREZ !!
ガロッ
SLAM
Preside
S-S-So sorry!! I didn't mean to barge in!!
FLAIL FLAIL
あた あた
Ah!
Right, well I brought our new club advisor ...
ダッ
DASH
HUH ?!!
Hey, wait!! Come back!!
ダッ
DASH
WHERE DO YOU THINK YOU'RE GOING ?!!

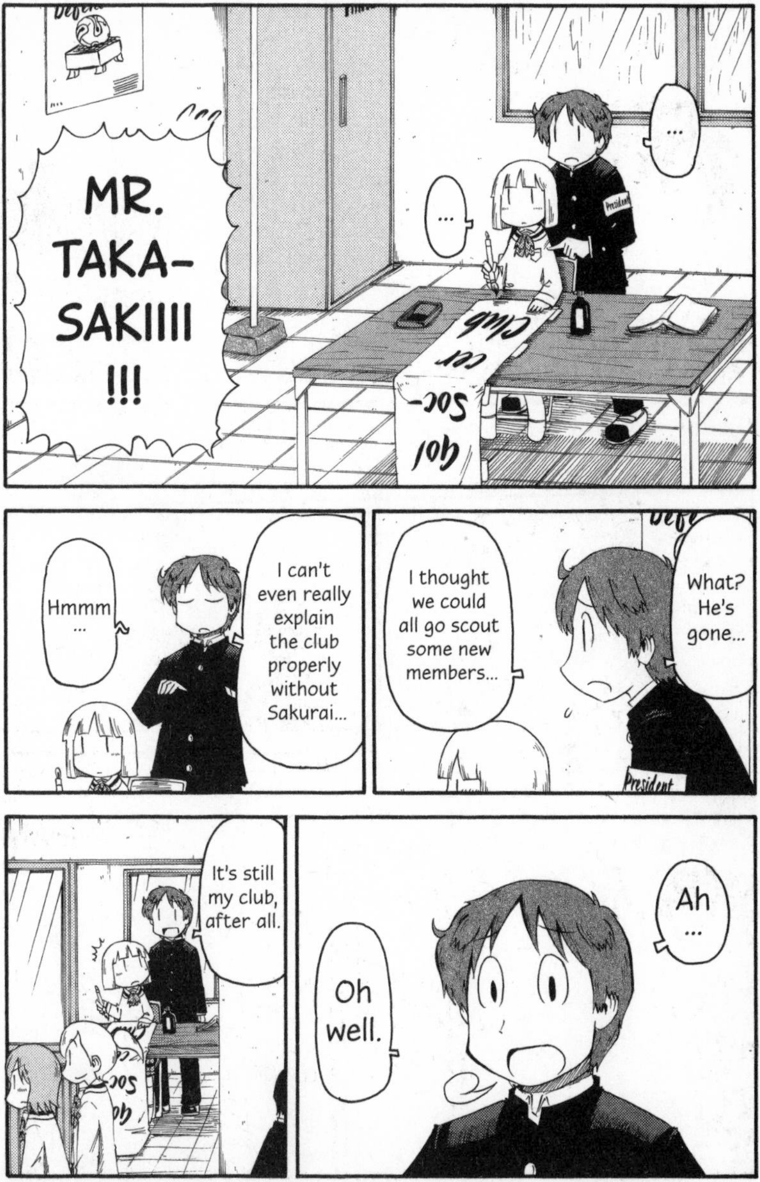
...
...
MR. TAKA-SAKIIIII!!!
What? He's gone...
I thought we could all go scout some new members...
I can't even really explain the club properly without Sakurai...
Hmmm ...
Ah ...
Oh well.
It's still my club, after all.

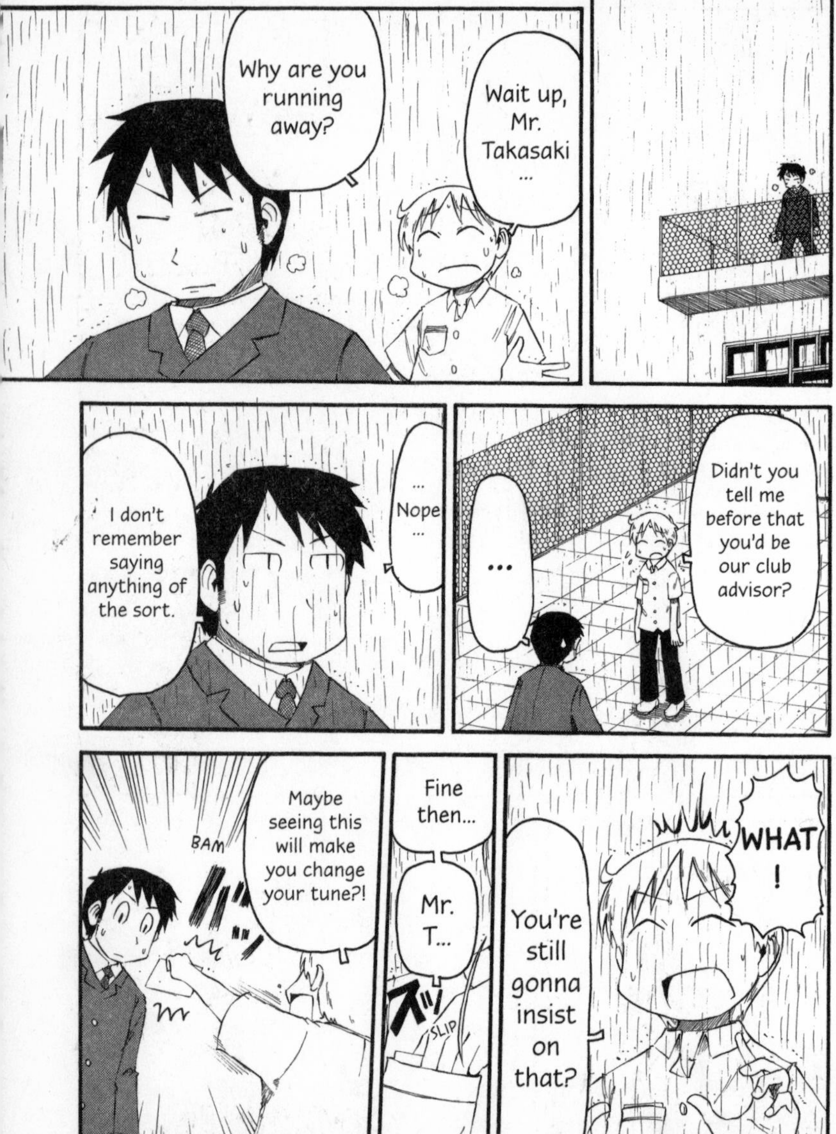
Wait up, Mr. Takasaki ...
Why are you running away?
Didn't you tell me before that you'd be our club advisor?
...
... Nope ...
I don't remember saying anything of the sort.
WHAT !
You're still gonna insist on that?
Fine then...
Mr. T...
SLIP
Maybe seeing this will make you change your tune?!
BAM

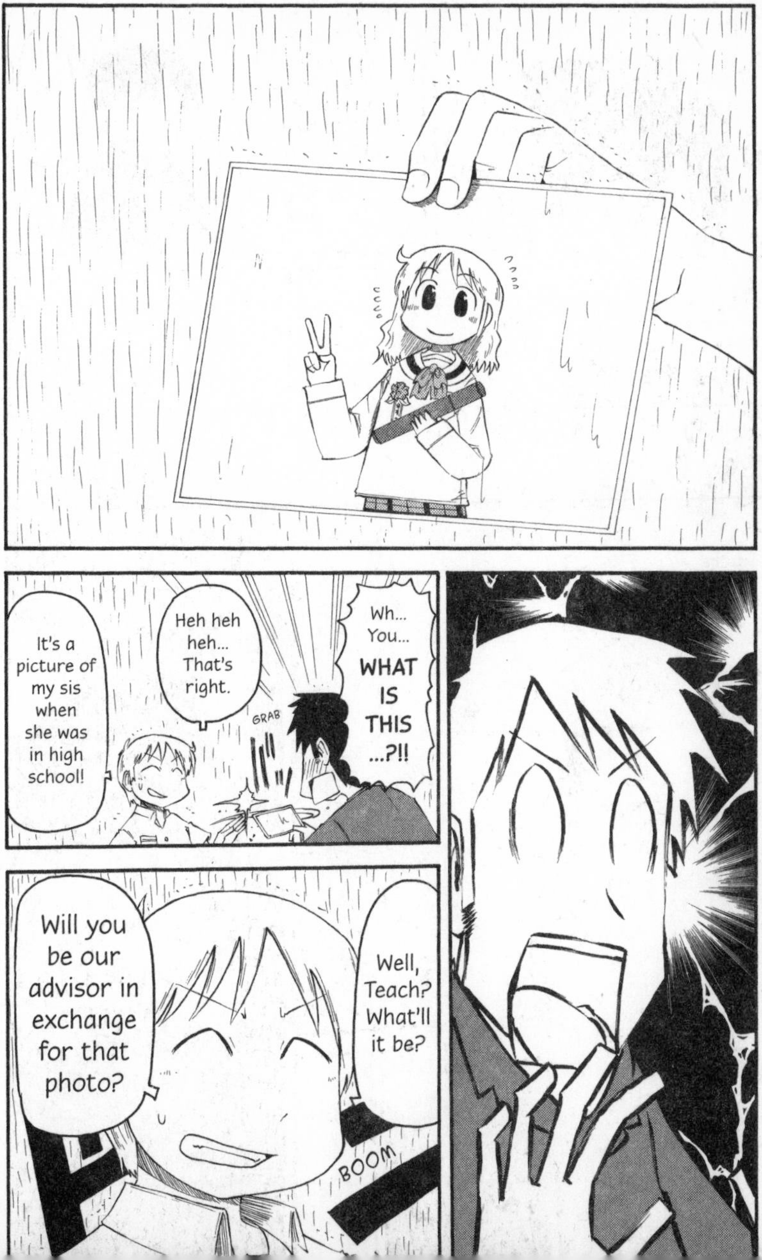
Wh... You... WHAT IS THIS ...?!!
Heh heh heh... That's right.
GRAB
It's a picture of my sis when she was in high school!
Well, Teach? What'll it be?
Will you be our advisor in exchange for that photo?
BOOM

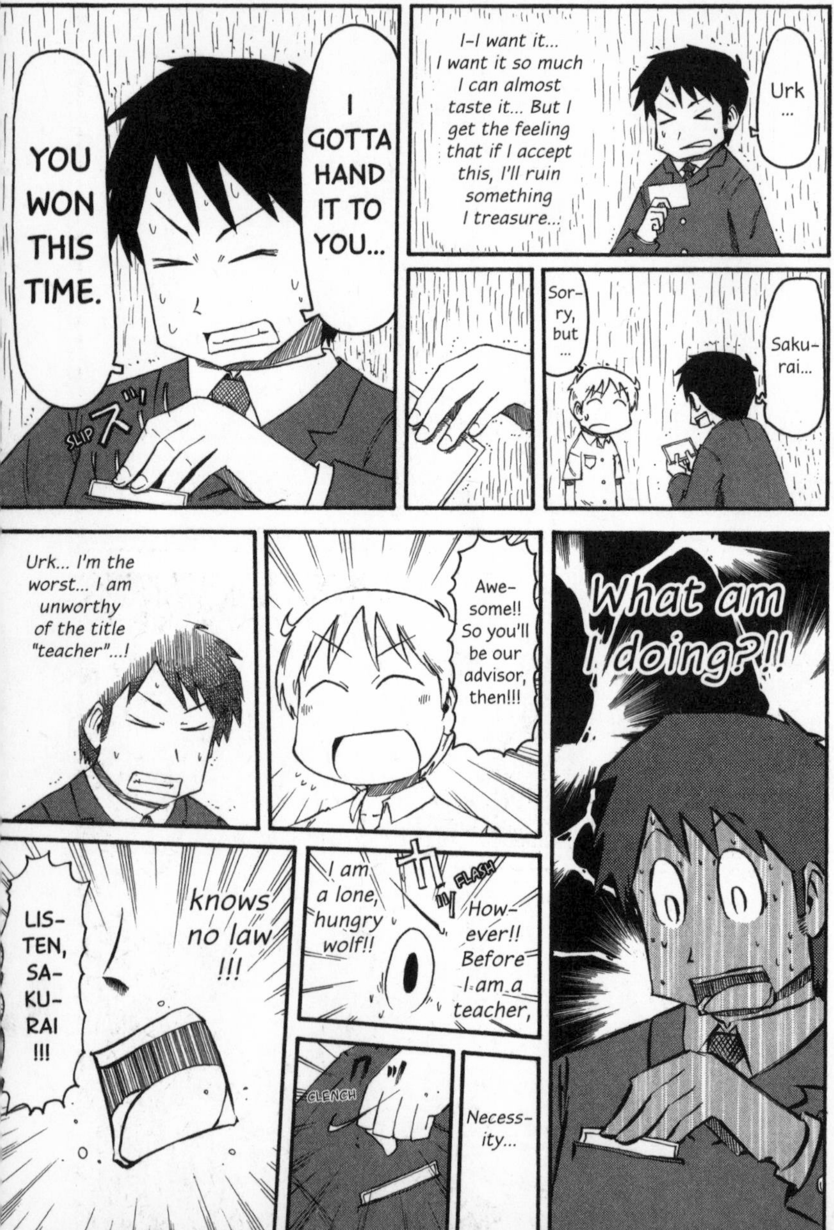
Urk ...
I-I want it... I want it so much I can almost taste it... But I get the feeling that if I accept this, I'll ruin something I treasure...
Saku-rai...
Sor-ry, but ...
I GOTTA HAND IT TO YOU...
YOU WON THIS TIME.
SLIP
What am I doing?!!
Awe-some!! So you'll be our advisor, then!!!
Urk... I'm the worst... I am unworthy of the title "teacher"...!
How-ever!! Before I am a teacher,
FLASH
I am a lone, hungry wolf!!
Necess-ity...
CLENCH
knows no law !!!
LIS-TEN, SA-KU-RAI !!!

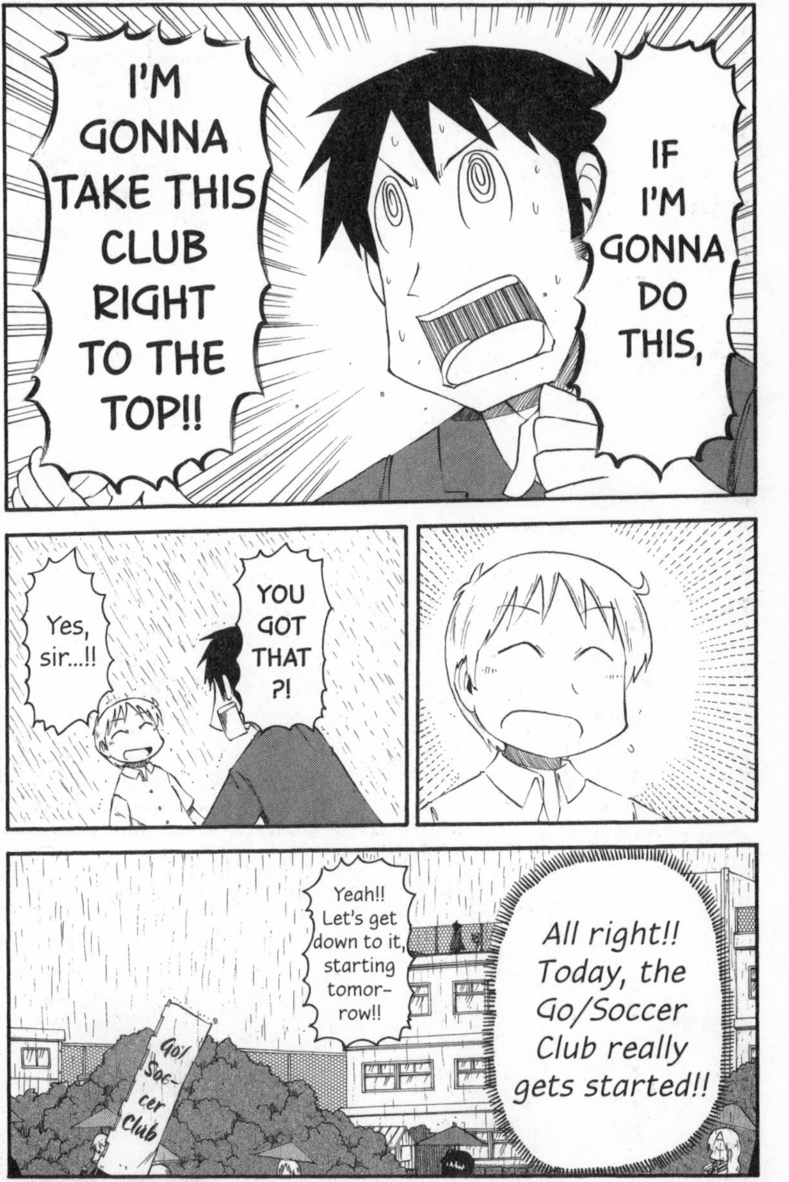
IF I'M GONNA DO THIS,
I'M GONNA TAKE THIS CLUB RIGHT TO THE TOP!!
YOU GOT THAT?!
Yes, sir...!!
All right!! Today, the Go/Soccer Club really gets started!!
Yeah!! Let's get down to it, starting tomor-row!!
Go/ Soc-cer Club

chapter 83: end

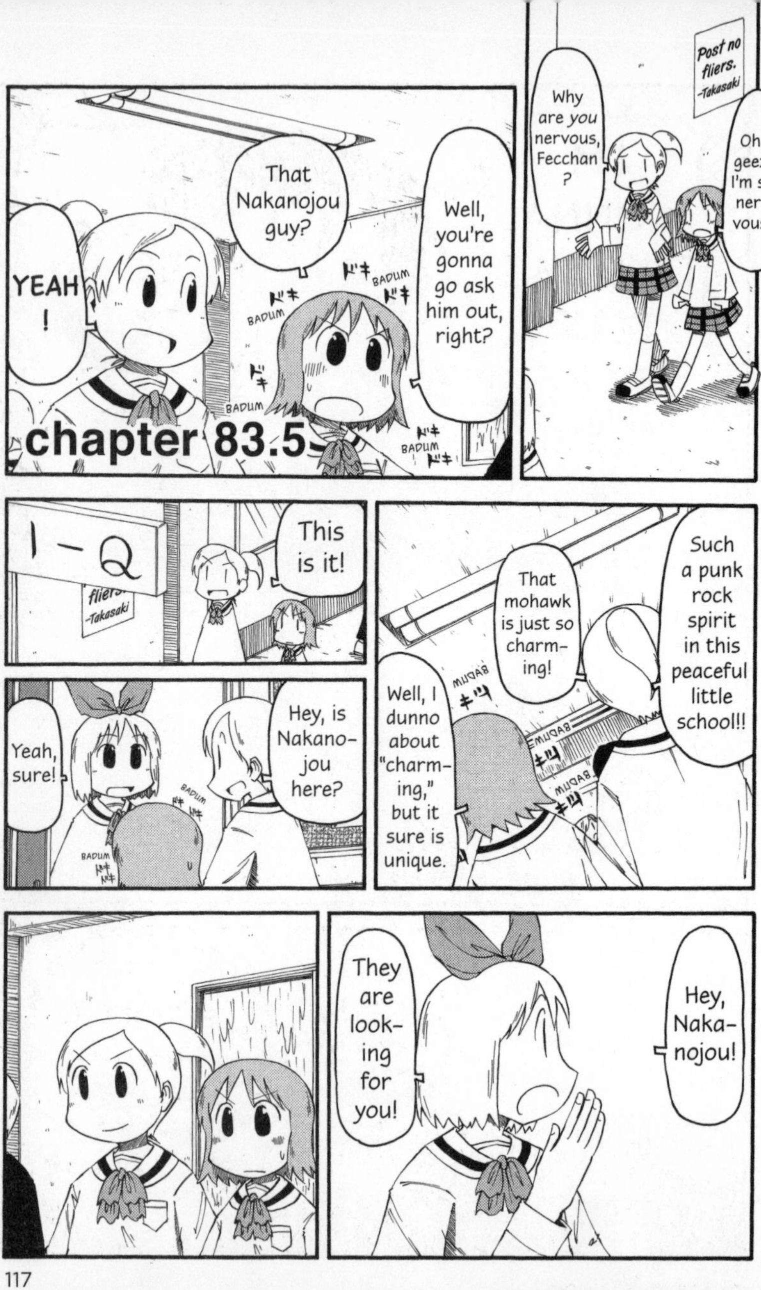
Post no fliers. -Takasaki
Oh, geez, I'm so ner-vous!
Why are you nervous, Fecchan?
Well, you're gonna go ask him out, right?
That Nakanojou guy?
ドキ BADUM ドキ BADUM ドキ BADUM
YEAH!
chapter 83.5
ドキ BADUM ドキ
Such a punk rock spirit in this peaceful little school!!
That mohawk is just so charming!
Well, I dunno about "charming," but it sure is unique.
ドキ BADUM ドキ BADUM ドキ BADUM
1-Q
fliers. -Takasaki
This is it!
Hey, is Nakano-jou here?
Yeah, sure!
BADUM ドキ ドキ BADUM ドキ ドキ
Hey, Naka-nojou!
They are look-ing for you!

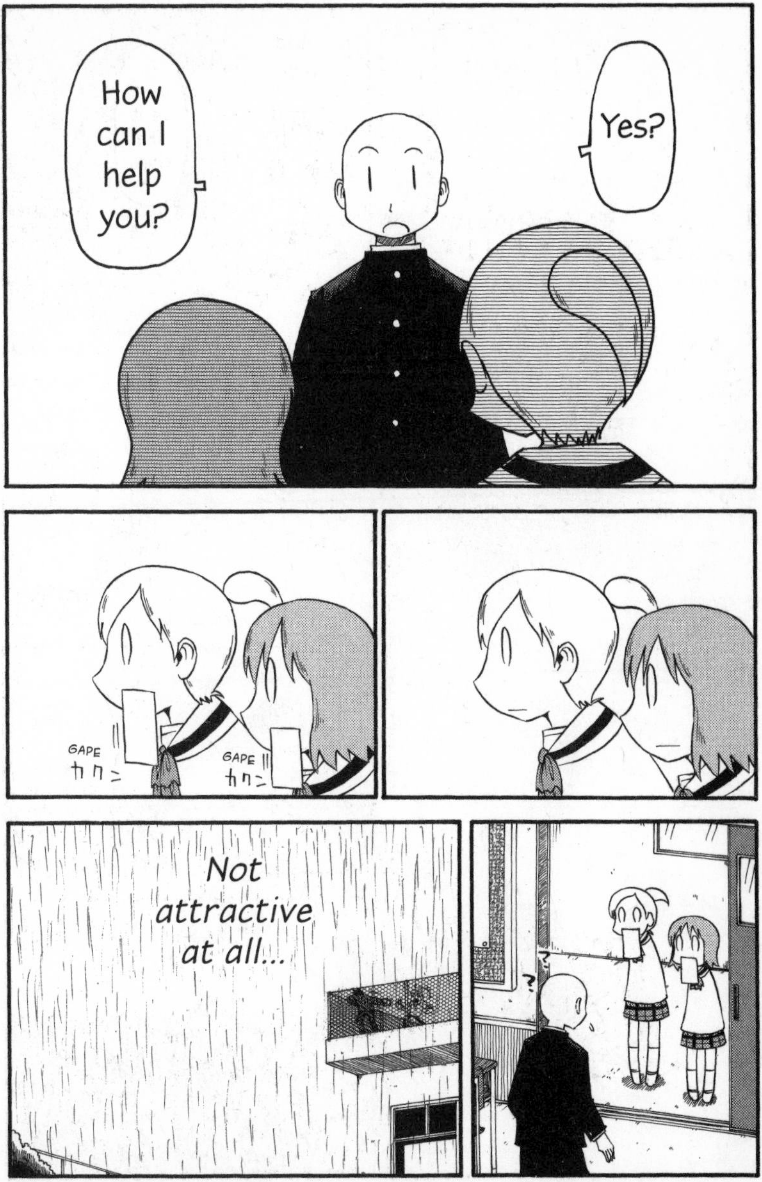
Yes?
How can I help you?
GAPE
カクン
GAPE
カクン
Not attractive at all...

chapter 83.5: end

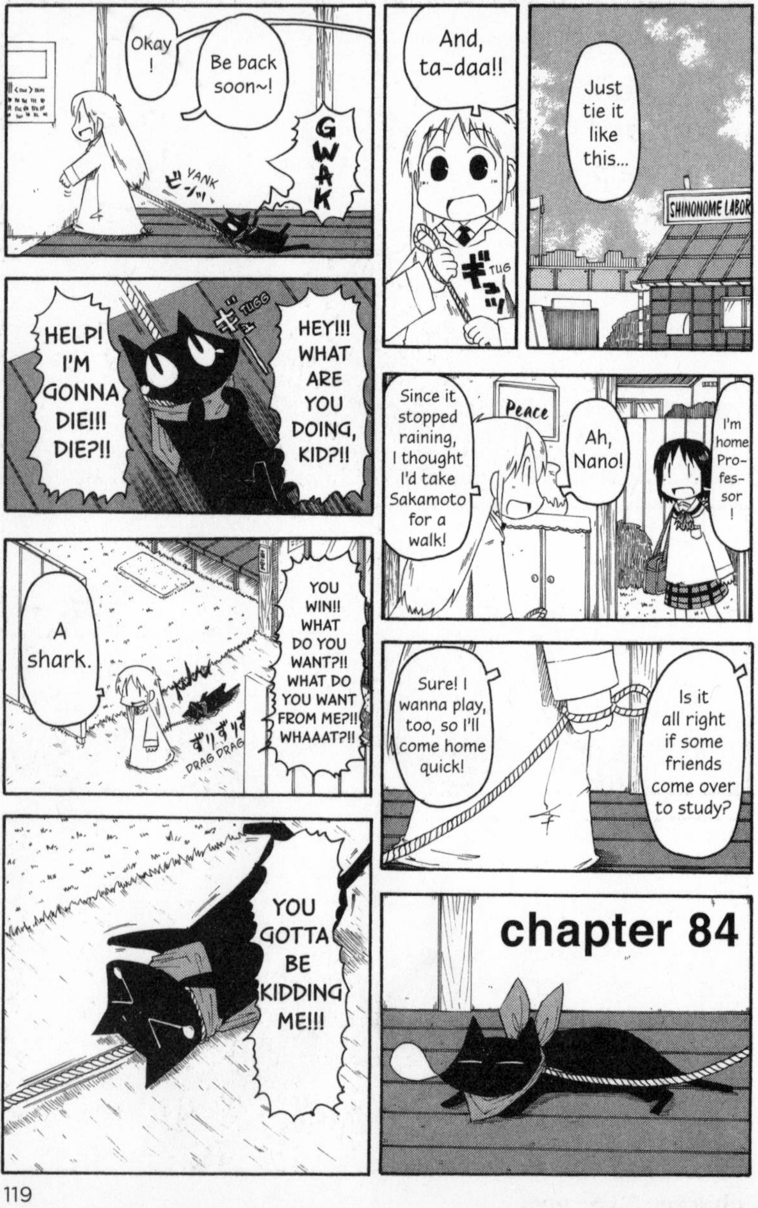
Just tie it like this...
SHINONOME LABOR
And, ta-daa!!
TUG
I'm home Professor!
Ah, Nano!
Peace
Since it stopped raining, I thought I'd take Sakamoto for a walk!
Is it all right if some friends come over to study?
Sure! I wanna play, too, so I'll come home quick!
chapter 84
GWAK
Be back soon~!
Okay!
YANK
HEY!!! WHAT ARE YOU DOING, KID?!!
TUGG
HELP! I'M GONNA DIE!!! DIE?!!
YOU WIN!! WHAT DO YOU WANT?!! WHAT DO YOU WANT FROM ME?!! WHAAAT?!!
A shark.
DRAG DRAG
YOU GOTTA BE KIDDING ME!!!

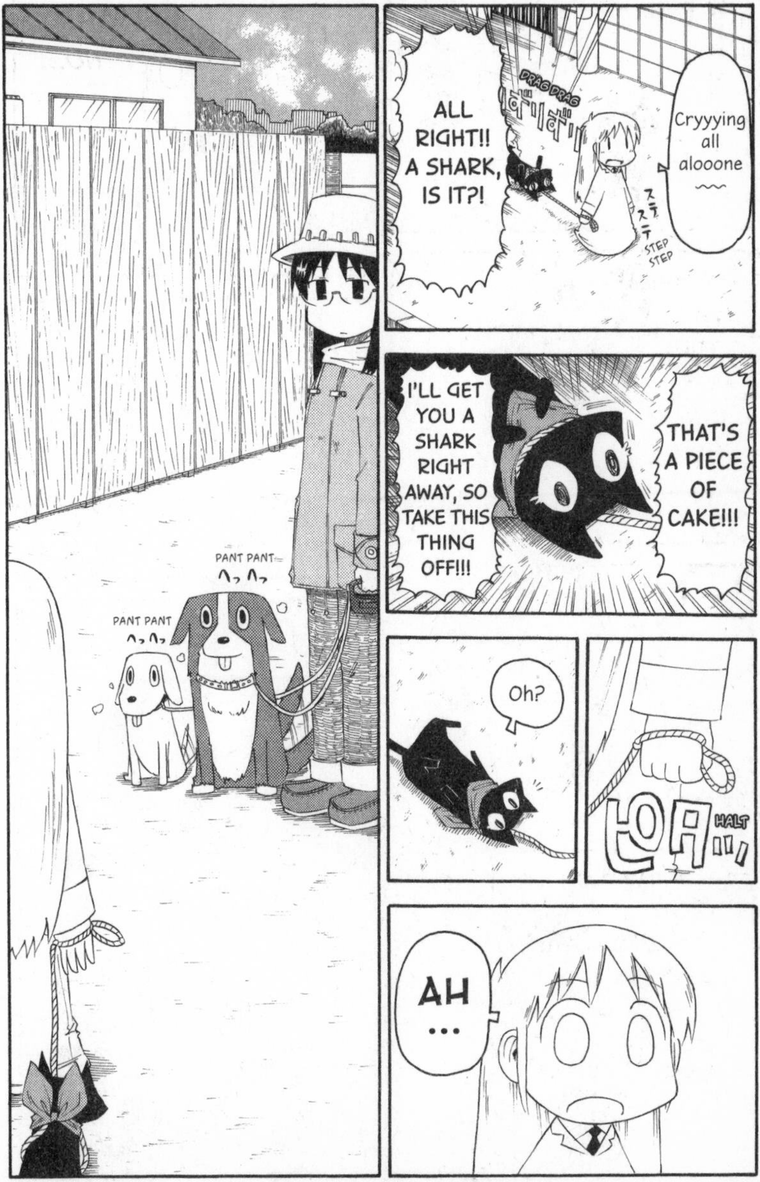
Cryyying all alooone ~~~
DRAG DRAG
ALL RIGHT!! A SHARK, IS IT?!
STEP STEP
THAT'S A PIECE OF CAKE!!!
I'LL GET YOU A SHARK RIGHT AWAY, SO TAKE THIS THING OFF!!!
HALT
Oh?
AH ...
PANT PANT
PANT PANT

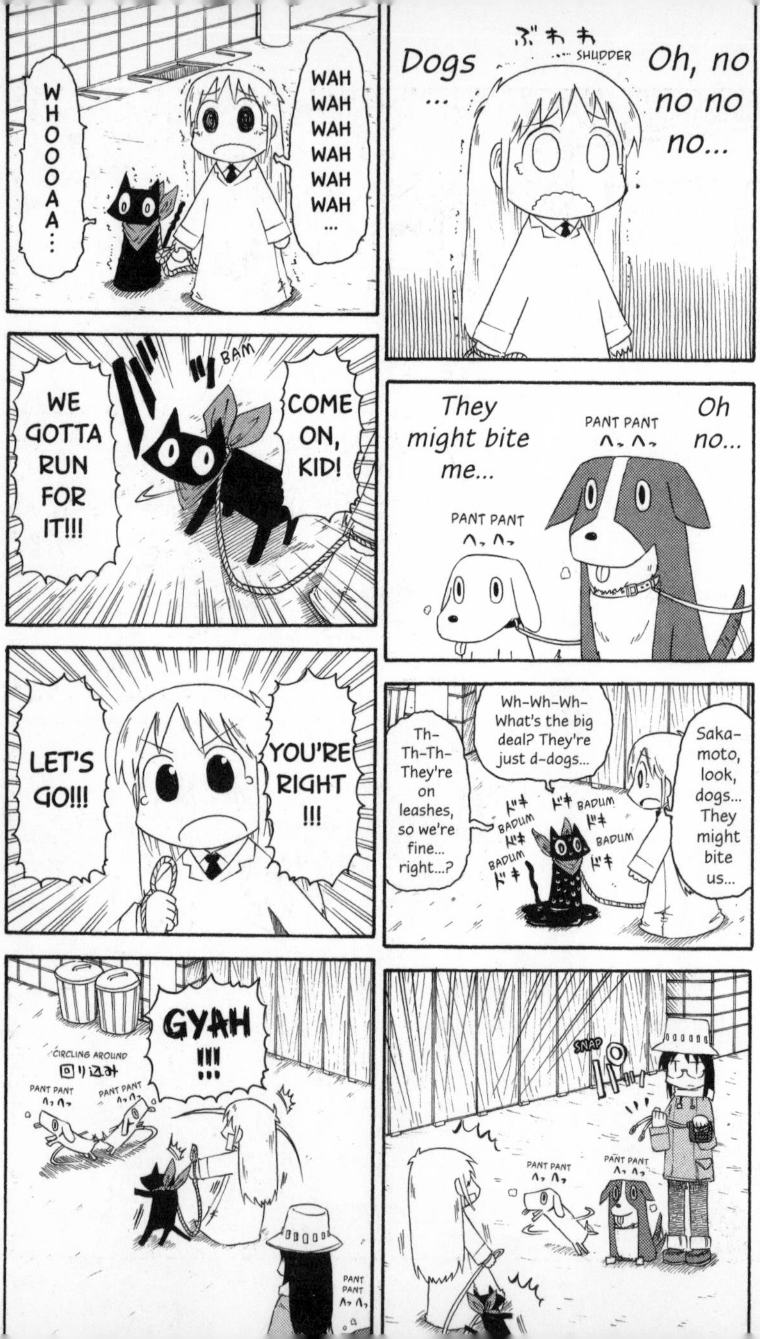
Oh, no no no no...
SHUDDER
Dogs...
WAH WAH WAH WAH WAH WAH...
WHOOOAA...
Oh no...
PANT PANT
They might bite me...
PANT PANT
BAM
COME ON, KID!
WE GOTTA RUN FOR IT!!!
Saka-moto, look, dogs... They might bite us...
Wh-Wh-Wh-What's the big deal? They're just d-dogs...
BADUM ドキ
BADUM ドキ
BADUM ドキ
BADUM ドキ
Th-Th-Th-They're on leashes, so we're fine... right...?
YOU'RE RIGHT!!!
LET'S GO!!!
SNAP
PANT PANT
PANT PANT
GYAH!!!
CIRCLING AROUND
回り込み
PANT PANT
PANT PANT
PANT PANT

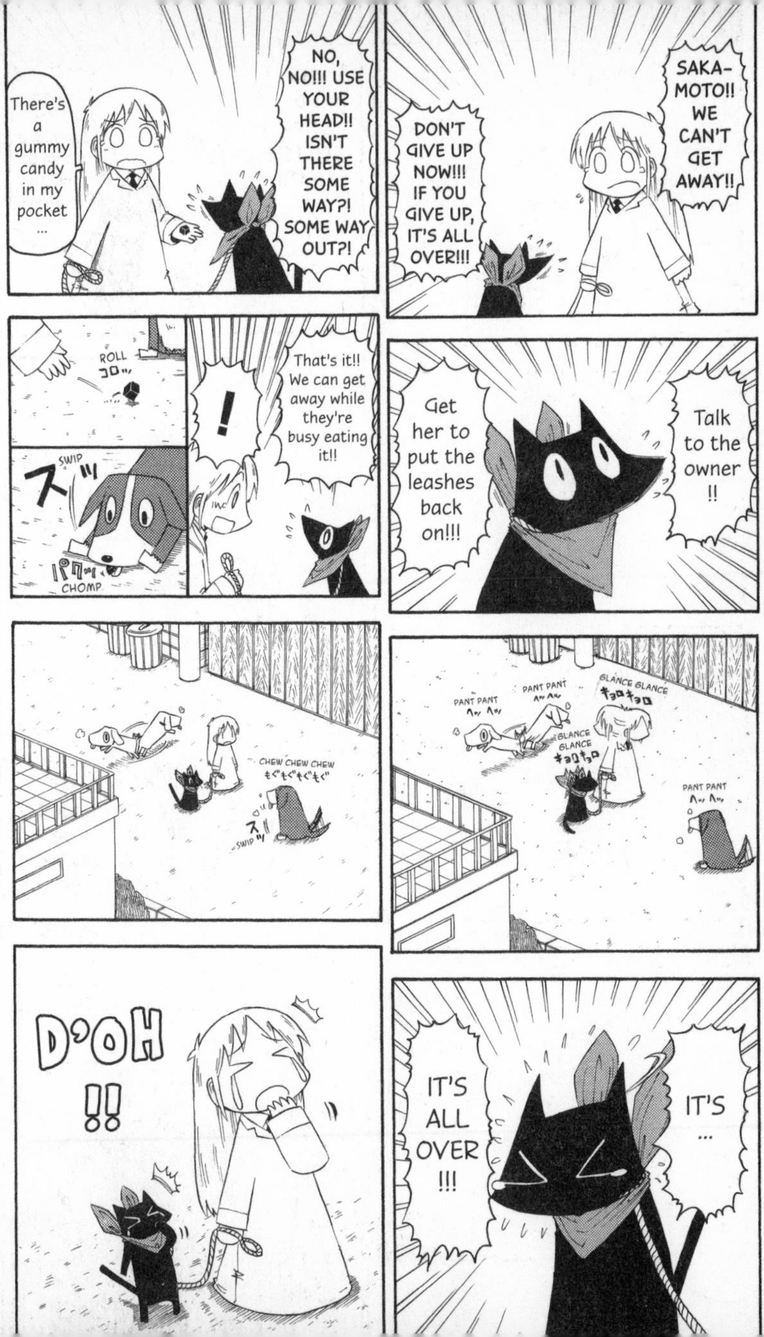
SAKA-MOTO!! WE CAN'T GET AWAY!!
DON'T GIVE UP NOW!!! IF YOU GIVE UP, IT'S ALL OVER!!!
NO, NO!!! USE YOUR HEAD!! ISN'T THERE SOME WAY?! SOME WAY OUT?!
There's a gummy candy in my pocket ...
Talk to the owner !!
Get her to put the leashes back on!!!
!
That's it!! We can get away while they're busy eating it!!
ROLL
コロッ
SWIP
スッ
パクッ
CHOMP
GLANCE GLANCE
キョロキョロ
PANT PANT
ヘッヘッ
PANT PANT
ヘッヘッ
GLANCE GLANCE
キョロキョロ
PANT PANT
ヘッヘッ
CHEW CHEW CHEW
もぐもぐもぐ
スッ
SWIP
IT'S ...
IT'S ALL OVER !!!
D'OH !!

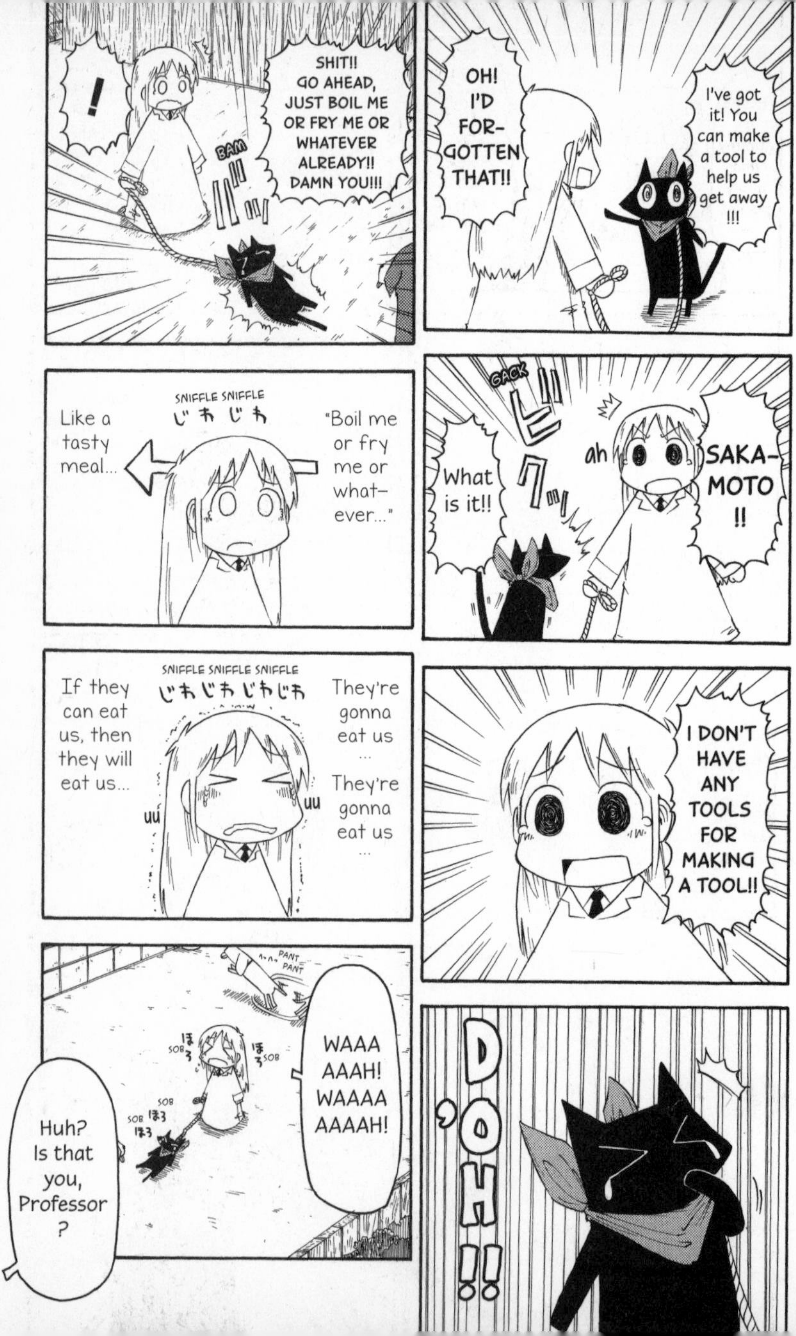
I've got it! You can make a tool to help us get away!!!
OH! I'D FORGOTTEN THAT!!
SAKAMOTO!!
ah
GACK
What is it!!
I DON'T HAVE ANY TOOLS FOR MAKING A TOOL!!
D'OH!!
SHIT!! GO AHEAD, JUST BOIL ME OR FRY ME OR WHATEVER ALREADY!! DAMN YOU!!!
BAM
!
"Boil me or fry me or whatever..."
SNIFFLE SNIFFLE
じわじわ
Like a tasty meal...
They're gonna eat us... They're gonna eat us...
SNIFFLE SNIFFLE SNIFFLE
じわじわじわじわ
uu
uu
If they can eat us, then they will eat us...
PANT PANT
WAAAAAAH! WAAAAAAAAH!
SOB ほろ
SOB ほろ
SOB ほろ
SOB ほろ
Huh? Is that you, Professor?

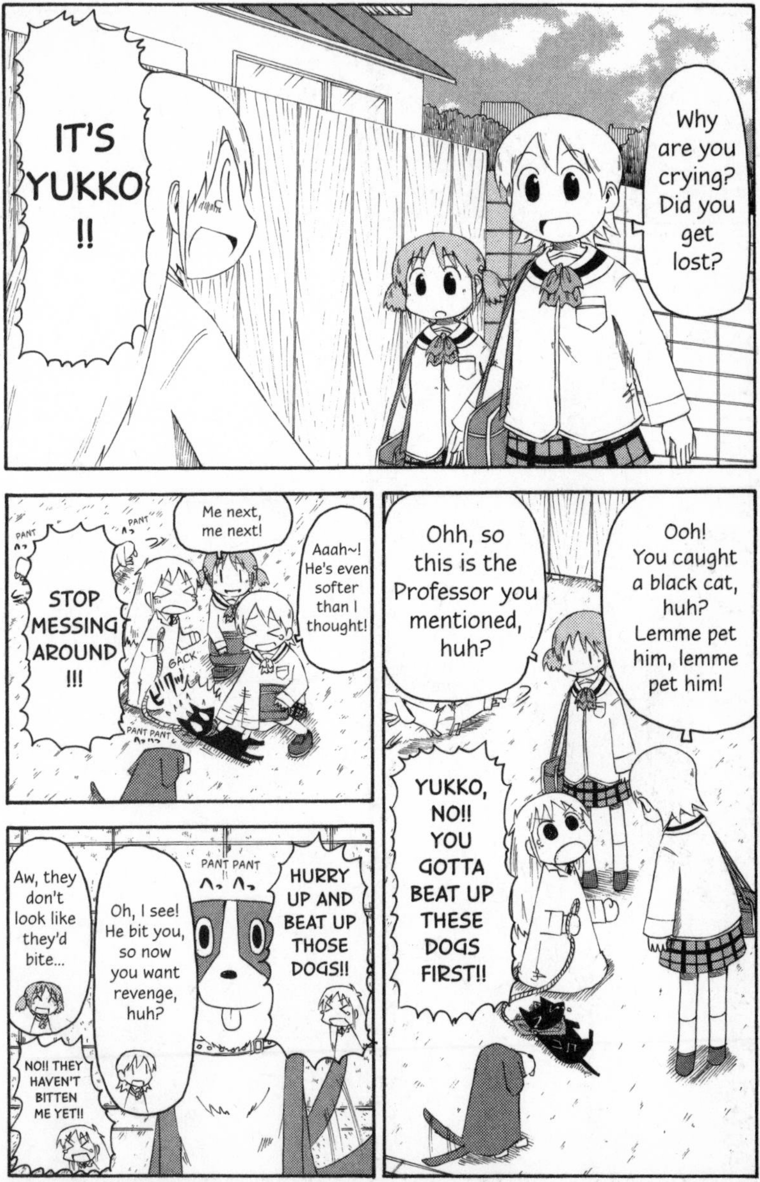
Why are you crying? Did you get lost?
IT'S YUKKO!!
Ooh! You caught a black cat, huh? Lemme pet him, lemme pet him!
Ohh, so this is the Professor you mentioned, huh?
YUKKO, NO!! YOU GOTTA BEAT UP THESE DOGS FIRST!!
Aaah~! He's even softer than I thought!
Me next, me next!
PANT PANT
PANT
STOP MESSING AROUND!!!
GACK
PANT PANT
HURRY UP AND BEAT UP THOSE DOGS!!
PANT PANT
Oh, I see! He bit you, so now you want revenge, huh?
Aw, they don't look like they'd bite...
NO!! THEY HAVEN'T BITTEN ME YET!!

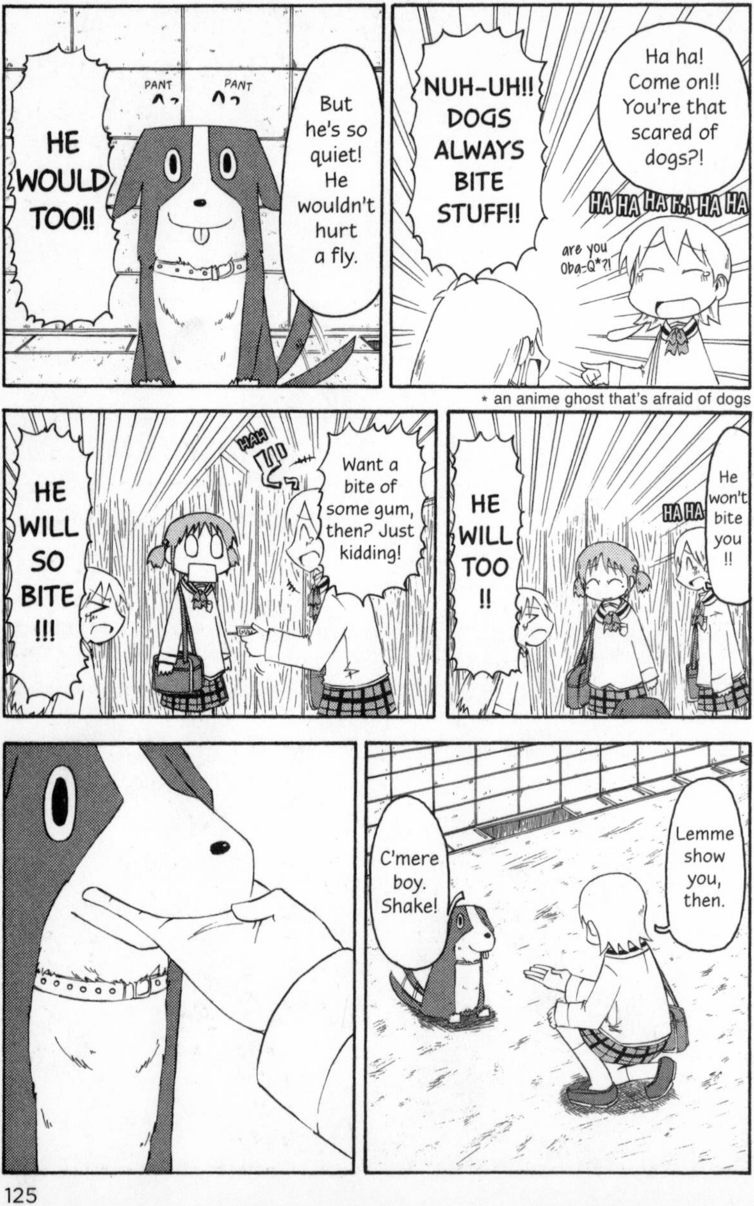
Ha ha! Come on!! You're that scared of dogs?!
HA HA HA HA HA HA
are you Oba-Q*?!
NUH-UH!! DOGS ALWAYS BITE STUFF!!
But he's so quiet! He wouldn't hurt a fly.
PANT
PANT
HE WOULD TOO!!
He won't bite you !!
HA HA
HE WILL TOO !!
Want a bite of some gum, then? Just kidding!
HAH
HE WILL SO BITE !!!
Lemme show you, then.
C'mere boy. Shake!

* an anime ghost that's afraid of dogs

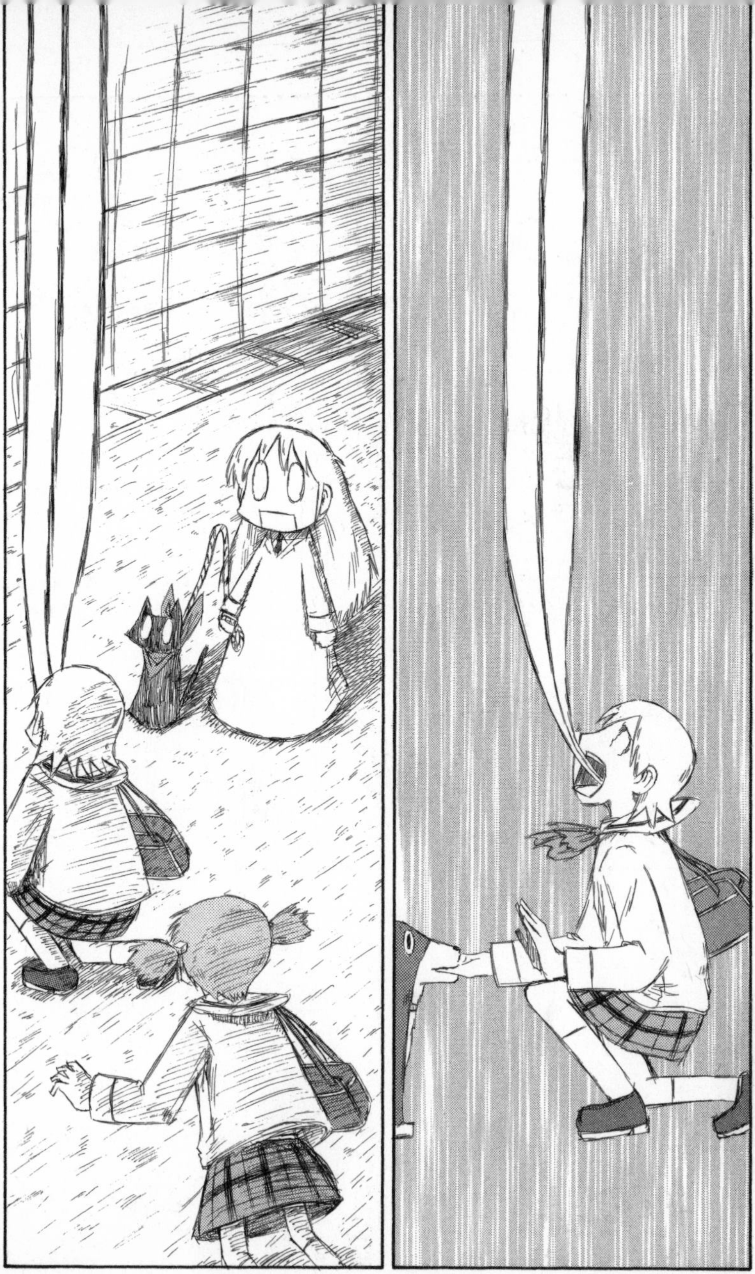

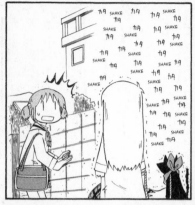

SHAKE SHAKE

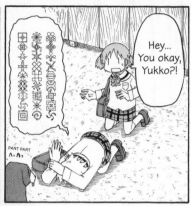

Hey... You okay, Yukko?!

PANT PANT

Okay?

... Okay.

Don't worry! She's just an idiot.

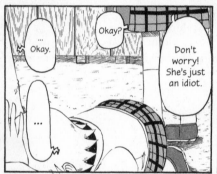

...

It's okay, he won't bite you unless you approach him...

Yuk-ko... Yuk-ko...

SHAKE SHAKE SHAKE SHAKE SHAKE SHAKE SHAKE SHAKE SHAKE SHAKE

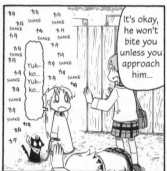

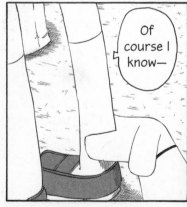

Of course I know—

! What? You know Nano, too?!

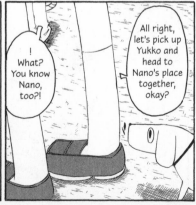

All right, let's pick up Yukko and head to Nano's place together, okay?

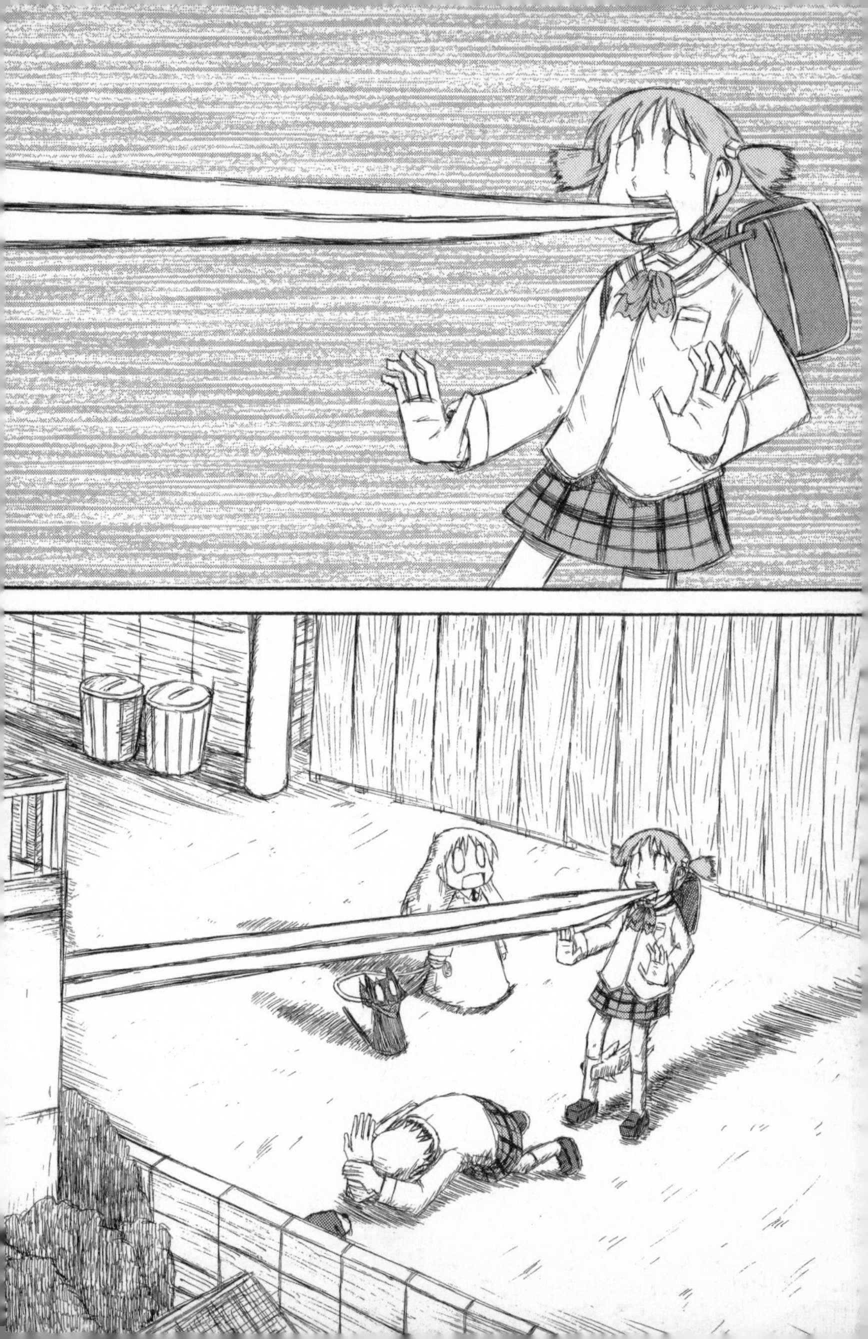

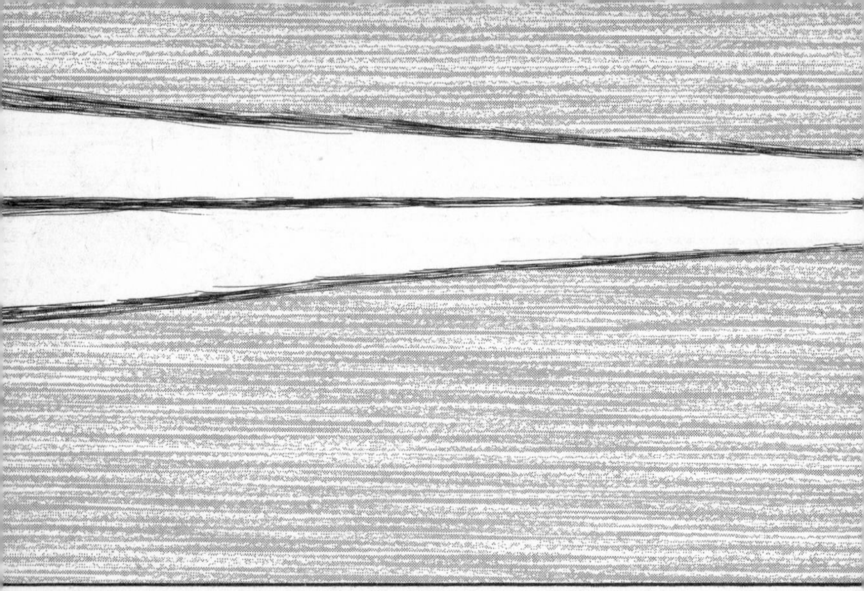
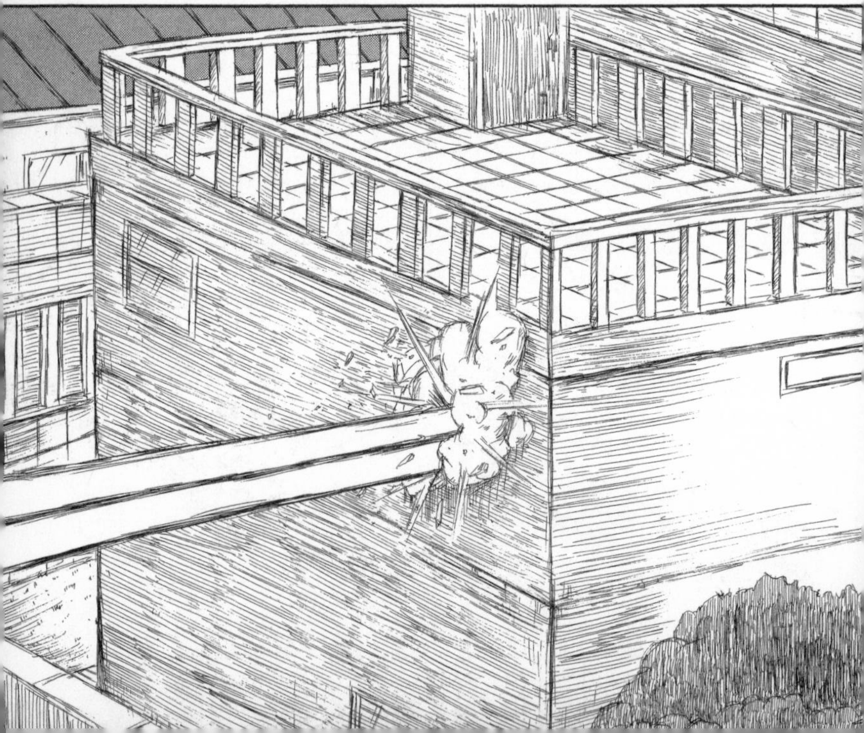

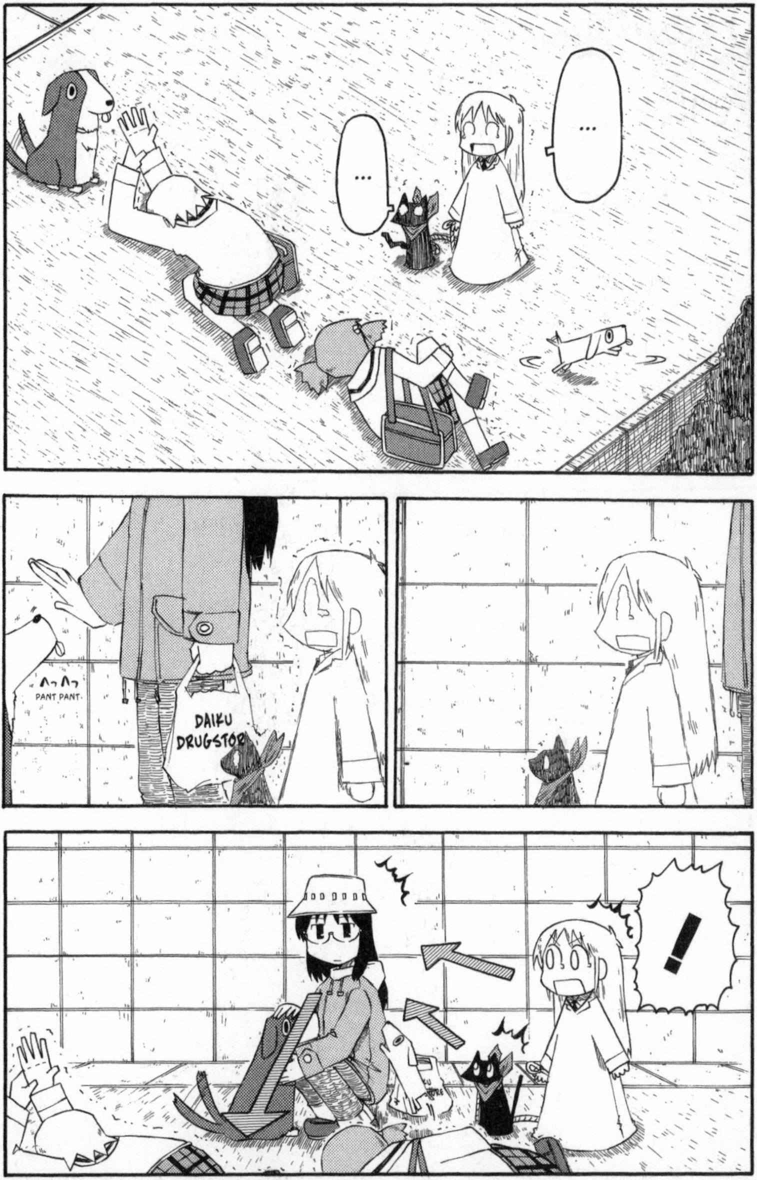
...
...
PANT PANT
DAIKU DRUGSTOR
!

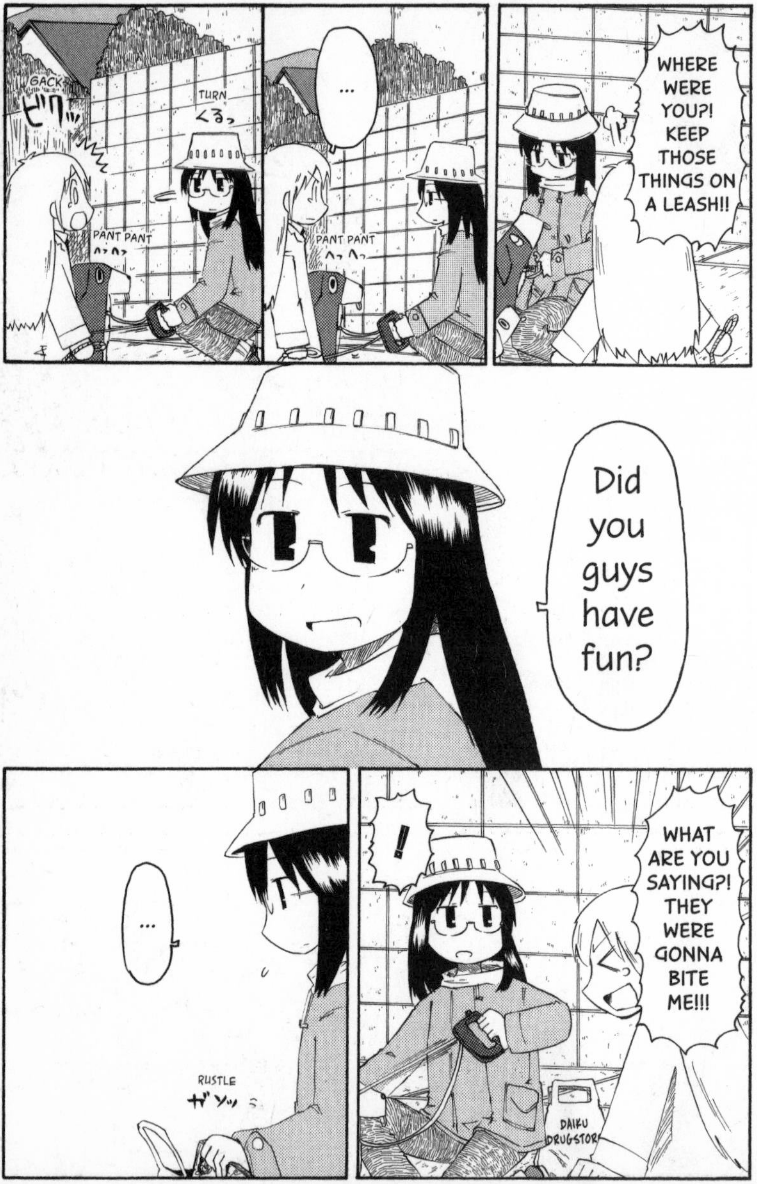
WHERE WERE YOU?! KEEP THOSE THINGS ON A LEASH!!
...
PANT PANT
へっへっ
GACK
ビクッ
TURN
くるっ
PANT PANT
へっへっ
Did you guys have fun?
!
WHAT ARE YOU SAYING?! THEY WERE GONNA BITE ME!!!
DAIKU DRUGSTOR
...
RUSTLE

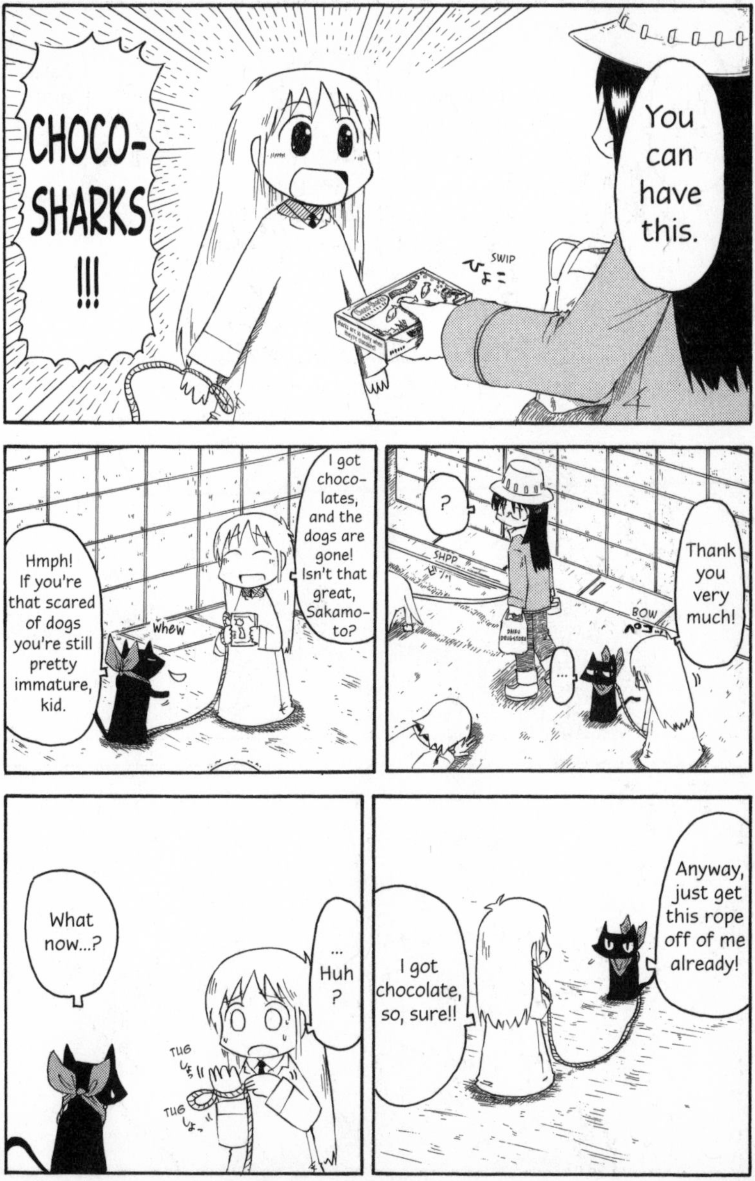
You can have this.
SWIP
ひょこ
CHOCO-SHARKS!!!
Thank you very much!
BOW
ペコー
?
SHPP
...
I got chocolates, and the dogs are gone! Isn't that great, Sakamoto?
Hmph! If you're that scared of dogs you're still pretty immature, kid.
Whew
Anyway, just get this rope off of me already!
I got chocolate, so, sure!!
... Huh?
What now...?
TUG
TUG

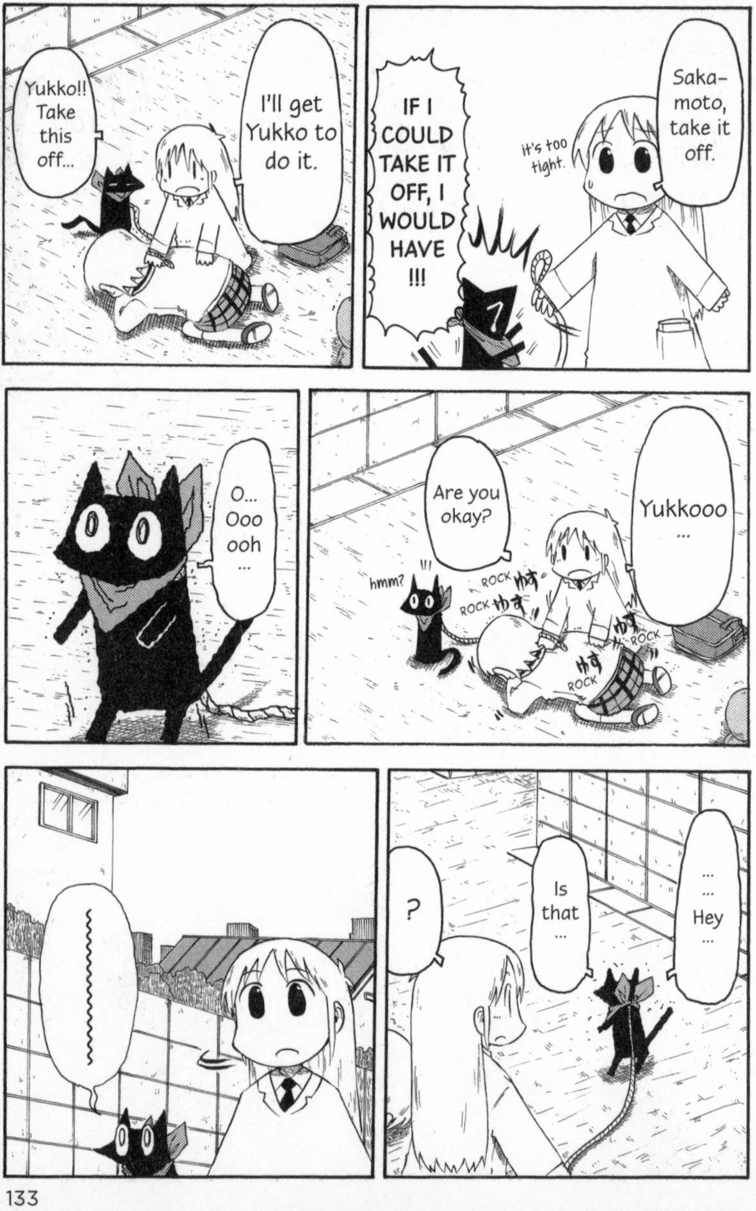
Saka-moto, take it off.
it's too tight.
IF I COULD TAKE IT OFF, I WOULD HAVE!!!
I'll get Yukko to do it.
Yukko!! Take this off...
Yukkooo ...
Are you okay?
hmm?
ROCK ゆす
ROCK ゆす
ゆす ROCK
ゆす ROCK
O... Ooo ooh ...
... ... Hey ...
Is that ...
?

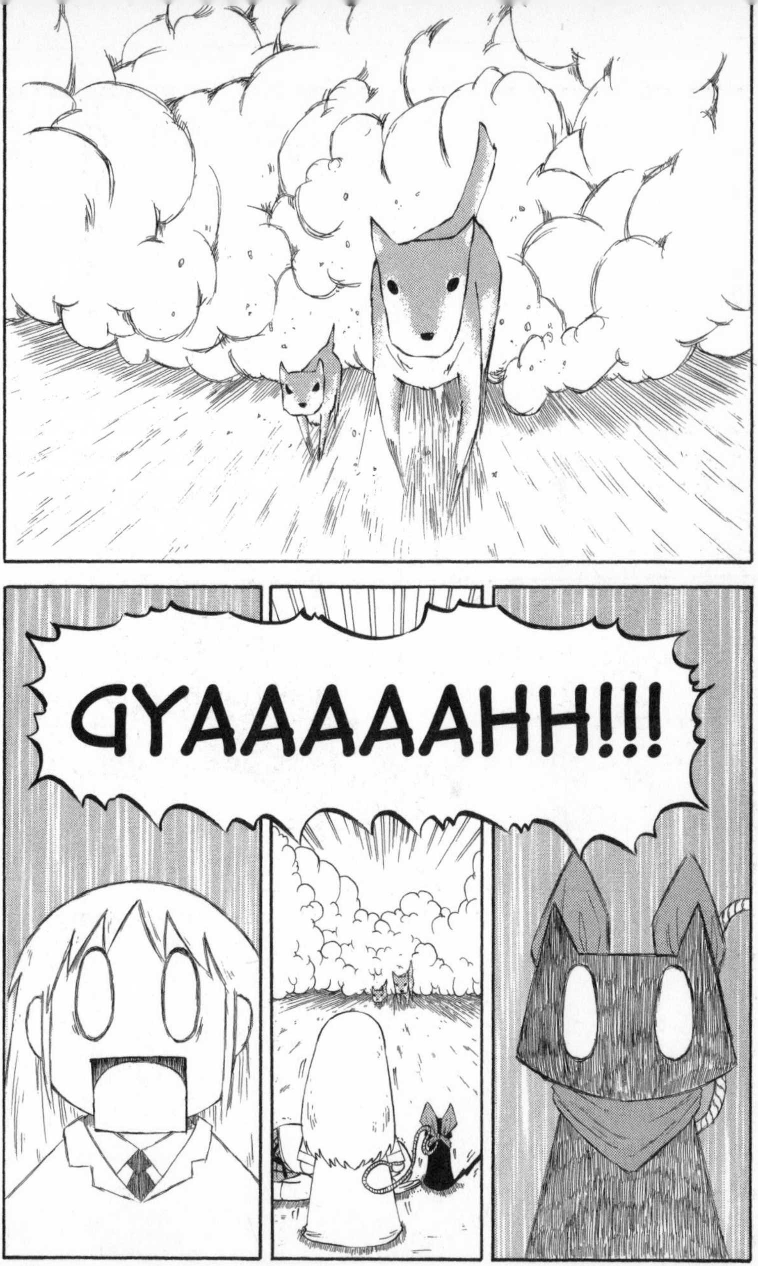
GYAAAAAHH!!!

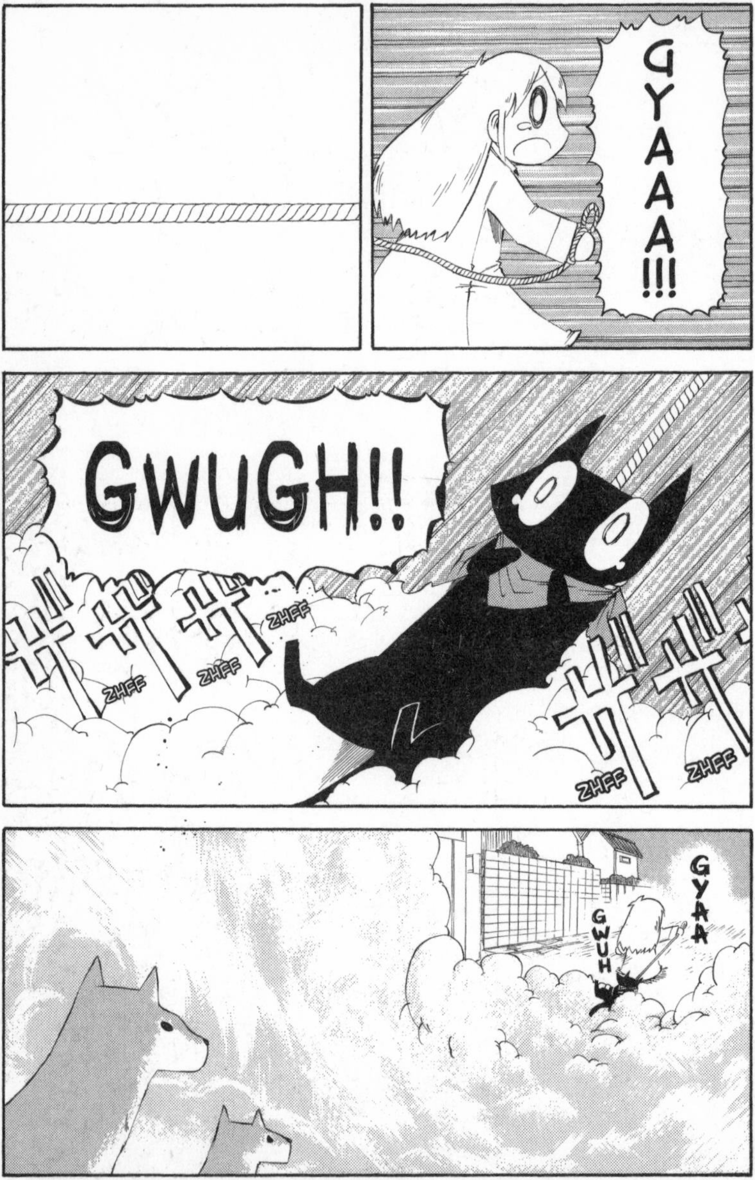
GYAAA!!!
GWUGH!!
ZHFF
ZHFF
ZHFF
ZHFF
ZHFF
GYAA
GWUH

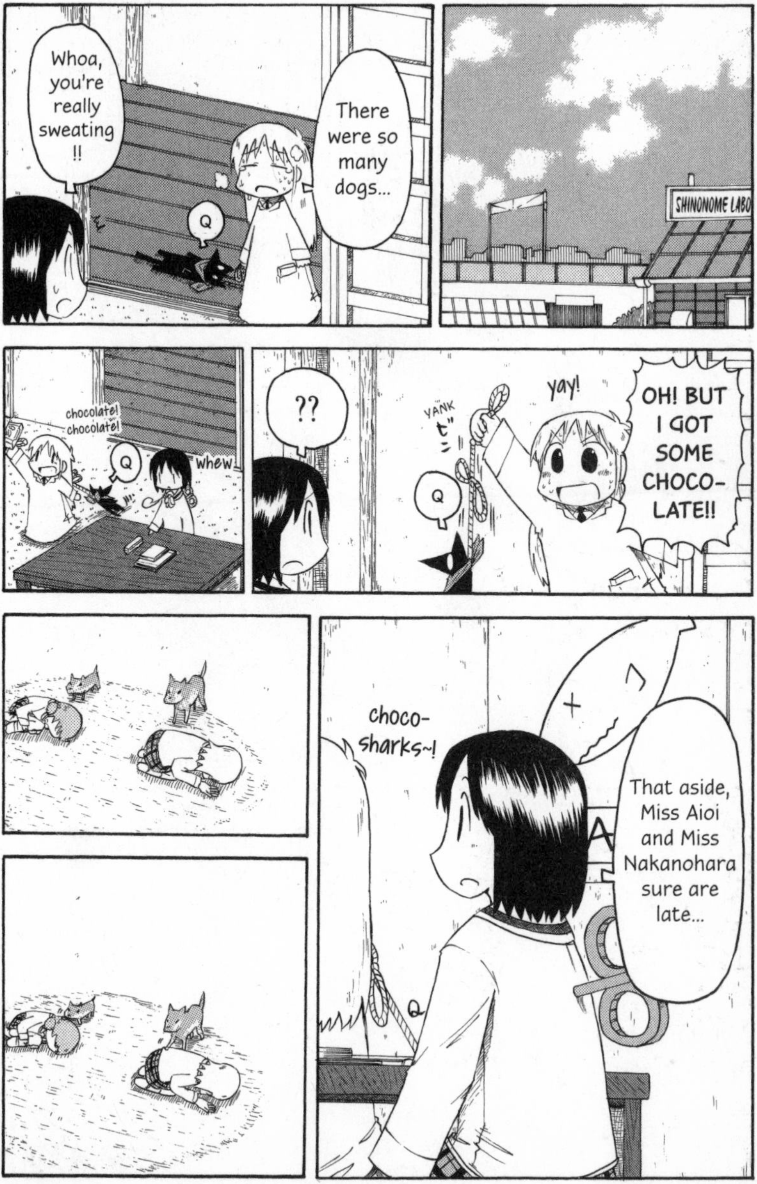
SHINONOME LABO
There were so many dogs...
Whoa, you're really sweating !!
Q
OH! BUT I GOT SOME CHOCO-LATE!!
yay!
YANK
Q
??
chocolate! chocolate!
Q
whew
That aside, Miss Aioi and Miss Nakanohara sure are late...
choco-sharks~!
Q

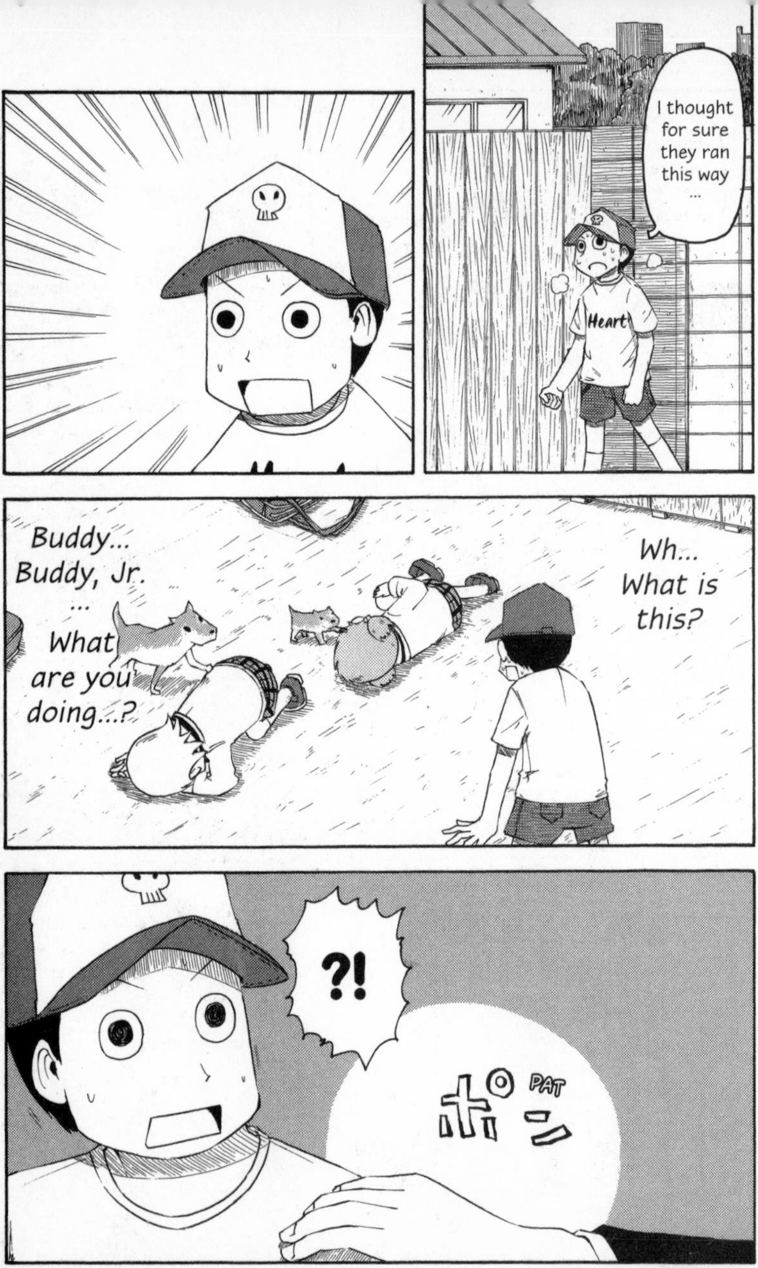
I thought for sure they ran this way ...
Wh... What is this?
Buddy... Buddy, Jr. ... What are you doing...?
?!
ポン
PAT

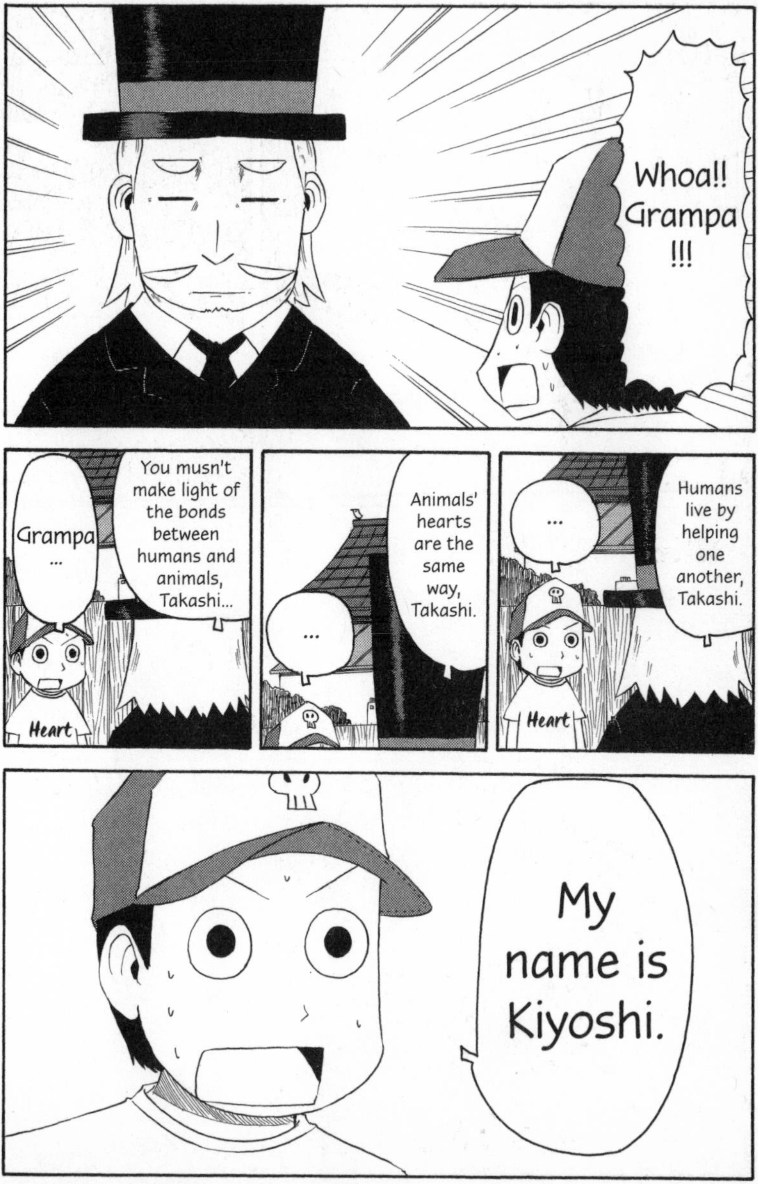
Whoa!! Grampa !!!
Humans live by helping one another, Takashi.
...
Heart
Animals' hearts are the same way, Takashi.
...
You musn't make light of the bonds between humans and animals, Takashi...
Grampa ...
Heart
My name is Kiyoshi.

chapter 84: end

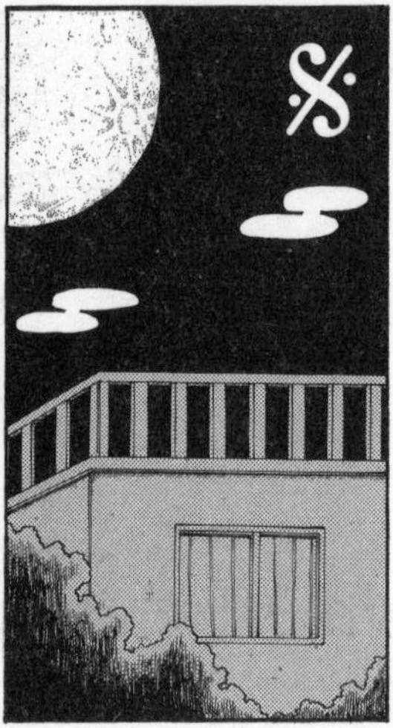

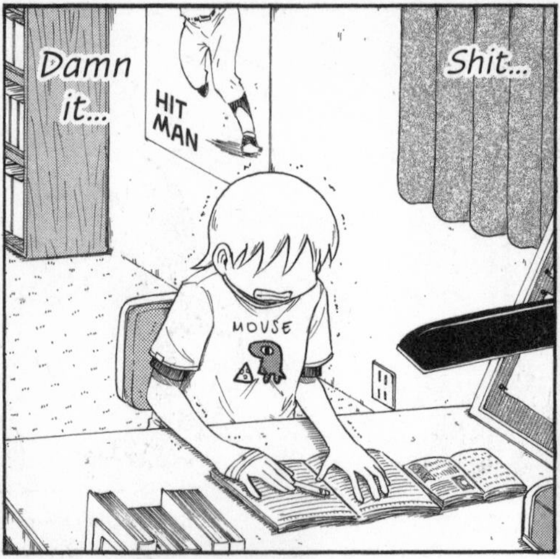
Shit...
HIT MAN
Damn it...
MOUSE

chapter 85

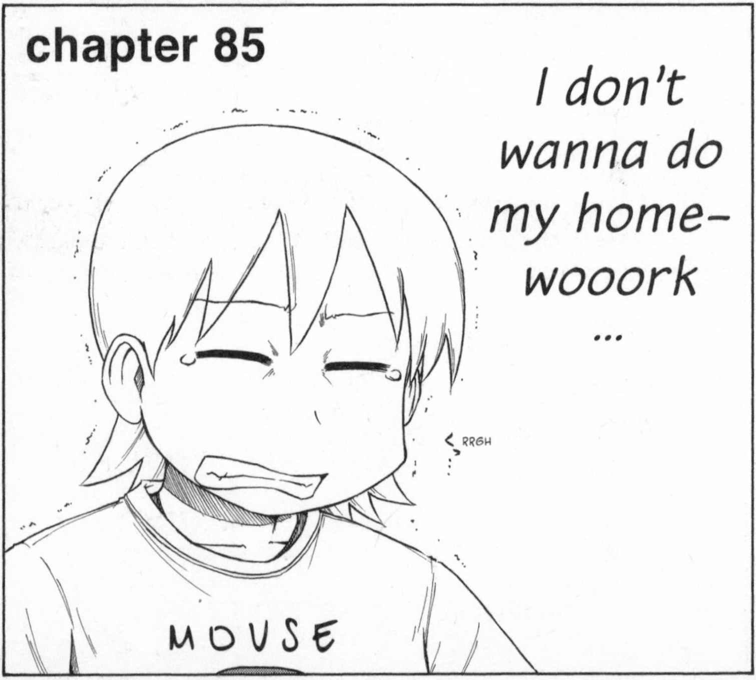
I don't wanna do my home-wooork ...
RRGH
MOUSE

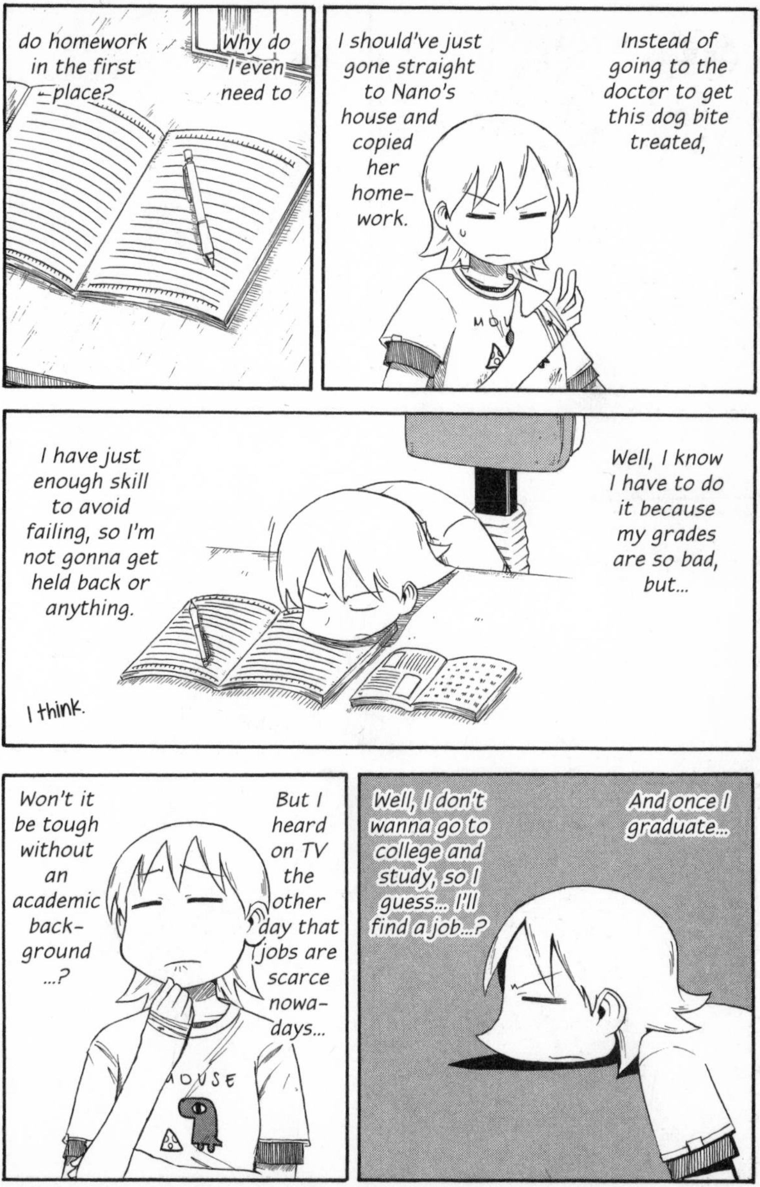
Instead of going to the doctor to get this dog bite treated,
I should've just gone straight to Nano's house and copied her home-work.
Why do I even need to
do homework in the first place?
Well, I know I have to do it because my grades are so bad, but...
I have just enough skill to avoid failing, so I'm not gonna get held back or anything.
I think.
And once I graduate...
Well, I don't wanna go to college and study, so I guess... I'll find a job...?
But I heard on TV the other day that jobs are scarce nowa-days...
Won't it be tough without an academic back-ground...?

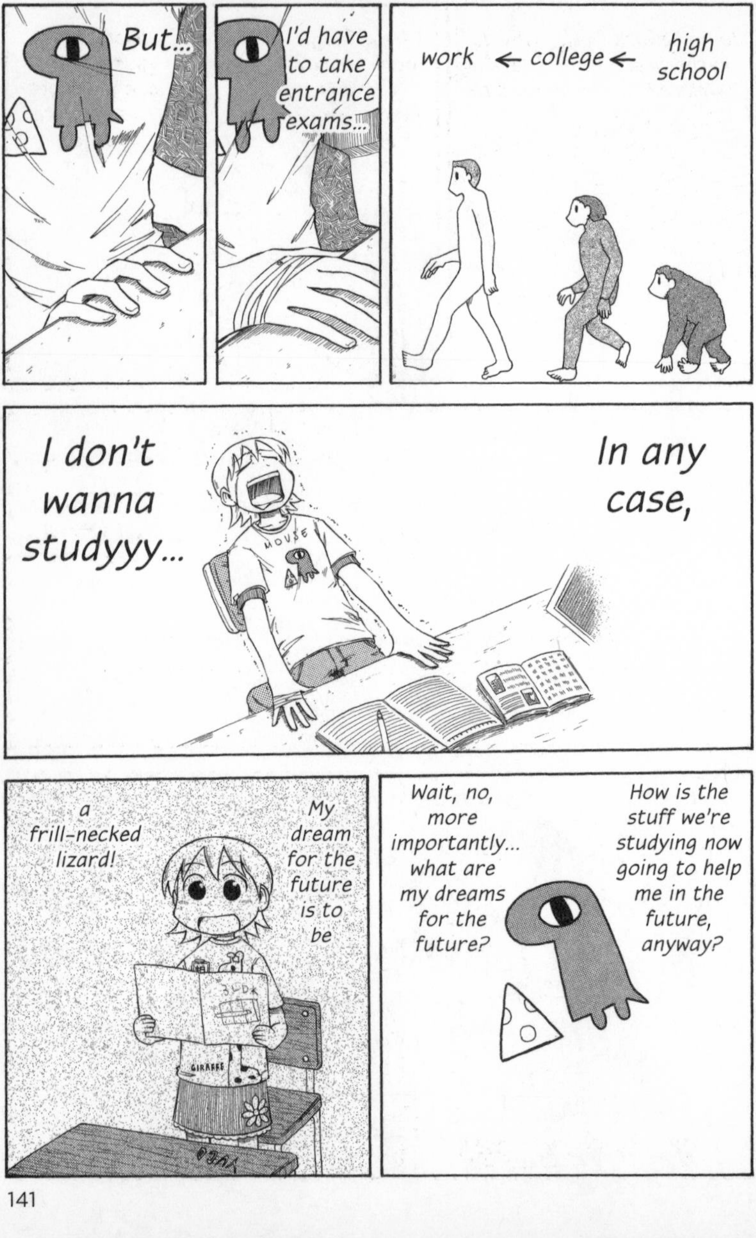

high school
college
work
I'd have to take entrance exams...
But...
In any case,
MOUSE
I don't wanna studyyy...
How is the stuff we're studying now going to help me in the future, anyway?
Wait, no, more importantly... what are my dreams for the future?
My dream for the future is to be
a frill-necked lizard!
GIRAFFE

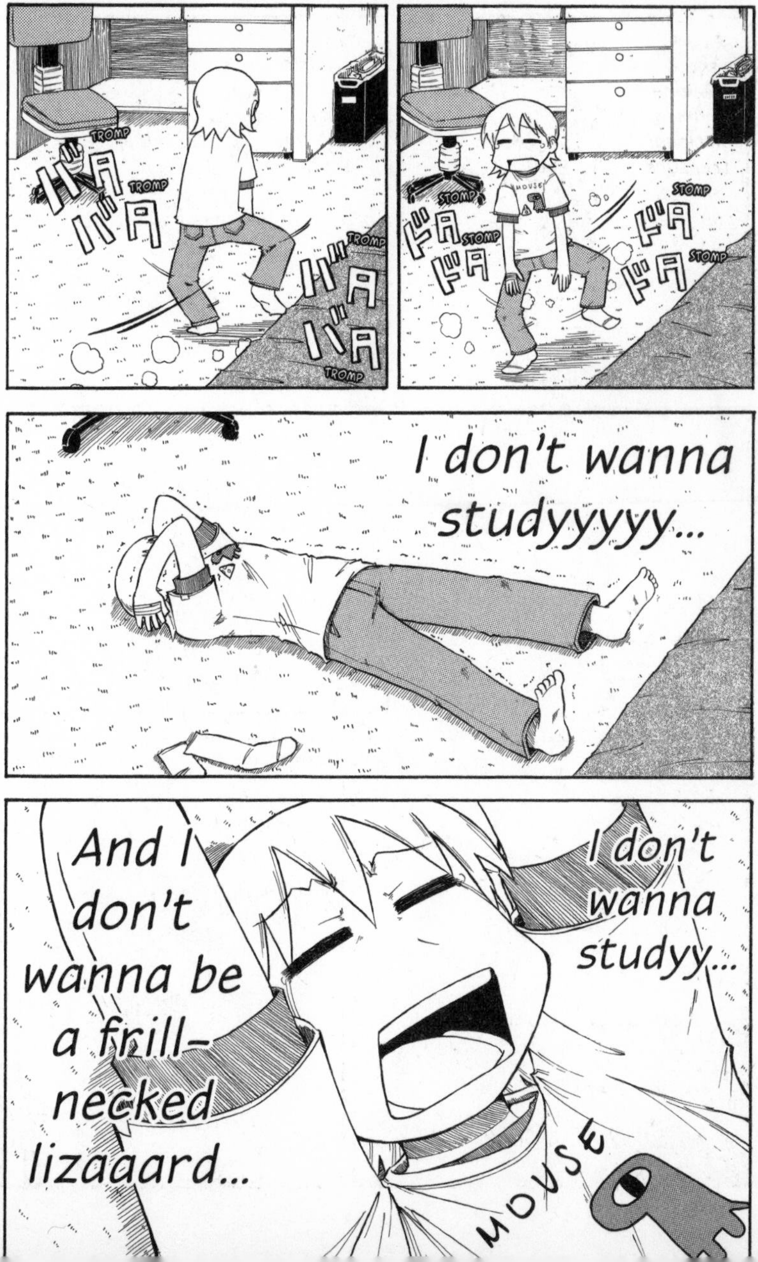

STOMP
ドタ
STOMP
ドタ
ドタ
STOMP
ドタ
STOMP
MOUSE
TROMP
バタ
TROMP
バタ
TROMP
バタ
バタ
TROMP
I don't wanna studyyyyy...
I don't wanna studyy...
And I don't wanna be a frill-necked lizaaard...
MOUSE

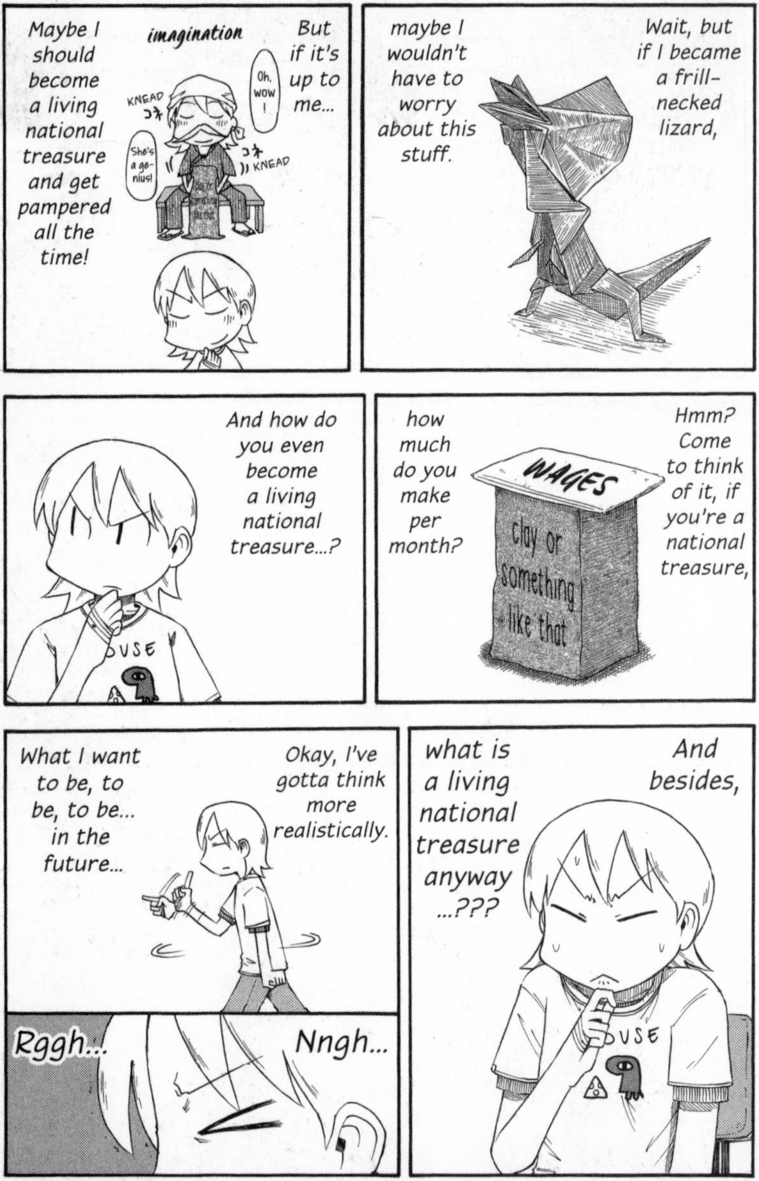
Wait, but if I became a frill-necked lizard,
maybe I wouldn't have to worry about this stuff.
But if it's up to me...
imagination
Oh, wow!
KNEAD コネ
KNEAD コネ
She's a genius!
Maybe I should become a living national treasure and get pampered all the time!
Hmm? Come to think of it, if you're a national treasure,
how much do you make per month?
WAGES
clay or something like that
And how do you even become a living national treasure...?
And besides,
what is a living national treasure anyway ...???
USE
Okay, I've gotta think more realistically.
What I want to be, to be, to be... in the future...
Nngh...
Rggh...

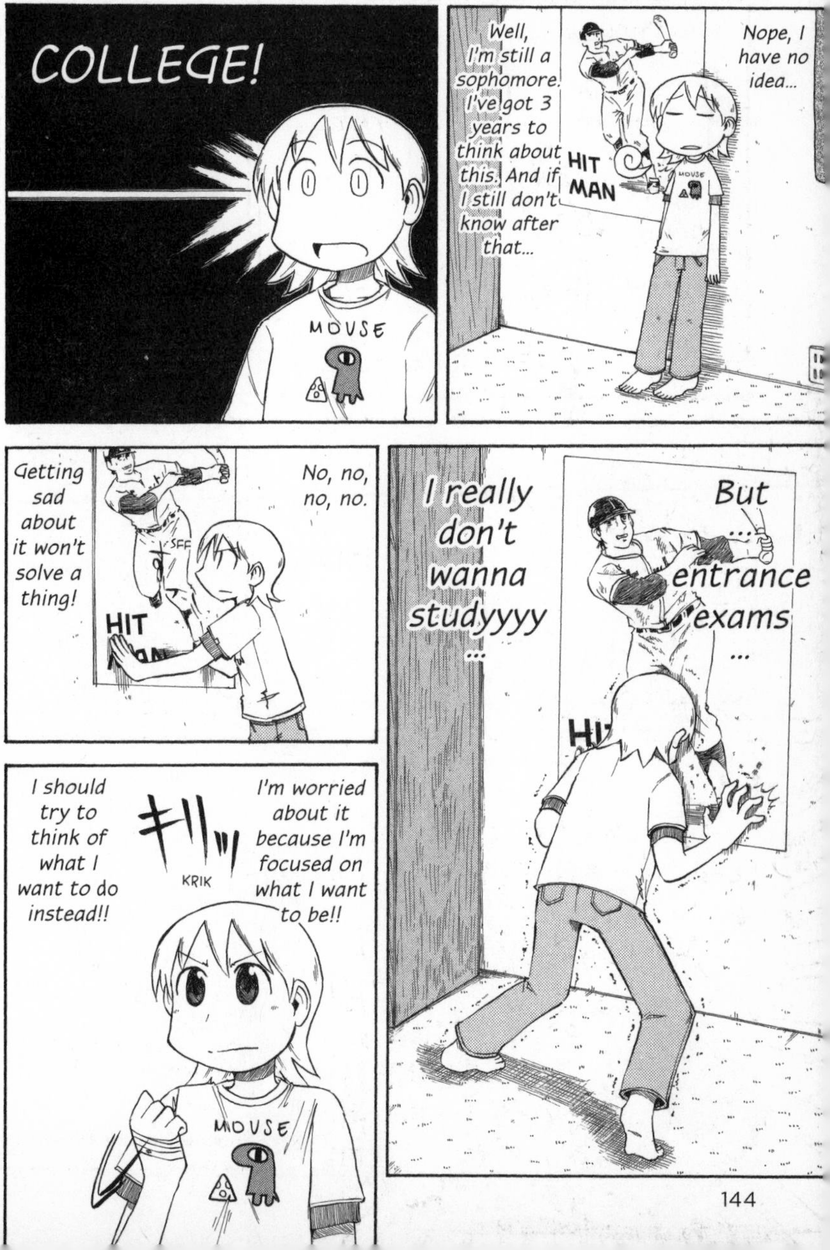

Nope, I have no idea...
Well, I'm still a sophomore. I've got 3 years to think about this. And if I still don't know after that...
HIT MAN
MOUSE
COLLEGE!
MOUSE
But... entrance exams...
I really don't wanna studyyyy...
No, no, no, no.
Getting sad about it won't solve a thing!
SFF
HIT
I'm worried about it because I'm focused on what I want to be!!
キリッ
KRIK
I should try to think of what I want to do instead!!
MOUSE

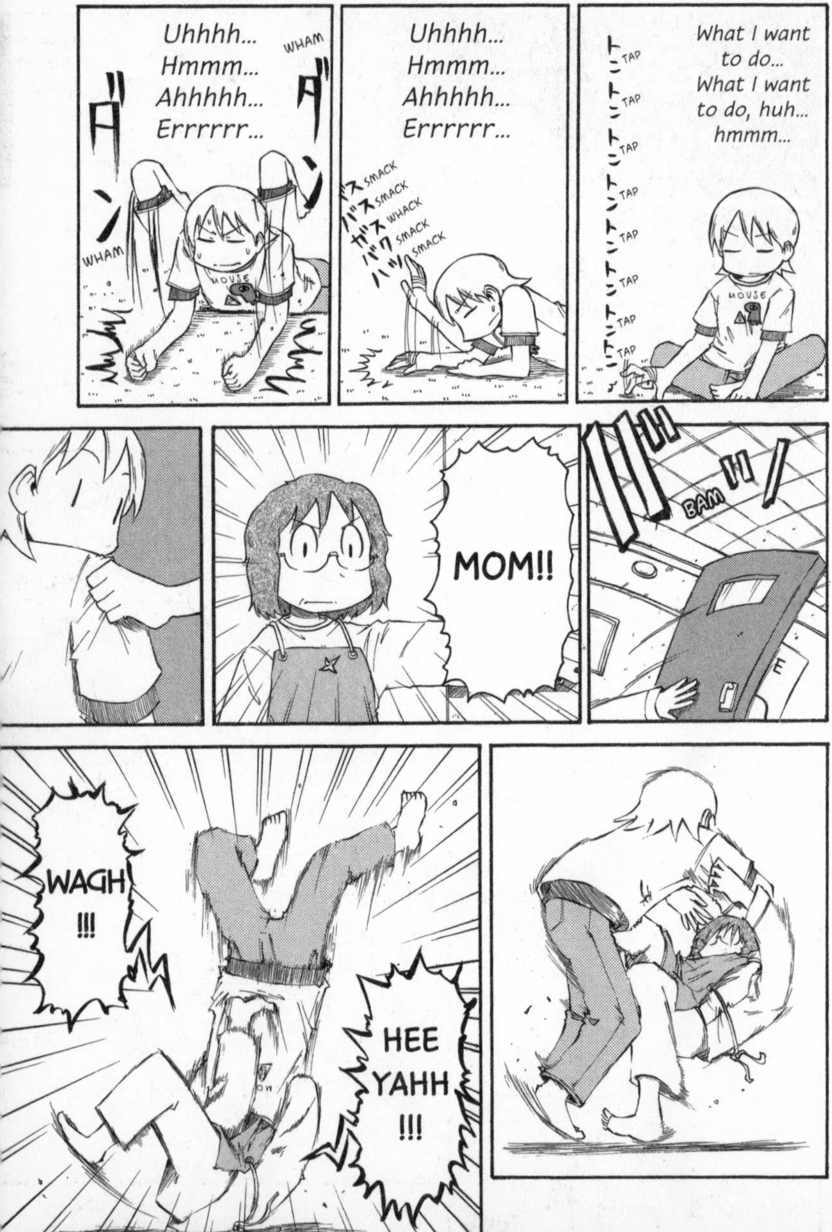
What I want to do... What I want to do, huh... hmmm...
TAP TAP TAP TAP TAP TAP TAP TAP
Uhhhh... Hmmm... Ahhhhh... Errrrrr...
SMACK SMACK WHACK SMACK SMACK
Uhhhh... Hmmm... Ahhhhh... Errrrrr...
WHAM
WHAM
BAM
MOM!!
WAGH !!!
HEE YAHH !!!

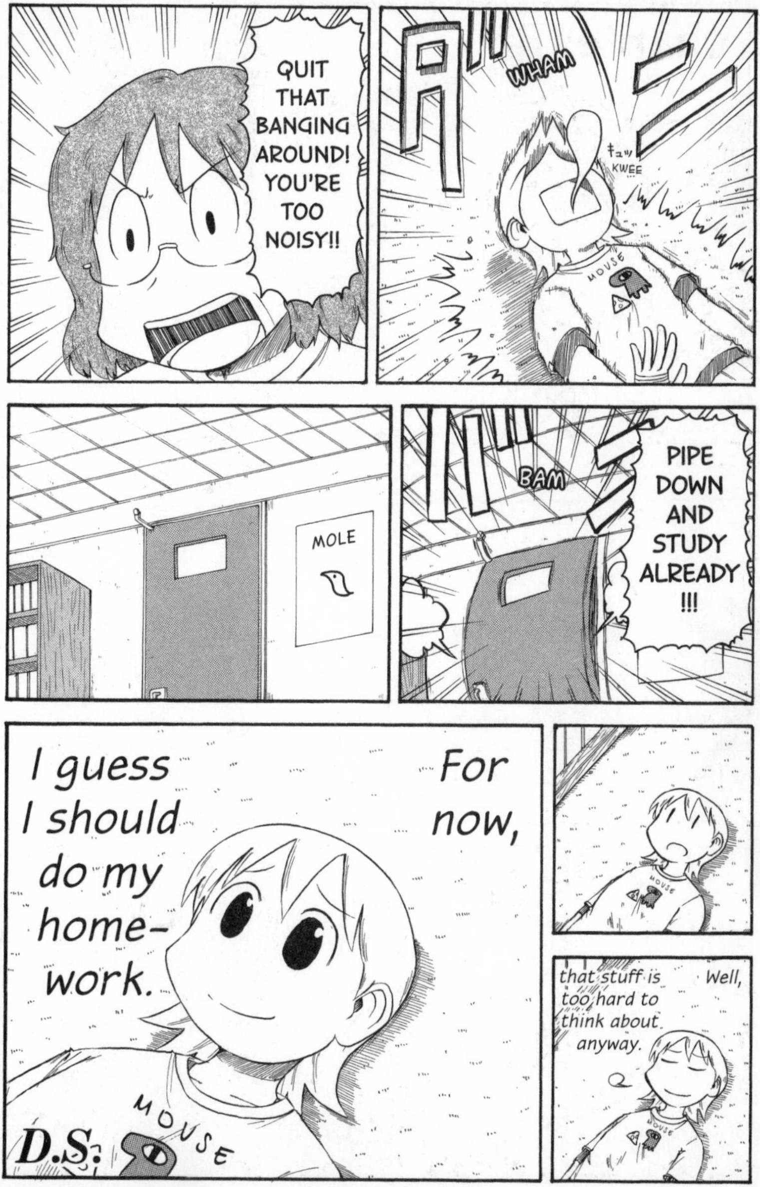

WHAM
キュッ
KWEE
MOUSE
QUIT THAT BANGING AROUND! YOU'RE TOO NOISY!!
BAM
PIPE DOWN AND STUDY ALREADY !!!
MOLE
MOUSE
Well,
that stuff is too hard to think about anyway.
MOUSE
For now,
I guess I should do my home-work.
MOUSE
D.S.

chapter 85: end

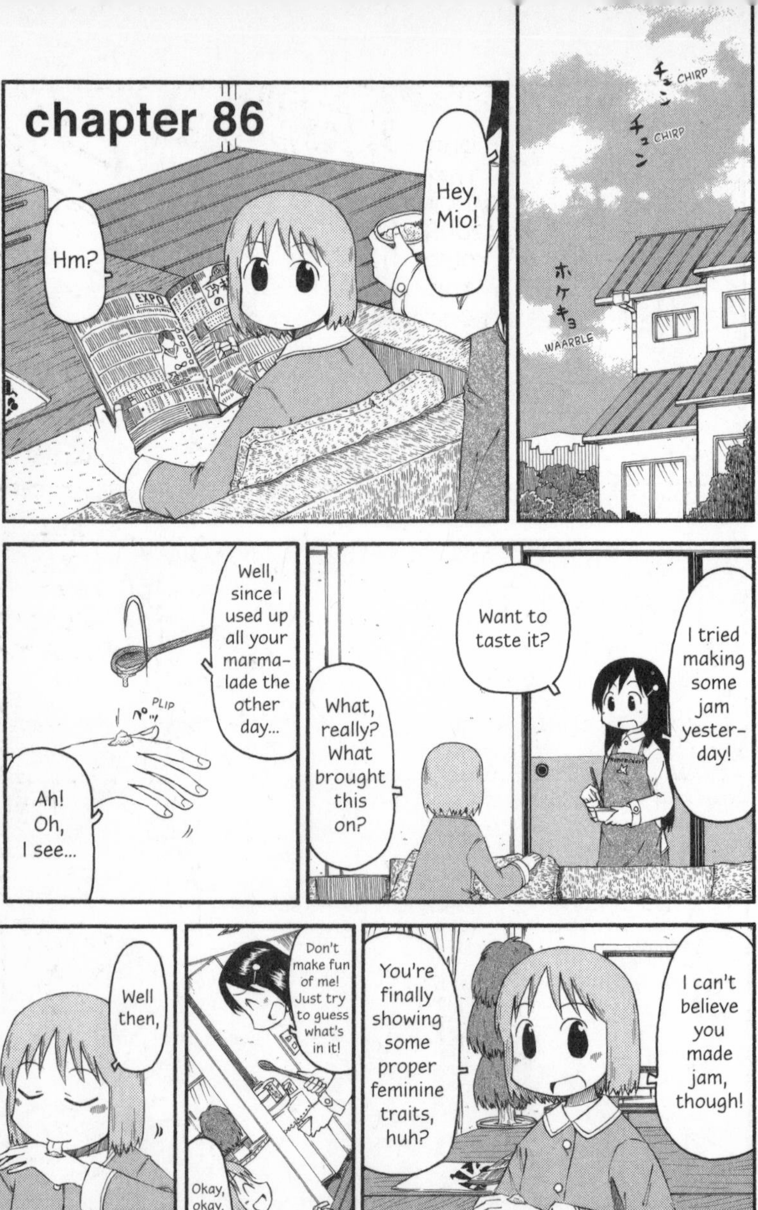
チュン CHIRP
チュン CHIRP
ホケキョ WAARBLE
chapter 86
Hey, Mio!
Hm?
I tried making some jam yesterday!
Want to taste it?
What, really? What brought this on?
Well, since I used up all your marmalade the other day...
ペッ PLIP
Ah! Oh, I see...
I can't believe you made jam, though!
You're finally showing some proper feminine traits, huh?
Don't make fun of me! Just try to guess what's in it!
Okay, okay.
Well then,
I'll try ...
ペロリ LICK

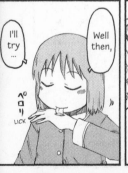

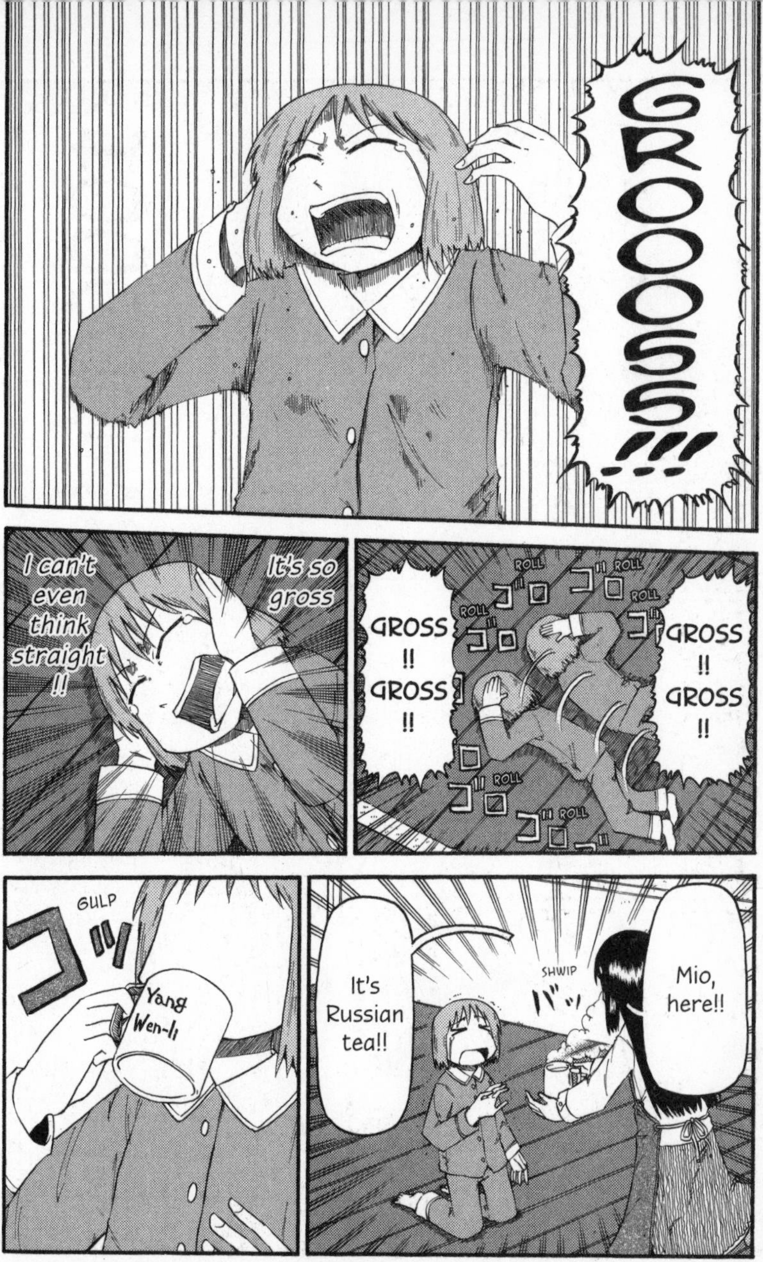
GROOOSS!!!
GROSS!! GROSS!!
ROLL
ROLL
ROLL
ROLL
ROLL
ROLL
GROSS!! GROSS!!
It's so gross
I can't even think straight!!
Mio, here!!
SHWIP
It's Russian tea!!
GULP
Yang Wen-li

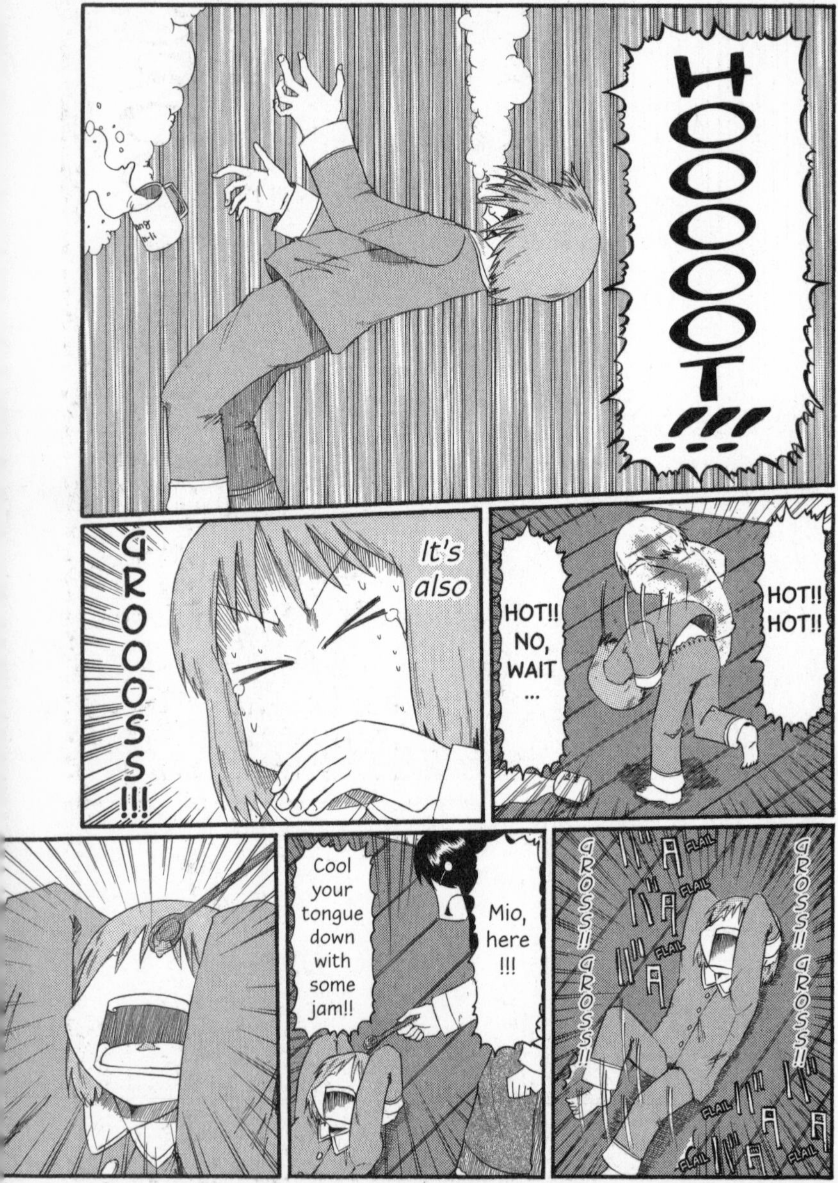
HOOOOOOT!!!
HOT!! HOT!!
HOT!! NO, WAIT ...
It's also
GROOOOSS!!!
GROSS!! GROSS!!
GROSS!! GROSS!!
FLAIL
Mio, here!!!
Cool your tongue down with some jam!!

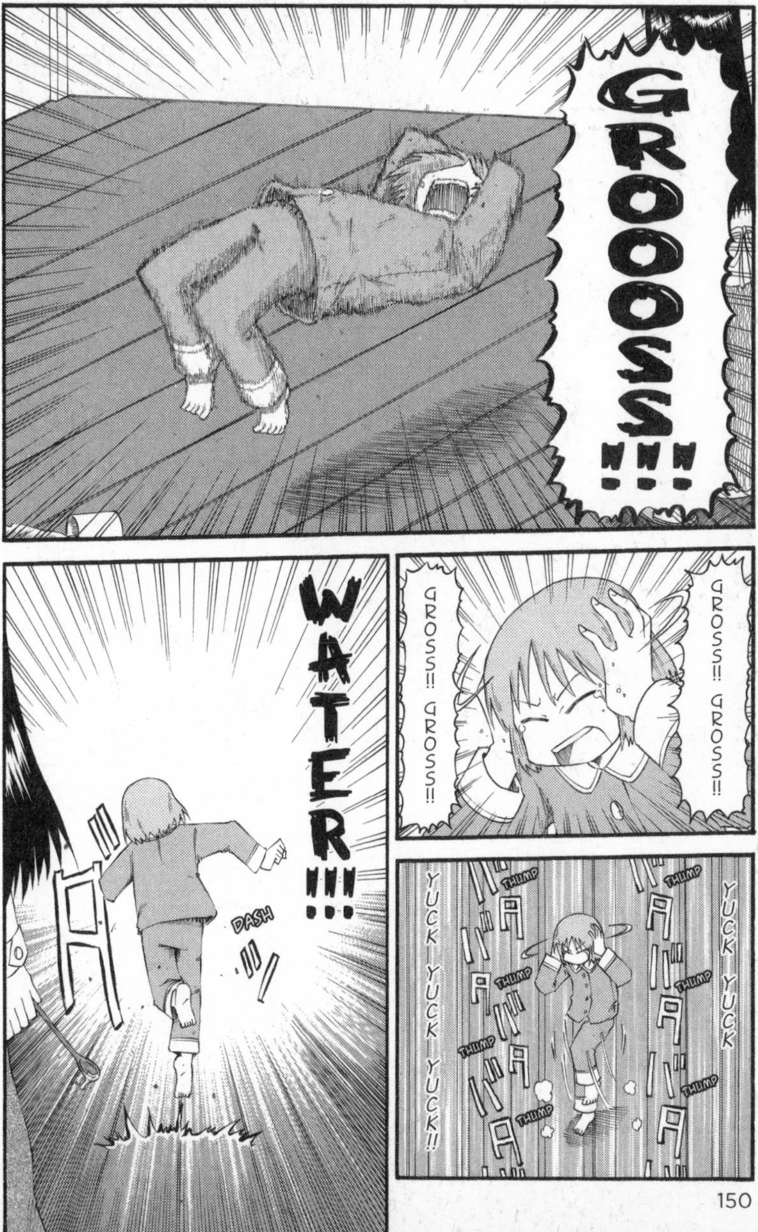
GROOOOSS!!!
GROSS!! GROSS!! GROSS!!
GROSS!! GROSS!!
YUCK YUCK YUCK
THUMP
THUMP
THUMP
THUMP
THUMP
THUMP
YUCK YUCK YUCK YUCK!!
WATER!!!
DASH

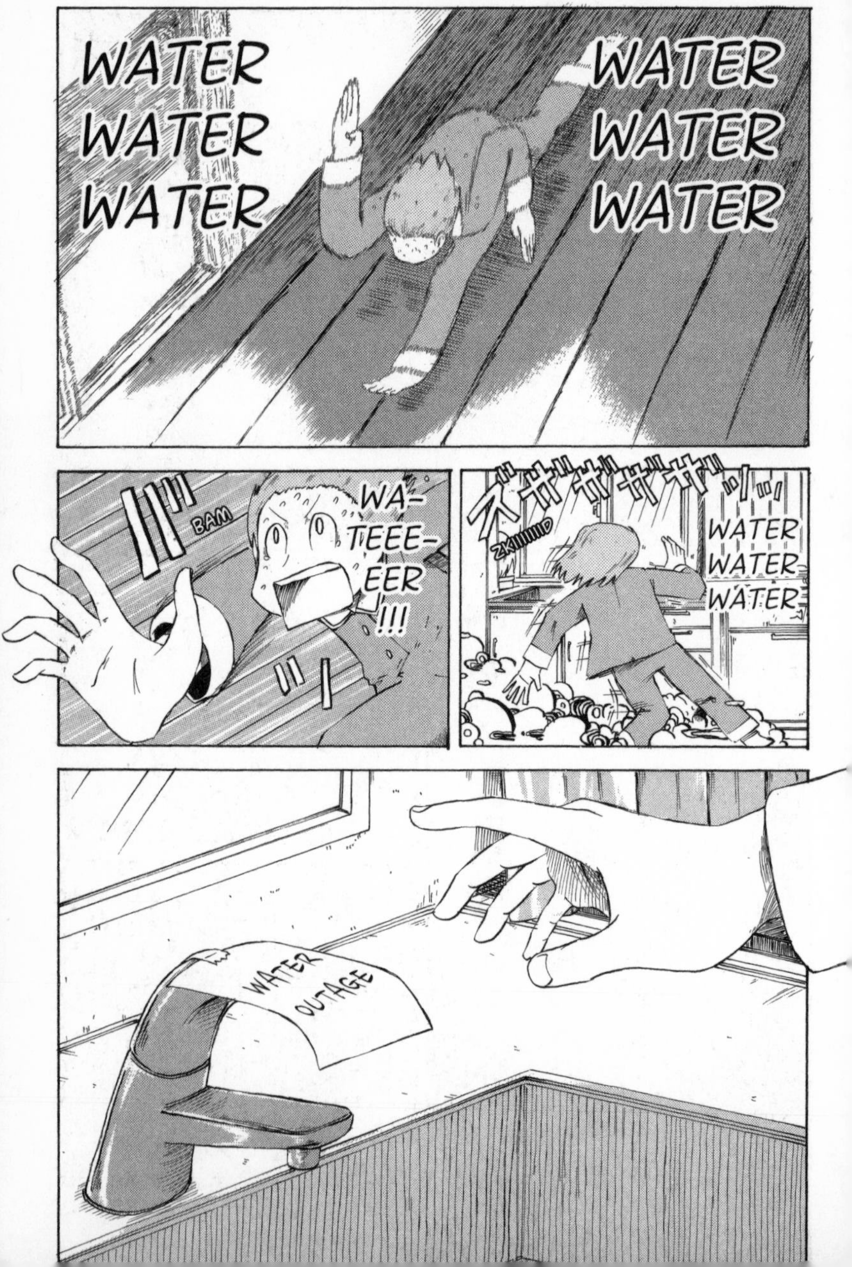

WATER WATER WATER
WATER WATER WATER
ZKIIIIIID
WATER WATER WATER
BAM
WA-TEEEE-EER!!!
WATER OUTAGE

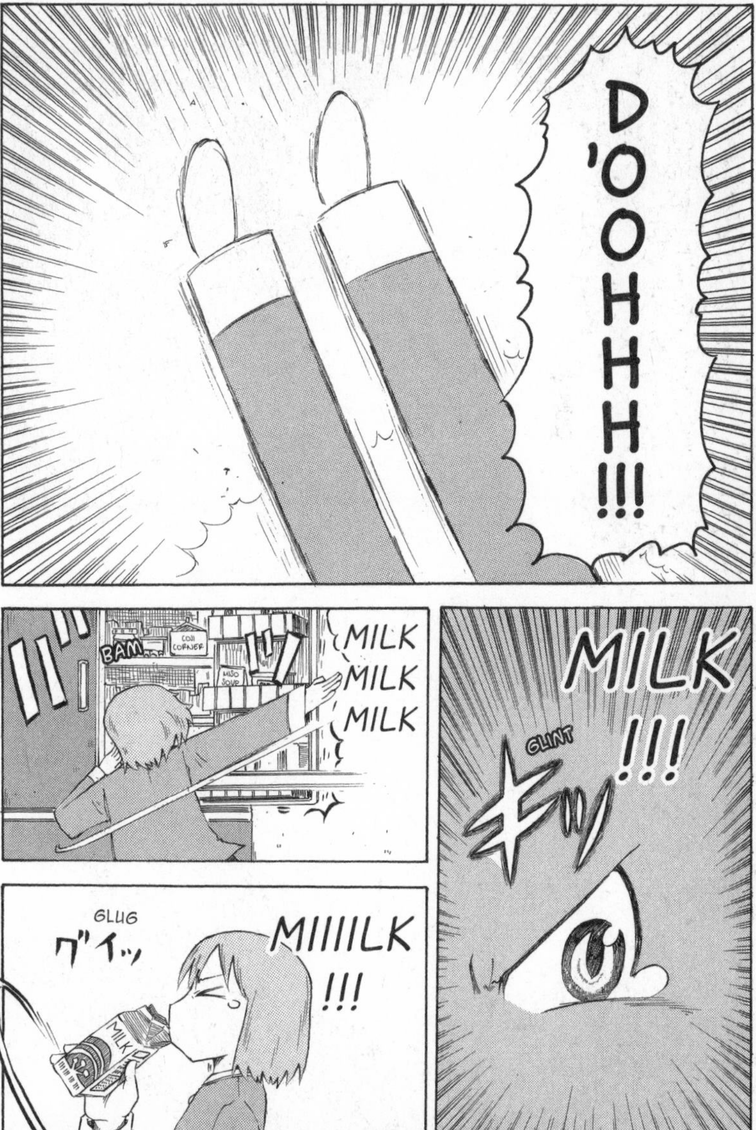
D'OOHH!!!
MILK!!!
GLINT
ギッ
MILK
MILK
MILK
BAM
COJI CORNER
MISO SOUP
MIIIILK!!!
GLUG
グイッ
MILK

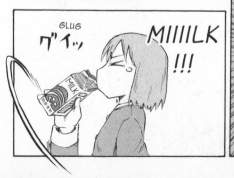

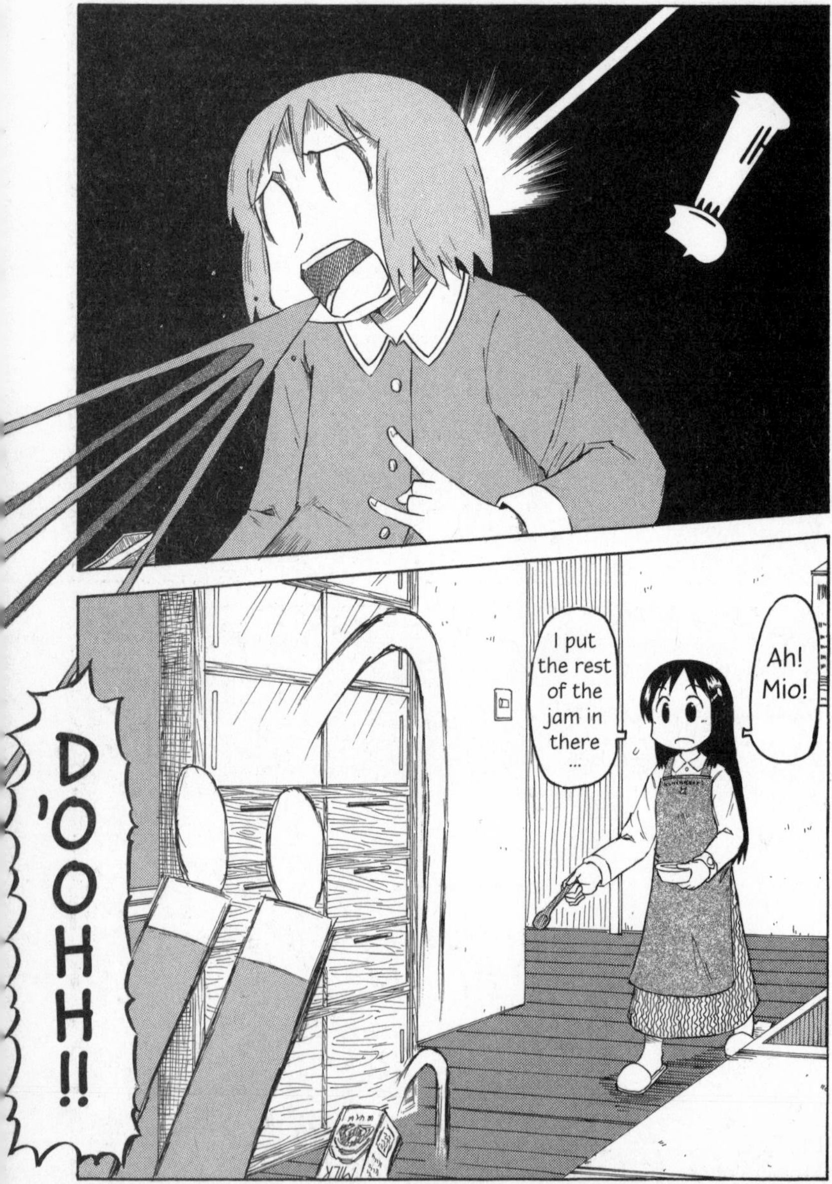
Ah! Mio!
I put the rest of the jam in there ...
D'OOHH!!

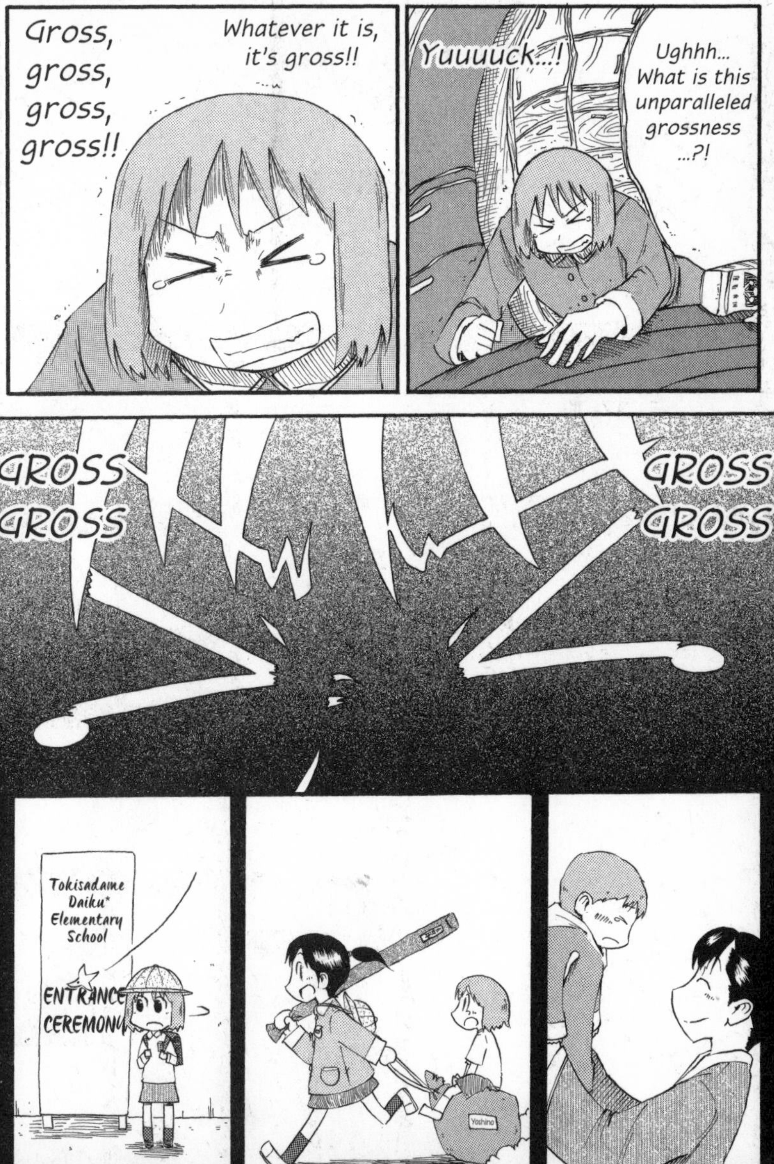
Yuuuuck...!
Ughhh... What is this unparalleled grossness ...?!
Whatever it is, it's gross!!
Gross, gross, gross, gross!!
GROSS GROSS
GROSS GROSS
Yoshino
Tokisadame Daiku* Elementary School
ENTRANCE CEREMONY

* homophone meaning "9th"

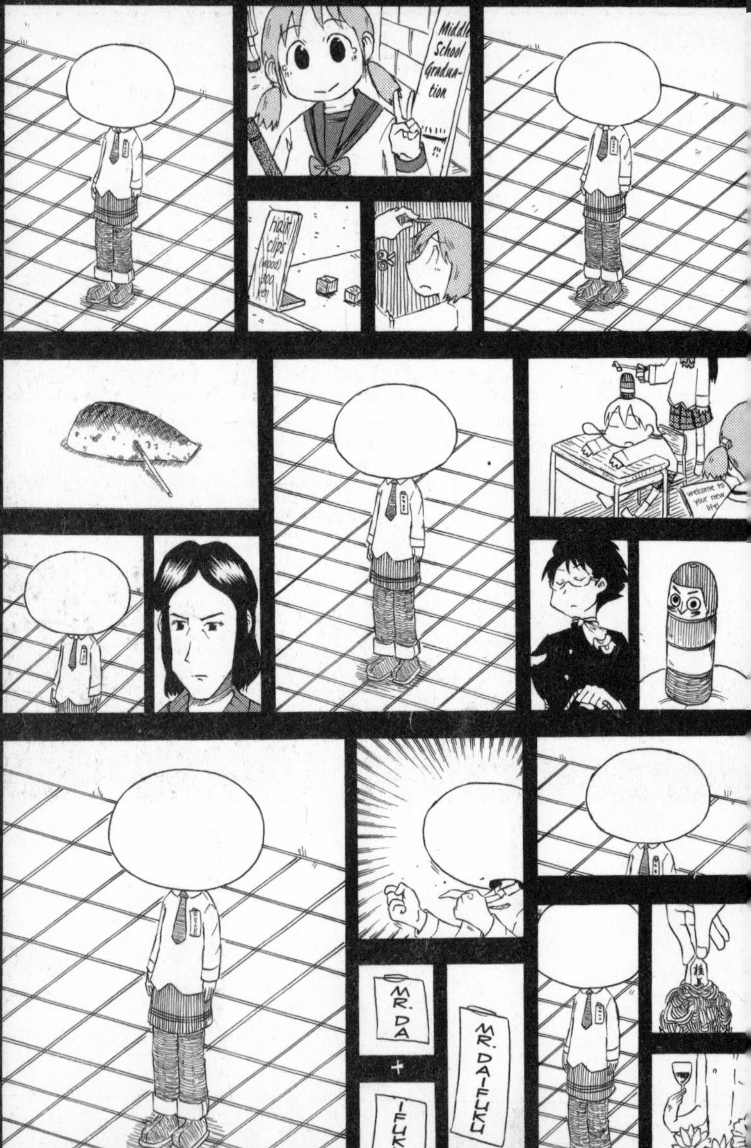
Middle School Graduation
hair clips (wood) 300 yen
welcome to your new life!
MR. DAIFUKU
MR. DA
+
IFUKU

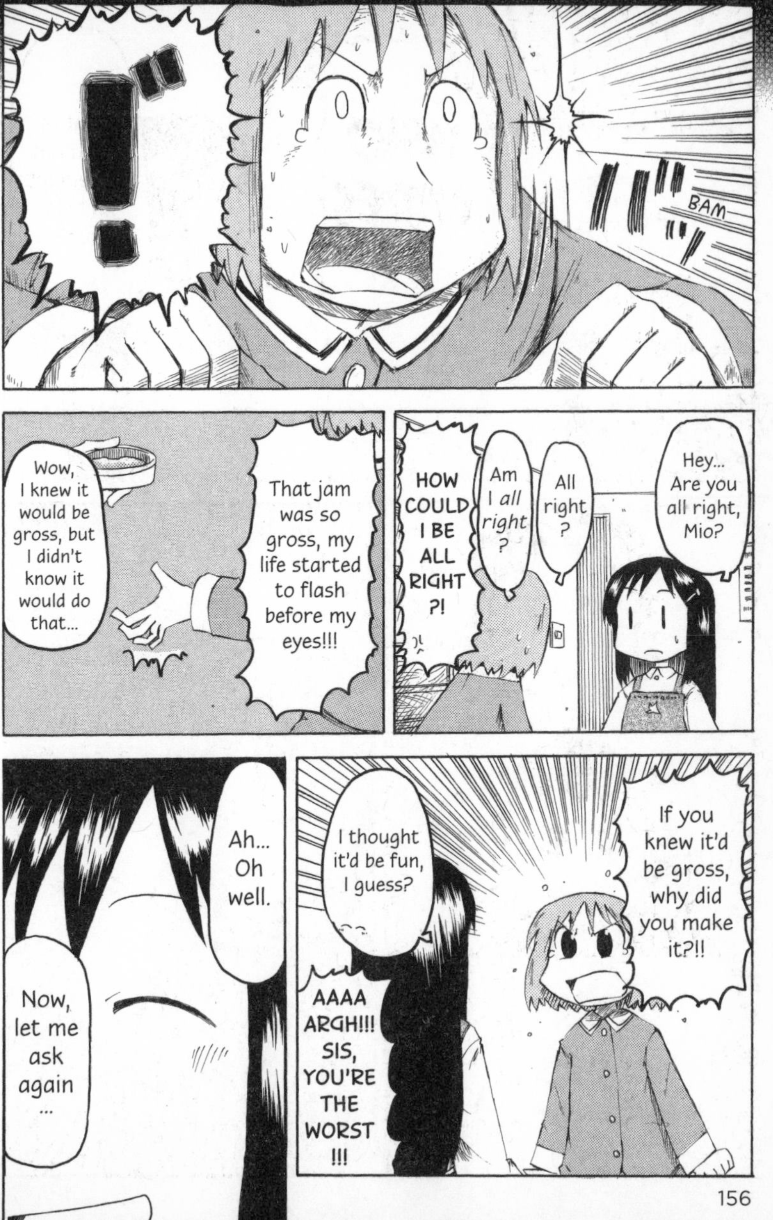
!"
BAM
Hey... Are you all right, Mio?
All right?
Am I *all right*?
HOW COULD I BE ALL RIGHT?!
That jam was so gross, my life started to flash before my eyes!!!
Wow, I knew it would be gross, but I didn't know it would do that...
If you knew it'd be gross, why did you make it?!!
I thought it'd be fun, I guess?
AAAA ARGH!!! SIS, YOU'RE THE WORST !!!
Ah... Oh well.
Now, let me ask again ...

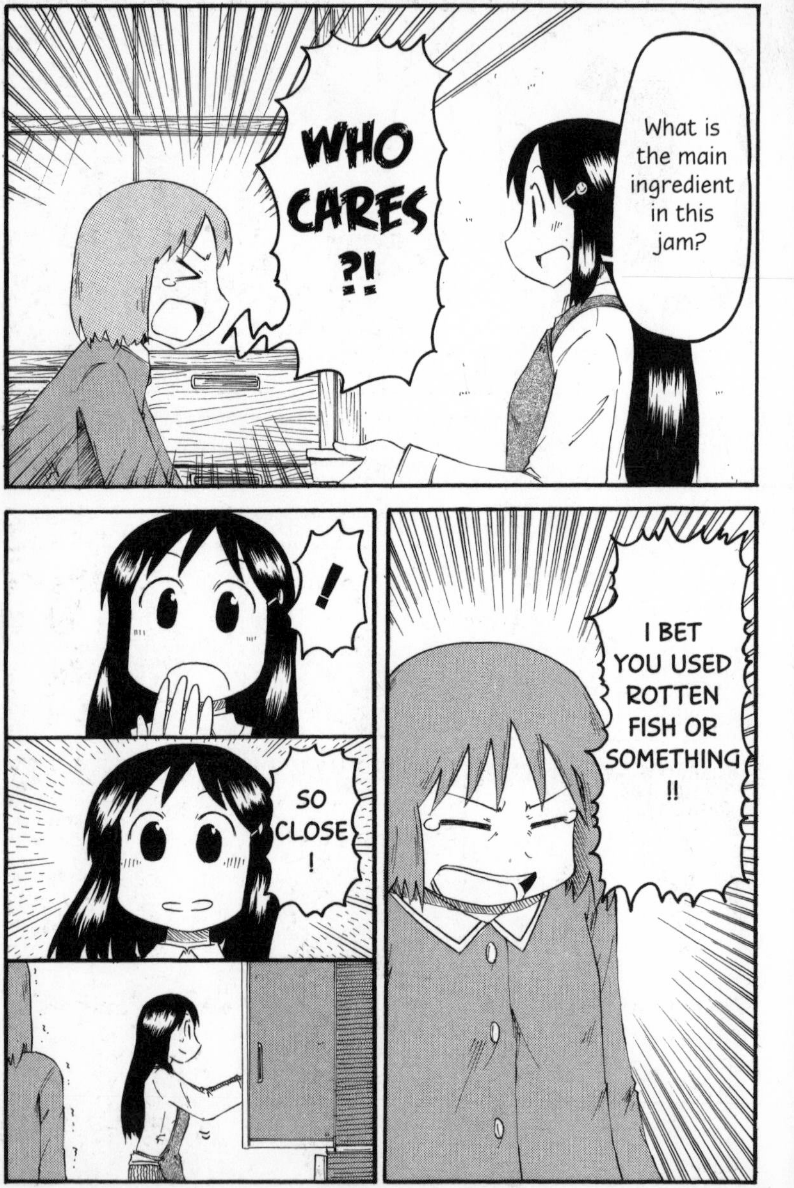
What is the main ingredient in this jam?
WHO CARES?!
I BET YOU USED ROTTEN FISH OR SOMETHING!!
!
SO CLOSE!

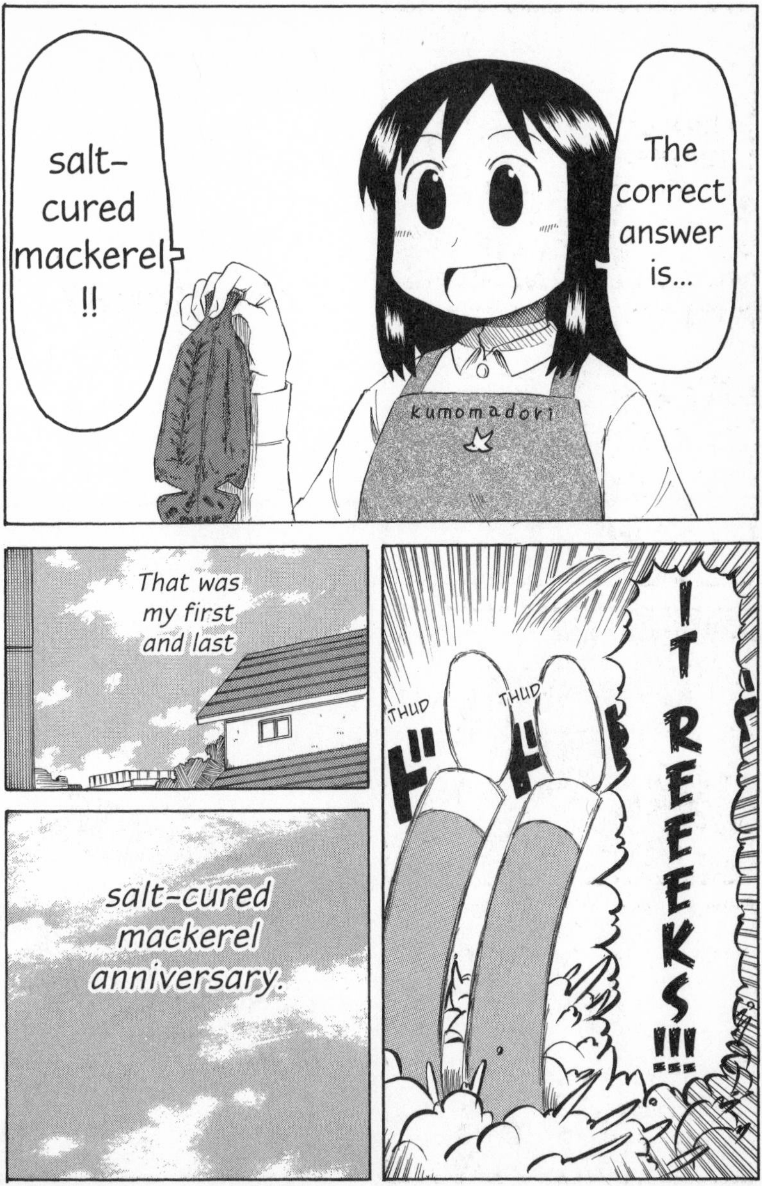
The correct answer is...
salt-cured mackerel!!
kumomadori
THUD
ド
THUD
ド
IT REEEKS!!!
That was my first and last
salt-cured mackerel anniversary.

chapter 86: end

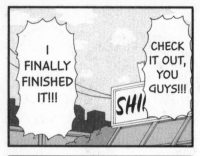

chapter 87

NICHIJOU

my ordinary life

Keiichi Arawi

CHECK IT OUT, YOU GUYS!!!
I FINALLY FINISHED IT!!!
This is Biscuit Mk-II !
TA-DAA
I am Biscuit Mk-II.
Ahh …
From the other day?
Zzz …
WHAT…
A WEAK REACTION !!!

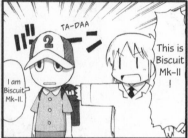

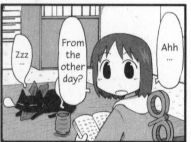

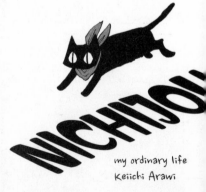

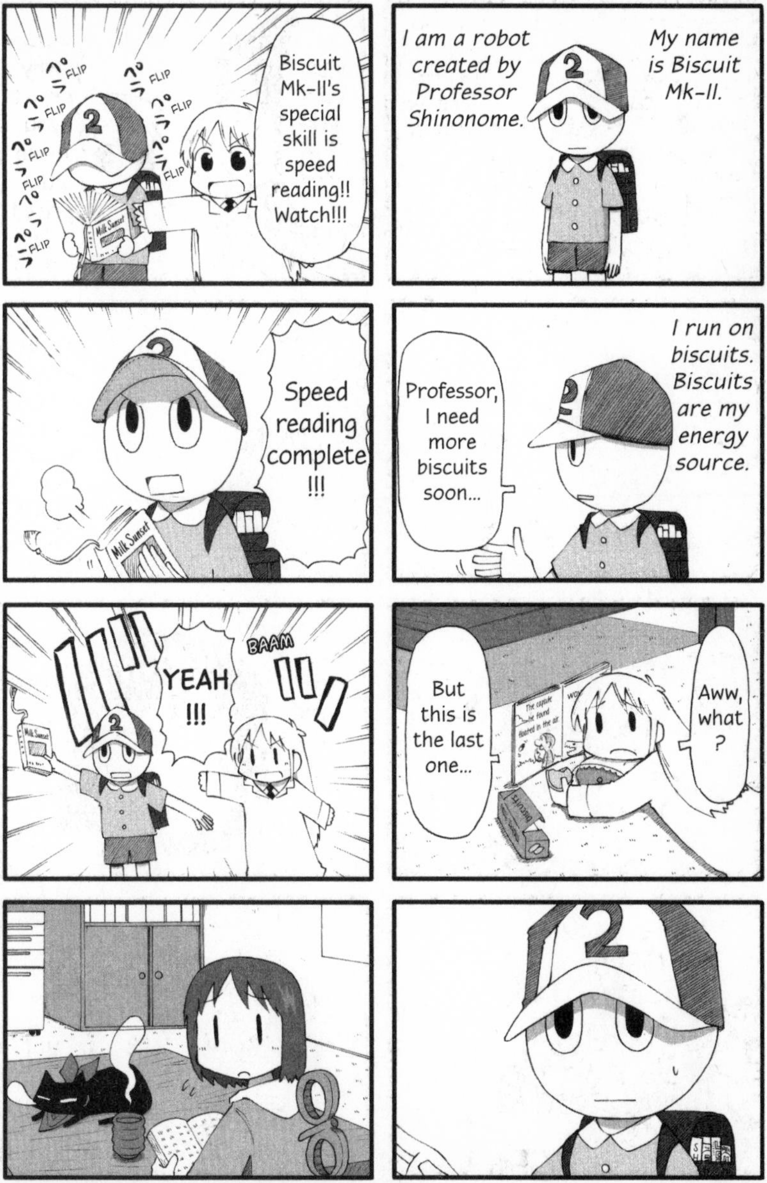

My name is Biscuit Mk-II.
I am a robot created by Professor Shinonome.
Biscuit Mk-II's special skill is speed reading!! Watch!!!
ぺら FLIP
ぺら FLIP
ぺら FLIP
ぺら FLIP
ぺら FLIP
ぺら FLIP
ぺら FLIP
ぺら FLIP
Milk Sunset
I run on biscuits. Biscuits are my energy source.
Professor, I need more biscuits soon...
Speed reading complete!!!
Milk Sunset
Aww, what?
But this is the last one...
The capsule he found floated in the air
Biscuits
BAAM
YEAH!!!
Milk Sunset

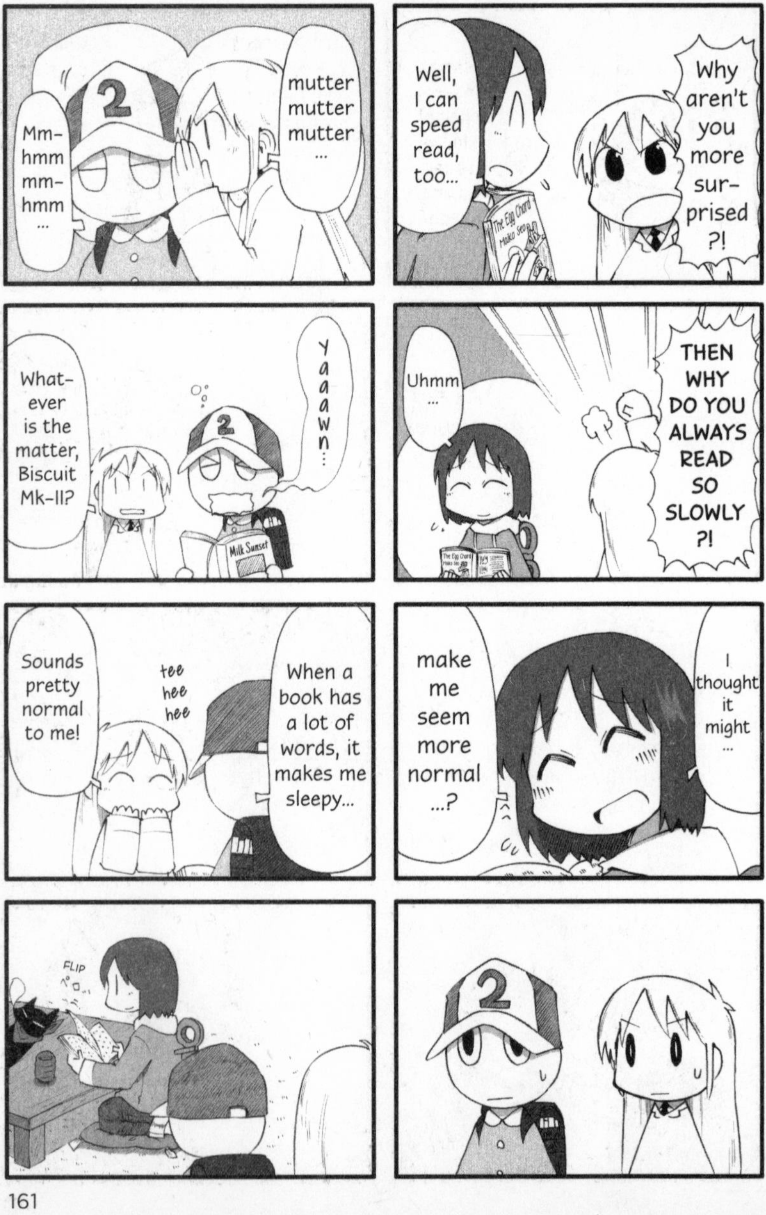
Why aren't you more sur-prised?!
The Egg Chord Maiko Seo
Well, I can speed read, too...
mutter mutter mutter ...
Mm-hmm mm-hmm ...
THEN WHY DO YOU ALWAYS READ SO SLOWLY?!
Uhmm ...
Yaaawn...
Milk Sunset
Whatever is the matter, Biscuit Mk-II?
I thought it might ...
make me seem more normal ...?
When a book has a lot of words, it makes me sleepy...
tee hee hee
Sounds pretty normal to me!
FLIP

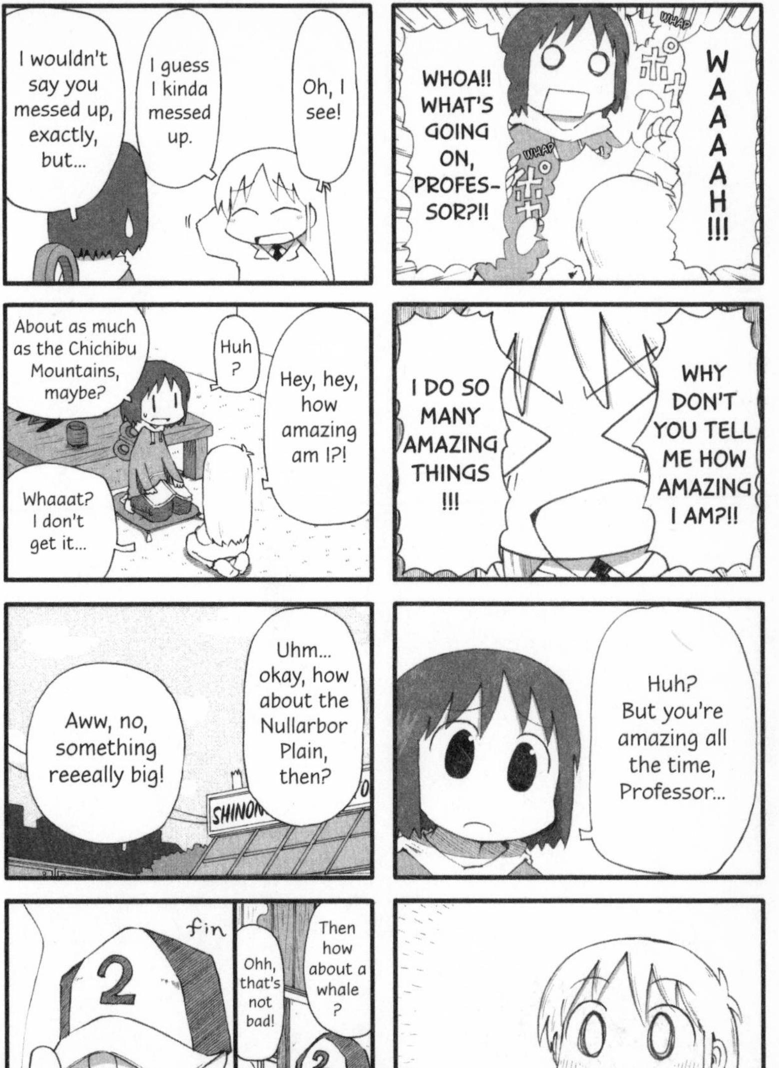
WHAP
WAAAAAH!!!
WHAP
WHOA!! WHAT'S GOING ON, PROFESSOR?!!
WHY DON'T YOU TELL ME HOW AMAZING I AM?!!
I DO SO MANY AMAZING THINGS!!!
Huh? But you're amazing all the time, Professor...
Oh, I see!
I guess I kinda messed up.
I wouldn't say you messed up, exactly, but...
Hey, hey, how amazing am I?!
Huh?
About as much as the Chichibu Mountains, maybe?
Whaaat? I don't get it...
Uhm... okay, how about the Nullarbor Plain, then?
Aww, no, something reeeally big!
Then how about a whale?
Ohh, that's not bad!
...
fin
...

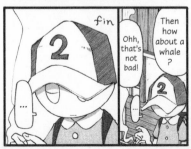

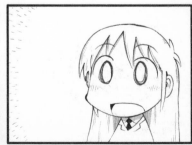

chapter 87: end

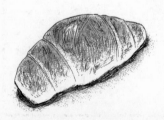

NICHIJOU

keiichi arawi

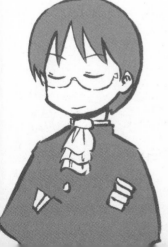
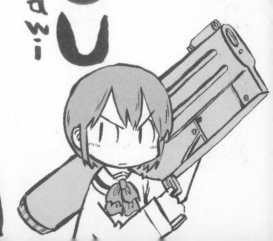

NICHIJOU

Keiichi Arawi

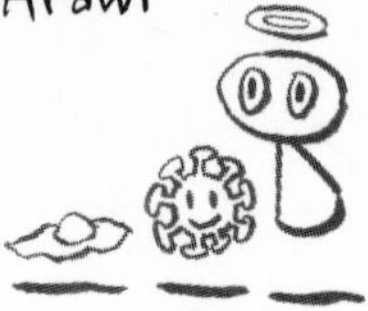

ORDINARY FACTS about TOKISADAME HIGH SCHOOL'S STAFF

Principal

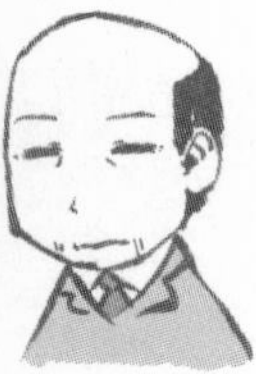

62 years old

- always doing his best for Tokisadame High School.
- apparently wants to reconcile with the vice principal.
- his hobby is buying presents for his grandchild.

Vice Principal

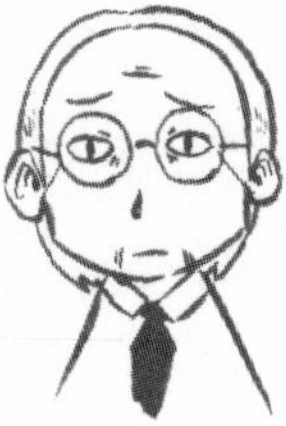

59 years old

- used to be the principal until the current principal was hired.
- apparently refuses to recognize either the Board of Education or the current principal.
- has a beloved pet rabbit.

Sakurai

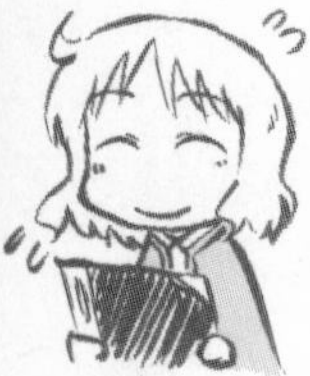

24 years old
(English teacher)

- guidance counselor
- always bright and cheerful.
- always seems nervous about something or other.

Takasaki

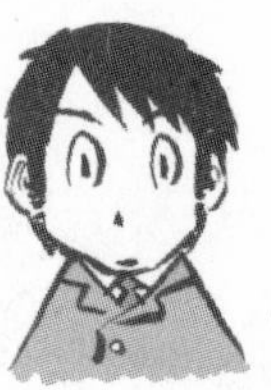

26 years old
(Japanese teacher)

- has a lot of pet theories about what a teacher should be.
- has a long history of being single.
- in love with Ms. Sakurai.

Akagi

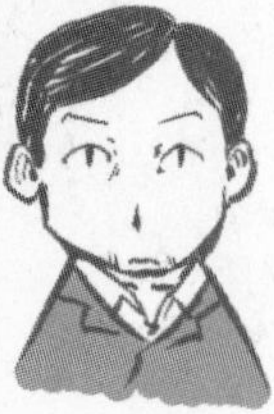

38 years old
(math teacher)

- feared by students, and will prod them with his binder if they mess up.
- his lectures are always difficult to follow.
- he actually wishes he could open up to his students more.

Tomioka

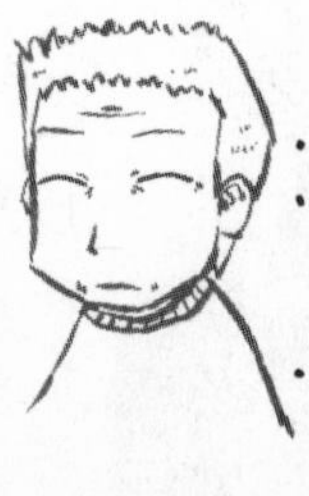

54 years old
(history teacher)

- a veteran teacher.
- Sasahara worries him a bit, but he doesn't worry all too much.
- his hobby is gambling (but never with real money).

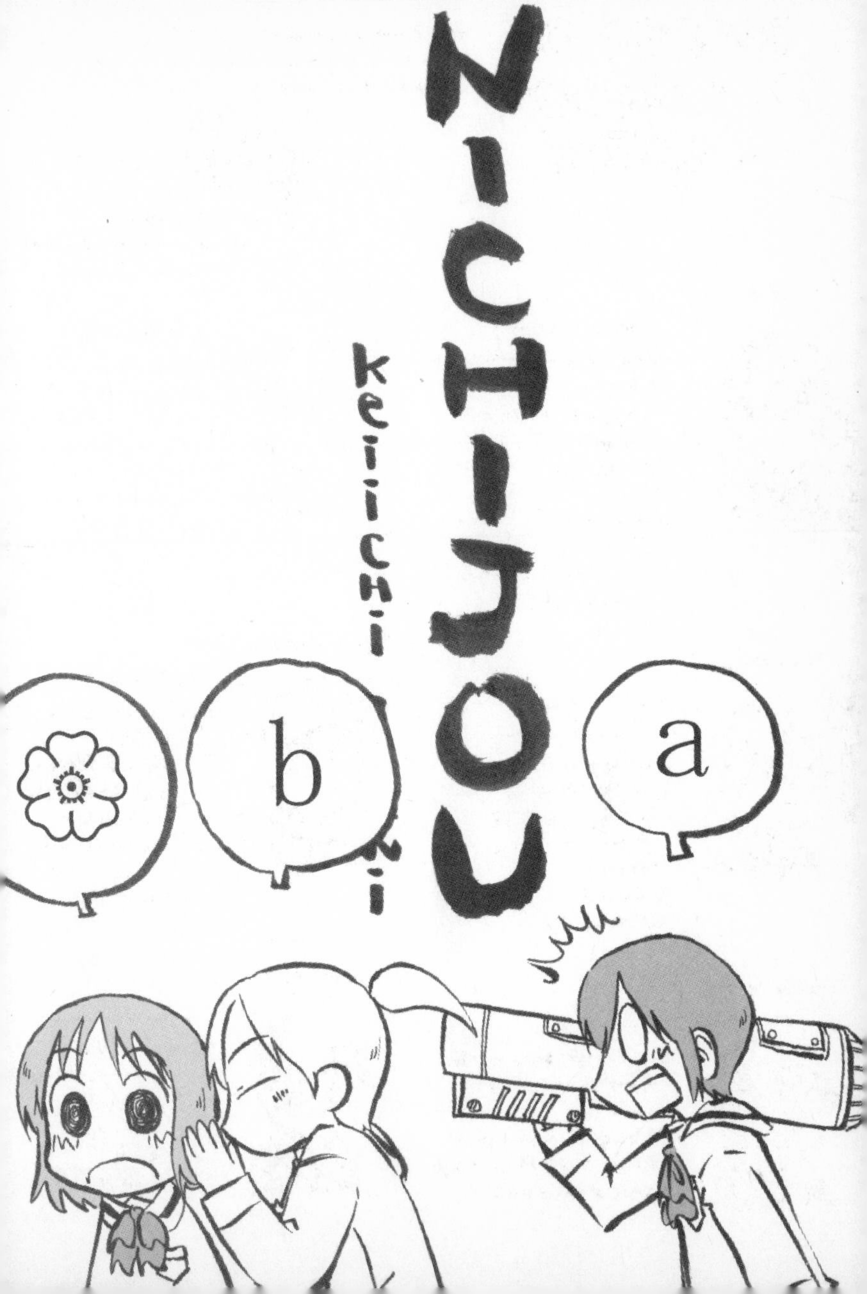
NICHIJOU
keiichi
b
a

RECORD OF FEY KINGDOM SOLDIERS

the flower does bloom
but after the fruit ripens,
surely it will burst.

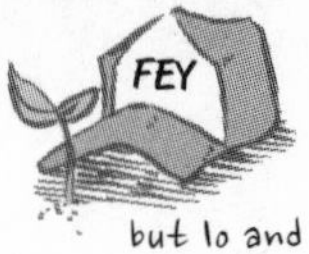
FEY

but lo and behold:
it will leave behind a seed.
— Keiichi Arawi

Number 6

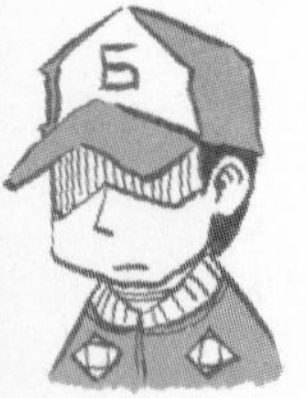
6

alias: Quizzical 6

- since elementary school, Number 6 thought of nothing but quiz games. he passed the enlistment test based solely on his interesting quizzes. however, those very same quizzes led to his death. his 26 years were spent laughing and crying over quizzes.

Aide

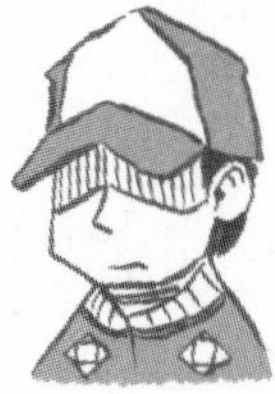

aide alias: Aide

- became the princess's aide in a game of rock-paper-scissors. nothing more or less. age at death: 35. had secretly taken a liking to Number 11.

Number 8

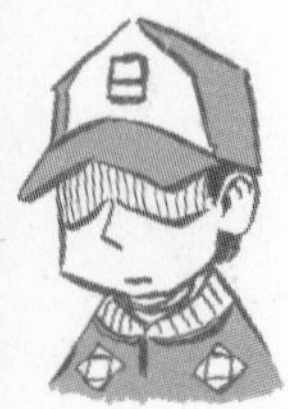
8

alias: Humorous 8

- an older brother-type figure who put those around him at ease with his humor. however, this very same humor led to his death. he loved potatoes. age at death: 28.

Number 13

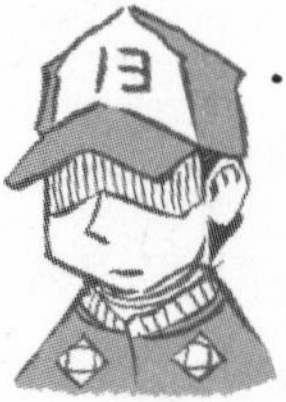
13

alias: Funny 13

- he was admired by the troops and the king alike for his fearless desire to get a laugh, but this was ultimately his undoing. he also had an interest in medical science, but nobody ever knew. age at death: 32.

Number 11

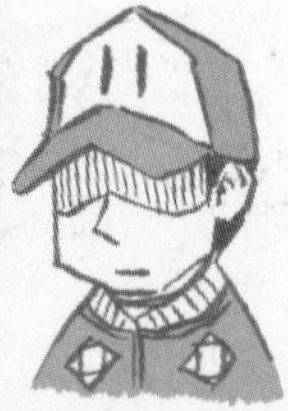
11

alias: none

- a soldier who looked up to Number 13, and so joined the troop.
- his constant imitation of Number 13 lead to his death. age at death: unknown.

Number 5

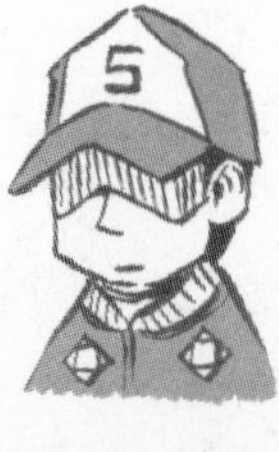
5

alias: Dominguez

- died without any particular distinction. he loved bread. he liked lasagna well enough. age at death: 29.

The Master of Killing Time

Toshinari Seki takes goofing off to new heights. Every day, on or around his school desk, he masterfully creates his own little worlds of wonder, often hidden to most of his classmates. Unfortunately for Rumi Yokoi, his neighbor at the back of the room, his many games, dioramas, and projects are often way too interesting to ignore; even when they are hurting her grades.

Volumes 1-8 available now!

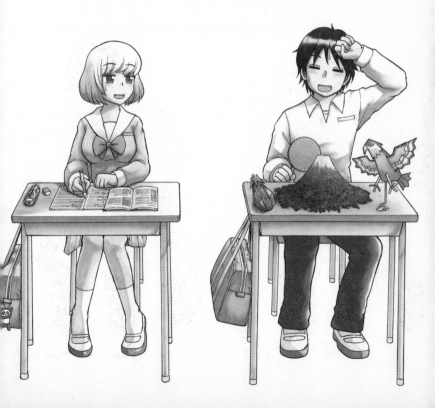

My Neighbor Seki

Tonari no Seki-kun

Takuma Morishige

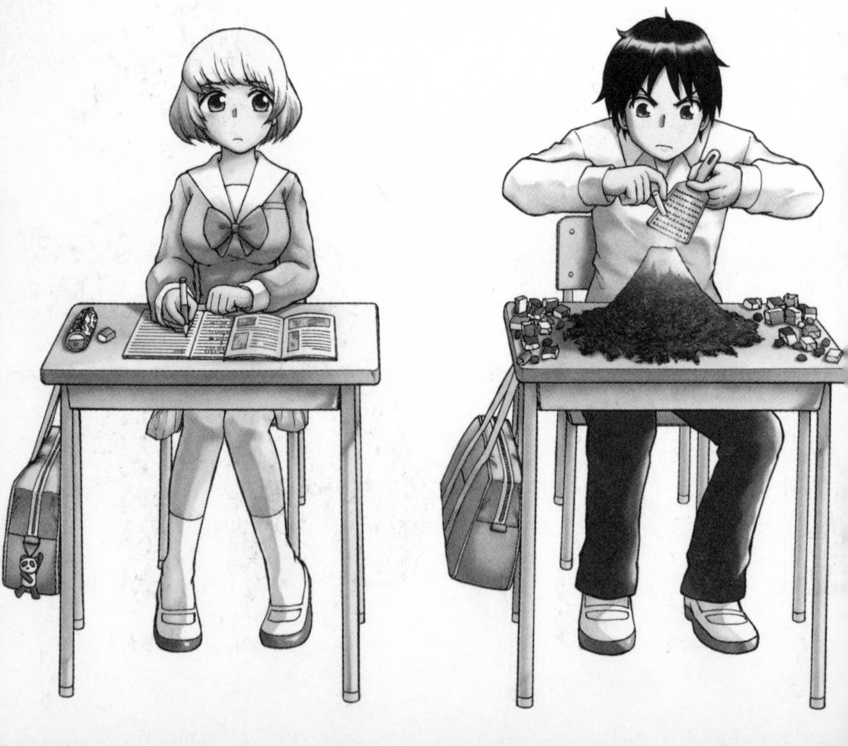

The Complete Chi's Sweet Home

Konami Kanata

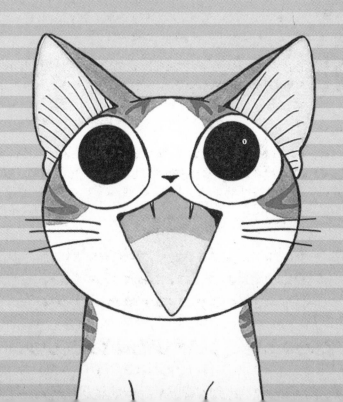

This Book is the Cat's Meow

Celebrating the conclusion of Konami Kanata's international megahit *Chi's Sweet Home*, **The Complete Chi** is a new edition that honors some of the best Japan has ever offered in the field of cat comics. A multiple *New York Times* Best Seller and two-time winner of the *Manga.Ask.com* Awards for Best Children's Manga, Konami Kanata's tale of a lost kitten has been acclaimed by readers worldwide as an excellent example of a comic that has truly been accepted by readers of all ages.

Presented in a brand new larger omnibus format each edition compiles three volumes of kitty cartoon tales, including two bonus cat comics from Konami Kanata's **FukuFuku** franchise, making **The Complete Chi's Sweet Home** a must have for every cat lover out there.

"*Chi's Sweet Home* made me smile throughout... It's utterly endearing. This is the first manga I've read in several years where I'm looking forward to the [next] volume."

—Chris Beveridge, *Mania.com*

"Konami Kanata does some pretty things with watercolor, and paces each of the little vignettes chronicling Chi's new life to highlight just the right moments for maximum effect... This is truly a visual treat." —*Comics and More*

Part 1 contains volumes 1-2-3
Part 2 contains volumes 4-5-6
Part 3 contains volumes 7-8-9

Parts 1 - 3 Available Now!

nichijou 5

my ordinary life

A Vertical Comics Edition

Translation: Jenny McKeon
Production: Grace Lu
           Hiroko Mizuno

© Keiichi ARAWI 2009
First published in Japan in 2009 by KADOKAWA CORPORATION, Tokyo.
English translation rights arranged with KADOKAWA CORPORATION, Tokyo
through TUTTLE-MORI AGENCY, INC., Tokyo.

Published by Vertical Comics, an imprint of Vertical, Inc., New York

Originally published in Japanese as *nichijou 5* by Kadokawa Corporation, 2009
nichijou first serialized in *Monthly Shonen Ace,* Kadokawa Corporation, 2006-2015

This is a work of fiction.

ISBN: 978-1-942993-34-6

Manufactured in Canada

First Edition

Vertical, Inc.
451 Park Avenue South
7th Floor
New York, NY 10016
www.vertical-comics.com

Vertical books are distributed through Penguin-Random House Publisher Services.